INVESTING IN WOMEN FOR AMERICA'S ECONOMIC BENEFIT

WOMEN'S STUDIES

Additional books in this series can be found on Nova's website under the Series tab.

Additional E-books in this series can be found on Nova's website under the E-book tab.

ECONOMIC ISSUES, PROBLEMS AND PERSPECTIVES

Additional books in this series can be found on Nova's website under the Series tab.

Additional E-books in this series can be found on Nova's website under the E-book tab.

WOMEN'S STUDIES

INVESTING IN WOMEN FOR AMERICA'S ECONOMIC BENEFIT

JAZMIN HENRICKSON

AND

LILLIAN O'CONNELL

EDITORS

Nova Science Publishers, Inc.

New York

NOTICE TO THE READER

The Publisher has taken reasonable care in the preparation of this book, but makes no expressed or implied warranty of any kind and assumes no responsibility for any errors or omissions. No liability is assumed for incidental or consequential damages in connection with or arising out of information contained in this book. The Publisher shall not be liable for any special, consequential, or exemplary damages resulting, in whole or in part, from the readers' use of, or reliance upon, this material. Any parts of this book based on government reports are so indicated and copyright is claimed for those parts to the extent applicable to compilations of such works.

Independent verification should be sought for any data, advice or recommendations contained in this book. In addition, no responsibility is assumed by the publisher for any injury and/or damage to persons or property arising from any methods, products, instructions, ideas or otherwise contained in this publication.

This publication is designed to provide accurate and authoritative information with regard to the subject matter covered herein. It is sold with the clear understanding that the Publisher is not engaged in rendering legal or any other professional services. If legal or any other expert assistance is required, the services of a competent person should be sought. FROM A DECLARATION OF PARTICIPANTS JOINTLY ADOPTED BY A COMMITTEE OF THE AMERICAN BAR ASSOCIATION AND A COMMITTEE OF PUBLISHERS.

Additional color graphics may be available in the e-book version of this book.

Library of Congress Cataloging-in-Publication Data

Investing in women for America's economic benefit / editors, Jazmin Henrickson and Lillian O'Connell.
    p. cm.
  Includes index.
  ISBN 978-1-62100-053-2 (hardcover)
  1. Sex discrimination in employment--United States. 2. Pay equity--United States. 3. Wages--Women--United States. 4. Sex discrimination against women--United States. I. Henrickson, Jazmin. II. O'Connell, Lillian. III. United States. Congress. Joint Economic Committee.
  HD6060.5.U5I58 2011
  331.40973--dc23
                    2011030121

Published by Nova Science Publishers, Inc. † New York

CONTENTS

PREFACE

As the nation charts a course out of the Great Recession and towards a brighter tomorrow, women's participation in the labor market and power over household purchases will be critical for economic growth. Women comprise half the workforce, and receive the majority of bachelor's degrees granted today. Women's earnings are crucial for family well-being, women's purchasing power drives the economy and women's leadership in the boardroom is a proven boon for businesses' bottom line. Because of all this and more, investing in women means investing in the nation as a whole. This book provides a comprehensive overview on women's position in the economy today. Decades of progress mean women are poised to lead the nation's next chapter of economic growth. Yet roadblocks remain and these blockades are hampering women's ability to reach their full economic potential.

Chapter 1- As the nation charts a course out of the Great Recession and towards a brighter tomorrow, women's participation in the labor market and power over household purchases will be critical for economic growth. Women comprise half the workforce, and receive the majority of bachelor's degrees granted today. Women's earnings are crucial for family well-being, women's purchasing power drives the economy, and women's leadership in the boardroom is a proven boon for businesses' bottom line. Because of all this and more, investing in women means investing in the nation as a whole.

Chapter 2- Equal Pay Day highlights an issue of social and economic significance: the gap between the earnings of men and women. In 2009, women working full-time earned 77 cents for every dollar earned by their male counterparts. That disparity has lasting consequences for the economic security of women that persist long after they have exited the labor force.

In: Investing in Women for America's Economic Benefit   ISBN: 978-1-62100-053-2
Editors: J. Henrickson and L. O'Connell   © 2012 Nova Science Publishers, Inc.

Chapter 1

INVEST IN WOMEN, INVEST IN AMERICA: A COMPREHENSIVE REVIEW OF WOMEN IN THE U.S. ECONOMY[*]

The Joint Economic Committee

December 2010

The Honorable Nancy Pelosi
Speaker of the House, House of Representatives Washington, DC

Dear Madam Speaker:

In 2009, you appointed me to serve as the first female Chair of the Joint Economic Committee (JEC), a bicameral Congressional committee created by Congress in 1946 to "make a continuing study of matters relating to employment, production and purchasing power" in the United States.

In the 111th Congress, as the JEC has examined ways to fuel our country's economic recovery, it has become clear that we must leave no stone unturned. One of our greatest assets in our effort to reinvigorate the country's economy is the know-how and talent of American women. As America steers its way out of the Great Recession, women's participation in the labor market, leadership in corporate boardrooms, and power over household purchases will be critical for economic growth. When we invest in women, we invest in the future of our economy.

In order to have a fuller understanding of the potential that women have to play a stronger role in our recovery, I asked the JEC Majority staff to produce a series of hearings and reports that together would provide a comprehensive assessment of women's role in the economy. It is my hope that this compendium, *Invest in Women, Invest in America: A Comprehensive*

---

[*] This is an edited, reformatted and augmented version of a A Report by the Majority Staff of the Joint Economic Committee Representative Carolyn B. Maloney, Chair, dated December 2010.

Review of Women in the U.S. Economy, and the facts, data, and forecasts relating to women and the economy it includes, become part of a public record that will help policymakers, economists, private-sector leaders, media, and everyday women and men determine whether policies promote or inhibit women's ability to be powerful contributors to economic growth.

In the ongoing effort to make women full and equal players in the United States economy – perhaps one of the biggest economic stories in this nation's history – the Joint Economic Committee has played a critical role in highlighting how women have fared in employment, earnings, education, jobs, and financial institutions. Since the 1970s, the JEC has analyzed the impact of the tax system, Social Security, and other social welfare institutions on women's economic well-being. It has chronicled the trends, challenges, and needs of American women workers as they seek to be part of a vibrant economy. The JEC's historic series of hearings in 1973 entitled *The Economic Problems of Women* and chaired by Representative Martha Griffiths, the House sponsor of the Equal Rights Amendment, set forth the economic rationale for women's equality. In 1983, a series of hearings, chaired by Senator Olympia Snowe (then a Member of the House of Representatives), explored the changing role of women in the workforce, especially their role in buffering families from the full impact of the 1980s recession. It is appropriate, therefore, that the JEC build on its previous work and prepare this compendium focused on women's contributions – and impediments to further contributions -- to the economy.

The 111th Congress took key actions to help with some of the challenges that women are facing in today's workplace. As the attached report highlights, one important issue confronting women is gender discrimination. Although women are important contributors to family income, they face gender pay discrimination, earning only 77 cents for every dollar earned by men. Additionally, women are underrepresented in management, especially in upper management, of our country's largest companies. The 111th Congress took action to help eliminate the gender pay gap by passing the Lilly Ledbetter Act of 2009. Additionally, the Dodd-Frank Wall Street Reform Act should boost women's representation in business leadership by establishing an Office of Minority and Women Inclusion at each federal financial services agency. The attached report also highlights other challenges facing women in today's economy that were addressed by the 111th Congress, including discriminatory pricing practices by health insurance companies, which were banned by the Affordable Care Act of 2010; unfair lending practices and lack of transparency in financial products, which were addressed by the Dodd-Frank Wall Street Reform Act of 2010; and the need for additional dollars for early care and education for the children of low-income women, which received a funding boost from the American Recovery and Reinvestment Act of 2009.

At a time when the goals of economic growth and prosperity are coupled with a heightened emphasis on fiscal responsibility, looking at the economy through a gendered lens is all the more critical. The decisions we make today will have dramatic impacts on our nation's future economic well-being, and we must carefully consider what those decisions will mean for women, both as consumers and as producers. For example, Social Security reforms that cut entitlements are likely to disproportionately impact women because of their longer life spans and lower lifetime earnings. Further, women are more often unpaid caregivers for family members and these responsibilities have an impact on their participation in the work force. Legislative action, such as the right to request a flexible work schedule and greater support for early care and education, would benefit American women, their families and the economy.

2010 marked the 90th anniversary of the 19th Amendment to the Constitution, which granted women the right to vote. It is my hope that this JEC report on women's economic well-being and labor force participation will shine a light on our path to full economic equality.

Sincerely,

Carolyn B. Maloney
Chair, Joint Economic Committee

PART I: INVEST IN WOMEN, INVEST IN AMERICA

Introduction

As the nation charts a course out of the Great Recession and towards a brighter tomorrow, women's participation in the labor market and power over household purchases will be critical for economic growth. Women comprise half the workforce, and receive the majority of bachelor's degrees granted today. Women's earnings are crucial for family well-being, women's purchasing power drives the economy, and women's leadership in the boardroom is a proven boon for businesses' bottom line. Because of all this and more, investing in women means investing in the nation as a whole.

This report provides a comprehensive overview on women's position in the economy today. Decades of progress mean women are poised to lead the nation's next chapter of economic growth. Yet roadblocks remain, and these blockades are hampering women's ability to reach their full economic potential. The cost of this log-jam is paid not only by women and their families, but by the economy as a whole. Jump-starting economic growth and putting the nation on a path to prosperity requires investing in women in order to allow them to meet their full economic potential. The result will be greater prosperity and progress for all.

A. Decades of Progress
for Women in the Workforce

For the first time in our nation's history, women comprise half of the U.S. workforce (49.8 percent). In 1970, women accounted for just over one-third (35.6 percent).[1] These figures alone highlight the stunning transformation of the U.S. economy over the last several decades, and women's profound role in that transformation.

Women today work in key industries throughout the economy. Women comprise 77.4 percent of workers in education and health services, the fastest growing sector of the U.S. economy. 59.3 percent of employees in the financial activities industry are women.[2] And at least half of the jobs in government, leisure and hospitality services, and other services are held by women. Female workers currently comprise the majority share of all but three of the fifteen occupations with the largest projected employment growth between 2006 and 2016.[3] In short, women play a critical role in many of the economy's key growth sectors.

Women have pulled ahead of men in educational attainment. While the fraction of men with four-year college degrees has stagnated, the share of women with four-year college degrees has grown exponentially. Today, women receive almost 60 percent of the bachelor's degrees granted in the United States, compared to just 40 percent in 1970.[4] Women's rise in educational attainment has accompanied a shift in the American economy, from an industrial economy dominated by manufacturing and construction to a post-industrial, "knowledge economy" dominated by service jobs. That same shift has meant a transition away from lower-skilled, manual work to more sophisticated work requiring a deeper skill set. Jobs requiring some form of post-secondary award or degree account for nearly half of all the new jobs projected to be created between 2008 and 2018.[5] In short, women are well-positioned to meet the demands of an increasingly sophisticated economy set to compete in the global marketplace.

Once upon a time, a working mother was an anomaly in most American communities. Today, only one in five married couples with children fit the "traditional" model of a breadwinner father and a stay-at-home mother.[6] In 1975, 44.7 percent of families with children fit that model. Likewise, in 1975, only 4 in 10 mothers (39.6 percent) with a child under age 6 worked outside the home. By 2008, that figure had risen to over 6 in 10 (64.3 percent). America's economy depends on women's work, as do America's families.

Women are co-breadwinners in many American families today. In the typical married household, the wife's paycheck accounts for over a third (36.0 percent) of the family's income.[7] In contrast, in 1970, wives' earnings comprised just over a quarter (26.6 percent) of family income.[8] Amongst all working wives in 2008, 38.1 percent earned as much or more than their husbands, compared to just 18.7 percent in 1967.[9] Amongst working wives ages 30 to 44, the share of wives earning as much or more than their husbands nearly tripled, from 11.9 percent in 1967 to 32.7 percent in 2008.

Women's earnings are critical for families' economic well-being. Between 1983 and 2008, families with wives in the paid labor force saw their income grow by 1.1 percent annually, on average, compared to a 0.2 percent annual decline in income for families where the wife did not work.[10] Families in which wives work are more likely to move up the income ladder or maintain their position over time when compared to those without working wives.[11] In 2009, women were the sole job-holders in one in three families with children (34.2 percent). In other words, 7.4 million mothers were their families' sole source of earnings.[12]

Many women with children who are their family's sole earner are single mothers. Over a quarter (26.0 percent) of working mothers are single moms, a group of women who have long been active labor market participants.[13] Over three-quarters (75.8 percent) of single mothers either worked or were actively seeking employment in 2009.

However, single mothers are not the only women whose earnings are a critical lifeline for their families. Married women's earnings play a particularly crucial role in light of the nature of the job losses that have characterized the Great Recession. Men experienced greater job losses than women over the course of the recession, because the hardest-hit industries were more likely to employ men. The share of married families where the husband was unemployed but the wife remains employed jumped sharply over the course of the recession.[14] Over the first five months of 2009, when job losses were heaviest, an average of

5.4 percent of working wives had an unemployed husband at home, compared to an average of 2.4 percent over the first five months of 2007. In other words, the share of married couples with an unemployed husband more than doubled over the course of the recession. In contrast, the share of working husbands with an unemployed wife remained much lower – just 3.3 percent in the first five months of 2009 compared to 1.6 percent in the first five months of 2007. Families with children were no exception: 5.7 percent of families with children under the age of 18 had an unemployed husband and an employed wife. This means that, in 2009, there were 1 million working wives with children at home, but an unemployed husband. For these families, women's earnings are a critical lifeline.

In no uncertain terms, women have made phenomenal progress over the course of the last several decades. Women are a vital force in the United States' economy, providing skills and labor in a diverse array of sectors. Women's paychecks have driven their families' standards of living upwards, and provide a key safety net during tough economic times.

B. Women's Potential Power

Women hold phenomenal potential to drive economic growth. Advertisers realized this basic fact ages ago, and products marketed specifically to women are recognizable to anyone with a passing familiarity with popular culture. Indeed, women control 73 percent of household spending.[15] This translates into over $4 trillion in annual discretionary spending. In an economy driven by consumption, this is a powerful role. In over half of middle- and upper-income families, women are more likely than men to handle daily money management tasks.[16] Yet women's power as an engine of economic growth extends beyond their role as consumers. Women have proven their potential as economic producers as well.

Take, for instance, women's role in business. Firm performance correlates directly with women's representation in corporate leadership. Companies with the most women on their boards of directors outperform those with the fewest women on their boards on myriad key performance measures – return on invested capital is 66 percent higher in firms with strong female representation, return on equity is 53 percent higher, and return on sales is 42 percent higher.[17] The link between women's representation on corporate boards and firm performance holds across industries. Fortune 500 firms with the best record of promoting women to senior positions, including their boards of directors, are more profitable than their peers.[18] The 25 firms with the best promotion records post returns on assets 18 percent higher, and returns on investments 69 percent higher, than the Fortune 500 median for their industry.

The link between gender diversity in corporate leadership and firm performance may stem from the talents that women are more likely than men to bring to the boardroom. Firms with female representation on their boards of directors are more likely to be highly attentive to corporate governance issues, which correlate with improved firm performance.[19] Women leaders are more likely than their male peers to demonstrate types of leadership behavior that positively affect corporate organizational performance, including participative decision-making, role modeling, inspiration, expectations and rewards, and mentoring.[20]

Female business owners are also a major driving force in the United States' economy. Women-owned businesses account for almost 30 percent of all non-farm, privately-held U.S. firms.[21] Growth in women-owned businesses outpaces that of male-owned business. Between 1997 and 2007, the number of women-owned businesses grew by 44 percent, twice the pace of male-owned businesses. These women-owned businesses added roughly 500,000 jobs between 1997 and 2007, when the rest of privately-held firms lost jobs.

Traditionally "female" occupations have expanded in economic importance over the last several decades, and are poised to grow exponentially in coming years. For instance, as of 2008, health care sector employment had grown by 25 percent over the last 9 years, compared to just 5 percent in all non-health care sectors combined.[22] Women comprise three-quarters (74.5 percent) of all health care practitioners, and 88.8 percent of all health care support occupations.[23] Within the health care sector, employment growth has been more rapid in the home health and hospice care sub-sectors than in the health care sector more generally. These are areas that are particularly saturated with female workers, who comprise the vast majority (88.7 percent) of home health aides. Projections into the future predict continued strong growth in the health care sector, particularly because of the aging baby boom population and the continued need for the "caring" professions that women predominate. For instance, forecasters predict that the economy will add 581,500 jobs for registered nurses between 2008 and 2018 – over one-third of the total growth in healthcare practitioner jobs.[24] As of 2008, 91.7 percent of registered nurses were female.

In addition to demographic changes favoring traditionally-female occupations, women's educational attainment means that millions of women are in a position to contribute meaningfully to the economy of the future. Women's impressive college graduation rate means that the up-and-coming cohort of young women are poised and ready with the skills and education necessary for creating economic value in the labor force of tomorrow.

Women are also in a position to influence the shape of the future labor movement in the United States. While total union membership has declined over the last quarter century, women's union membership has been on the rise.[25] In 1984, women made up just over one-third (34.0 percent) of all union members. In 2008, women comprised 45.0 percent of all union members. The growing importance of women in the labor movement is likely due to the expansion of female-concentrated sectors such as health care, education, and the service sector, combined with the contraction of male-concentrated sectors such as manufacturing.

C. What's Holding Women Back?

Women's prospective economic power is substantial – as both consumers and producers, women hold the keys to revving up the economy's engine and driving the nation towards a future of prosperity. Yet women face serious constraints to achieving their full potential. A persistent wage gap not only cheats women and their families out of the earnings they deserve, but artificially constrains the purchasing power of women, and therefore hampers the American economy as a whole. Women's continued underrepresentation in corporate leadership means that America's companies are missing out on the proven economic value to having women in the boardroom and the C-suite. A patchwork social support system – particularly in the work-family arena, where the United States offers virtually no institutionalized support for working families – means that America's economy suffers as women struggle to balance demands from work and demands from home. And a retirement system that disadvantages women means that too many hard-working women spend their elder years on the precipice of economic disaster.

A Persistent Gender
Wage Gap

The gender wage gap remains substantial today. Women working full-time, year-round earn only 77 cents for every dollar earned by men, and virtually no progress has been made in closing the gap since 2001.[26] In 2009, the most recent year for which data is available, median annual earnings of women ages 15 and older working full-time, year-round were just $36,278 compared to $47,127 for their male counterparts. New calculations from the JEC show that the gender wage gap is even greater for older women. In 2009, median weekly wages for women over 50 were just 75 percent of their male colleagues' earnings.[27]

The gender wage gap persists across a wide spectrum of occupations.[28] Female attorneys earn just 80.5 cents for every dollar earned by their male counterparts, and female physicians and surgeons earn 64.4 cents on the dollar. Women in retail sales earn 70.6 cents for every dollar earned by men in retail sales, and female truck drivers earn just 76.4 cents on the dollar. A recent Government Accountability Office (GAO) study requested by Chair Maloney and Representative John Dingell examined the pay gap amongst women and men employed in management occupations, and found that full-time female managers earn 81 cents for every dollar earned by their male manager peers.[29] This figure accounts for many observable differences between male and female managers, so the remaining 19 cent gap between men and women may be attributable to discriminatory practices. The gender pay gap amongst managers remained persistent between 2000 and 2007, the most recent year of available data.

The pay gap is not limited to the private sector. Even within the federal government, which ought to be a model employer, a substantial unexplained pay gap persists. In response to a request by Chair Maloney and Representative Dingell, the GAO examined the gender pay gap in the federal government and found that women federal employees earn 89 cents for every dollar earned by their male peers.[30] After accounting for observable differences between men and women (including education, experience, and occupation), that gap narrows to 93 cents on the dollar. The remaining 7 cent pay gap may be attributable to discriminatory practices.

Women earn less than men across all educational levels.[31] In 2009, female high school graduates earned 69.6 cents for every dollar earned by their male counterparts; median earnings amongst female high school graduates is $22,468 compared to $32,272 for male high school graduates. Amongst college graduates, the gender wage gap is similarly substantial, with female college graduates earnings 70.9 cents for every dollar earned by their male counterparts; median earnings for female college graduates is $40,098 compared to $56,566 for men. The gender pay gap for workers with a professional degree is the largest across the education spectrum: professional women earn 57.9 cents for every dollar earned by professional men, or $67,245 as compared to men's $116,136.

The pay gap amongst college graduates grows substantially over the course of a woman's career.[32] Just one year out of college, women earn about 80 percent of what their male classmates earn. Ten years after graduation, women have fallen further behind, earning just 69 cents for every dollar earned by their male classmates. Similarly, recent research suggests that the pay gap between male and female professional degree-holders grows steeper over time. For instance, a study tracking the earnings of graduates of the University of Chicago's MBA program finds that the gap between male and female MBA's earnings grows from 11 percent at graduation (i.e. 89 cents on the dollar) to 31 percent at five years out (i.e. 69 cents on the dollar) to a whopping 60 percent at ten years or more (i.e. 40 cents on the dollar).[33] A second study tracking male and female MBA recipients found that women averaged $4,600 less in their first job, even after controlling for job level.[34] Women started at lower levels than men and were outpaced in salary growth, even after controlling for career aspirations and parenthood status. The salary growth gap intensified over time. While women and men step off the corporate track at equal rates, women pay a greater penalty in terms of compensation and position than do men when they return to corporate life.

Mothers face an additional wage penalty, on top of the basic penalty paid simply by virtue of being a woman in the labor force. Much research has shown that working mothers earn less than non-mothers.[35] Even after accounting for differences in work experience, job characteristics, human capital such as education, and other individual attributes, mothers pay a 7 percent wage penalty per child, relative to non-mothers.[36] A GAO report requested by Chair Maloney and Representative Dingell found that while mothers incurred at 2.5 percent earnings penalty for each child, fathers enjoyed a 2.1 percent earnings boost for each child.[37]

Other studies provide detail on the depth of the motherhood wage penalty. A GAO report requested by Chair Maloney and Representative Dingell found that mothers who are managers earn 79 cents for every dollar earned by fathers who are managers, and that pay gap has not budged since 2000.[38] The pay gap for mothers is larger than the pay gap for childless female managers, who earn 83 cents for every dollar earned by childless male managers. While the pay gap for childless women narrowed slightly between 2000 and 2007, the pay gap for "manager moms" remains stuck at 79 cents on the dollar. These figures compare full-time workers, and account for many factors that might explain the discrepancy between men and women, including age, education and other variables. Another study sent out over 1,200 fictitious resumes to employers in a large Northeastern city, and found that female applicants with children were significantly less likely to be hired (and, if hired, were offered a lower salary) than identical male applicants with children.[39] In no uncertain terms, a preponderance of evidence suggests that women are penalized in the workforce when they have children, despite no evidence that their productivity suffers.

As detailed above, full-time, full-year female workers earn less, on average, than full-time, full-year male workers. This problem persists across occupations and industries, and is particularly pernicious for mothers. Yet the problem does not stop there. The wage gap for part-time workers exacerbates the existing problem.[40] The "part-time penalty" means that part-time workers are paid an average of 58 cents on the dollar compared to the hourly wages of their full-time peers. In other words, while the part-time employee and the full-time employee are likely doing the same work, the part-time worker faces a wage penalty simply for being a part-timer. Women are far more likely than men to be employed part-time – nearly two-thirds (64 percent) of part-time workers are women, and one in four (26 percent) of all employed women work part-time. Therefore, the part-time wage penalty is an additional factor exacerbating the gender pay gap.

The cost of the pay gap to women and their families is enormous, particularly when measured over the course of a career.[41] In the first five years of her career, between ages 25-29, the average woman loses $8,510 to the pay gap. Because the pay gap widens as women progress through their careers, her losses grow progressively larger. By the time she retires at 64, she's lost over $430,000 to the pay gap.[42] When individual women's losses due to the pay gap are aggregated across all working women for a generation, the results are staggering – for instance, as a group, young college-educated women who entered the workforce between 1984 and 2004 have lost $1.7 trillion.

The gender wage gap comes at a cost to the economy as a whole. Women's phenomenal purchasing power and critical role as financial decision-makers for their households means that when a woman is cheated out of a portion of her paycheck, the whole economy suffers. Fewer take-home dollars means fewer purchases, which in turn means a more sluggish economy and slower economic growth. Closing the gender pay gap therefore has the potential to have salutary effects not only for women and their families, but for the nation's future economic health as well.

Underrepresentation in
Corporate Leadership

Despite the clearly demonstrated economic rewards that accrue to companies with women in corporate leadership, women remain dramatically underrepresented in corporate boardrooms and executive suites.[43] While women comprise 46.4 percent of all employees in Fortune 500 companies, they make up just 15.7 percent of board seats, 14.4 percent of executive officers, 7.6 percent of top earning executive officers, and 2.4 percent of chief executive officers (CEOs). Women lag men in Fortune 500 leadership across all industries, including female-prevalent industries. The percentage of women-held board seats and corporate officer positions are quite similar across industries, even in fields such as retail and finance, where women represent a greater share of total employees. The only fields where women's leadership is markedly lower than average are utilities, mining, and quarry extraction and oil and gas extraction, where women's overall representation is much lower.

Women's representation in Fortune 500 leadership has remained stagnant over time. Women have made little progress in representation as CEOs, corporate officers, or board members over the last several decades.[44] The last five years have been particularly flat periods for progress. For instance, between 1996 and 2003, women's representation on corporate boards increased from 10.2 percent to 15.2 percent, but it has remained stalled at 15.2 percent for the last six years.

The underrepresentation of women in corporate leadership – in the boardroom and the executive suite – may mean that U.S. companies are not reaching their full potential. Corporate performance correlates directly with women's representation in corporate leadership. Companies with the most women on their boards of directors outperform those with the least women on their boards on myriad key economic performance measures, and the link between women's representation on corporate boards and firm performance holds across industries.[45] Fortune 500 firms with the best record of promoting women to senior positions, including their boards of directors, are more profitable than their peers.[46] A lack of gender diversity in corporate leadership may be hindering corporate profits, and holding back future economic growth.

An out-of-Date Framework
for Social Support

Our nation's public policies are still rooted in the antiquated assumption that families rely on a single male breadwinner, and therefore have a wife at home to care for the young, the sick, and the elderly. The reality is that most families depend on two breadwinners, and many struggle to patch together care for their loved ones in order to continue to make ends meet. The absence of social supports for working families spans a wide range of policy areas impacting families from birth until death.

No Paid Leave

Perhaps the most important advance in social support for working families was the Family and Medical Leave Act of 1993, but even this major legislative accomplishment only allows 12 weeks of unpaid job-protected family or medical leave to about half of all workers in the United States. The United States' approach stands in stark contrast to our peers. The OECD average length of job-projected leave for new parents is 18 weeks, compared to the U.S.'s 12 weeks. Beginning in January 2011, the United States will be the only OECD nation with no paid parental leave.[47] As a result of the lack of paid parental leave, many families incur serious financial hardship upon the birth of a child.

The lack of paid parental leave means the economy pays, too. Paid parental leave can serve as a powerful retention tool: new mothers who are able to take a paid leave are more likely to return to the same employer than are those without paid leave. The cost of turnover is substantial, with turnover costs estimated at between 25 and 200 percent of employee compensation.[48] Those costs stem from direct expenses such as recruiting, interviewing, hiring, training, and supervising new employees, but also from indirect costs such as lost sales due to consumer dissatisfaction, new employee errors, and reduced morale of employees charged with training new hires.

The absence of a federal paid sick leave policy also places a special burden on women. Currently, more than one-third (37 percent) of working women in establishments with 15 or more workers lack access to paid sick leave.[49] The actual share of working women with no access to paid sick leave may be substantially larger, since smaller establishments are less likely to provide workplace benefits and women may be more likely to be work in smaller establishments as compared to men. The absence of paid sick leave means that millions of women are vulnerable to income and job loss when an illness requires that they stay home from work. Despite women's mass movement into the labor force, mothers still bear the primary responsibility for their children's health, regardless of whether or not that mother works. Half of all working mothers must miss work if their child is sick, compared to 30 percent of working fathers, and half of these mothers who stay home with their sick child report that they do not get paid when they stay home to provide care. The lack of access to paid sick leave is of particular harm to working women because of the double burden they face – both self-care and care for an ailing child.

The absence of a federal paid leave policy takes a toll on the economy, too. Employers pay substantial wages to workers who go to work ill, known as "presenteeism." Workers who report to work sick are typically about half as productive as usual, and that productivity slowdown exacerbating productivity problems. The cost of presenteeism averages between $217 and $1,567 per employee per year.[51]

Inflexible Work Arrangements

The absence of access to flexible work arrangements is another factor holding women back from achieving their full economic potential. Busy working women face responsibilities at home and at work, and flexible work arrangements can offer a win-win solution that allows for an easier balancing act. For the millions of women who are working longer hours in the aftermath of the Great Recession in order to help their families make ends meet, added flexibility would be of particular use.

Only 50 percent of American workers agree they have the flexibility they need in order to successfully manage their work and family life, despite the fact that the vast majority of Americans rate flexibility as a very important job quality.[52] Research shows that workers with a high-quality work-life "fit," a summary metric of job quality that includes several important measures of flexibility, are better employees – they are more likely to remain in their current job, more highly engaged, in better health, and less stressed than workers with a poor work-life fit. Flexible work arrangements promoting better work-life fit could boost economic performance by promoting lower levels of job turnover, higher employee satisfaction, and lower levels of absenteeism.

Studies provide evidence of precisely this effect. Employees respond to flexibility with enhanced loyalty and commitment, which increases productivity and makes businesses more competitive. In the tight labor markets of the 1990s and early 2000s, a major advantage of flexibility was reduced turnover. Access to flexible work arrangements motivated productive performers to stick with the current employer, which meant that the employer saved money searching for and training new employees.[53] For example, 96 percent of AstraZeneca employees claimed that flexibility influenced their decision to remain with the company. Deloitte estimated that the firm saved $41.5 million in 2003 due to reduced turnover attributable to their flexibility policies.

Moreover, in the absence of broadly available flexible work arrangements, women may work in positions that are more flexible but less well-suited for their skills and talents. This skills mismatch may drag down productivity and waste valuable human capital, thereby slowing economic growth.

Undervalued Early Care and Education Sector

The workplace is not the only arena where federal policies have failed to keep up with the changing reality of American family life. Prior to the mass movement of women into the labor force, mothers were more likely to provide early care and education for their own children. The movement of women into the labor force means that child care arrangements are a necessity for most American families. Yet the early care and education system in the United States remains under-developed and underfunded.

This failure not only hurts working women, who bear the primary responsibility for caring for children. It also hurts the workers employed in the care sector – child care workers and early educators, who are primarily women and remain under-valued and under-paid. Moreover, it hurts the economy as a whole, because under-funded early care and education has meaningful consequences for children's health, well-being, and human capital. The failure to invest in early care and education is a strategic error that is holding back the American economy from achieving its full potential not only today, but in the future as well.

Quality, affordable early care and education – child care centers and pre-kindergarten programs – remain in short supply across the United States. As a result, access to quality, affordable care for young children presents a major source of financial and emotional stress for working parents. The cost of full-time, center-based child care for an infant is nearly half (49 percent) of the annual income for two-parent family living at the federal poverty threshold ($18,310/year in 2009), and nearly one quarter (24 percent) of the annual income for a two-parent family living at 200 percent of the federal poverty threshold ($36,620/year in 2009).[54] In all but one state, the average cost of pre-school is more than the average annual cost of public college tuition. In many cities, preschool costs twice as much as college tuition.[55]

This burden is particularly high for low-income families, especially single mothers who simply do not have the option of staying home to provide care for their own children. While the Head Start and Early Head Start programs are meant to provide subsidized child care for low-income families, demand far outstrips the supply of slots in these programs, and many families are simply not able to access these resources. Moreover, many working families' incomes are too high to allow them to qualify for federal programs but too low to comfortably afford safe, secure, and high-quality child care arrangements.

The lack of access to quality early care and education for children comes at substantial cost. Working families – particularly the women who bear the primary responsibility for child care and well-being – are under extraordinary financial and emotional pressure as they struggle to make sure that their children are safe and nurtured. Yet the problem extends beyond the private stresses of families scrambling to provide for their children. Government investments in early childhood education provide a proven bang-for-the-buck. On the flip side, therefore, a failure to invest in children yields an economy that is failing to reach its full potential. Early interventions – early child care, pre-kindergarten, and other similar programs – can promote educational attainment, raise the quality of the workforce, and enhance the productivity of schools, in addition to reducing crime, teenage pregnancy, and welfare receipt. In terms of earnings alone, investing in early care and education provides a return on dollars invested as high as 17 percent.[56]

Despite a large body of research suggesting strong returns on the investment in children, federal policy has consistently under-funded children's programs in comparison to other spending priorities. Spending on children as a share of domestic federal spending has been decreasing for nearly 50 years.[57] In 1960, spending on children comprised 20.2 percent of all domestic spending. By 2000, that figure was just 16.2 percent, and spending on children as a share of all domestic spending is projected to dip to just 13.8 percent by 2018.[58] This continued under-investment in early care and education is a drag on our nation's future economic well-being.

Tenuous Retirement Support

Elderly women are far more likely than elderly men to struggle financially. 11.7 percent of women over the age of 75 are poor, compared to just 7.4 percent of men.[59] Older women are struggling to get by with today's retirement system.

Despite the substantial increase in women's education, employment, and earnings over time, women still tend to experience shorter and more interrupted career trajectories than do men. The demands of child birth, child rearing, elder care, and other factors mean that women's employment patterns are not as even as men's. Because our nation's retirement system is built on the assumption of consistent, stable work, women's retirement security remains precarious.

Women's role as the main caregivers in American society extends across their lifespans. Even childless women are likely to take some time out of the labor force to care for aging parents or other infirm relatives. Over 82 percent of all care for the frail elderly is unpaid, and women account for two-thirds of these unpaid caregivers.[60] Daughters account for about seven in ten of adult children who help their frail parents, and five of every six who assume primary responsibility for their personal care. The aging of the Baby Boom cohort translates into a growing elderly population that will require care in the coming years, and much of that care will be provided by women. As a result, more women are likely to curtail work to provide care.[61] Moreover, while women spend more time out of the labor force than men, they also have more substantial retirement income needs, because women live longer than men.

This time spent out of the labor force combines with the gender pay gap to make saving for retirement and accruing Social Security benefits a challenge for many women. Women reach retirement with smaller balances in their individual retirement accounts than their male colleagues, in part because of the gender pay gap and in part because of career interruptions. The median female worker neared retirement with a 401k or IRA plan valued at $34,000, compared to her male counterpart's $70,000 in 2004.[62]

Social Security plays a uniquely important role for women because it provides a guaranteed source of retirement income. Without it, over half of all women over the age of 65 would be poor.[63] Yet lower earnings and time out of the labor force mean that women's Social Security contributions are consistently lower than those of men. Because the Social Security system does not recognize unpaid care as "work," women's contributions to the well-being of their children and parents remains unremunerated. When workers reduce their employment due to transitions from full- to part-time employment, or from withdrawal from the labor force, their future retirement streams suffer. Yet women's care contributions have sizeable economic value. For instance, family unpaid elder care constitutes an economic value of between $45 billion to $200 billion annually.[64] The failure of the current system to recognize this fact means that older women face a constant challenge to their economic security.

D. Potential Solutions – 21st Century Economic Equity

The economic status of women has progressed tremendously over the last half-century. Yet, as the above section explains, women's full economic potential has yet to be realized. Investments in women, and in policies that advance women's economic status, are more than investments in individual and family well-being. They are also investments in the economy as a whole, because women's potential for contributing to economic growth and prosperity is enormous. A wide variety of policy solutions aimed at fostering economic equity in the 21st century could harness that potential and push America forward into a new era of economic prosperity.

Stronger Protections against
Wage Discrimination

The Lilly Ledbetter Fair Pay Act reversed the recent Supreme Court decision in *Ledbetter v. Goodyear Tire & Rubber Co.,* ensuring that workers – all workers who are discriminated against, not just women – have 180 days from the most recent instance of discrimination to file a complaint. The Ledbetter Act was an important victory for workers' rights, but it simply restores anti-discrimination legislation to where it stood prior to the Supreme Court's creation of the Ledbetter standard. Additional protections against discrimination are necessary for closing the gender pay gap, and the Paycheck Fairness Act would do just that.

The Paycheck Fairness Act would update and strengthen the original Equal Pay Act. The Paycheck Fairness Act (PFA) prohibits employers from punishing employees for sharing salary information with their co-workers. It toughens the remedies provisions of the Equal Pay Act by allowing prevailing plaintiffs in gender discrimination cases to receive compensatory and punitive damages, just as prevailing plaintiffs in race and ethnicity discrimination cases currently do. By making discrimination costly, the Paycheck Fairness Act would add teeth to the Equal Pay Act and dissuade employers from discriminatory behavior. The Paycheck Fairness Act closes a number of additional loopholes in the Equal Pay Act, includes a number of new data-gathering requirements for the federal government, aimed at assisting the Equal Employment Opportunity Commission (EEOC) to identify and respond to wage discrimination claims and assisting the Department of Labor in detecting wage discrimination, and creates a competitive grant program to develop training programs for women and girls on how to negotiate compensation packages, as well as an award to recognize and promote the achievements of employers who have made strides in eliminating pay disparities.

Repeated studies have shown persistent unexplained gender pay gaps, suggesting that discriminatory practices remain a problem in today's workforce. Robbing women of the wages they are owed not only cheats those women and their families, but also cheats the economy as a whole, because those stolen dollars might otherwise have gone back into the economy in the form of women's consumer spending. Updating and strengthening legislation aimed at protecting against gender wage discrimination is a key policy for advancing economic equity and prosperity in the future.

Health Reform

The Affordable Care Act of 2010, the health care reform legislation passed by Congress and signed into law by President Obama in March 2010, has the potential to pave the way toward a more equitable, prosperous future for both women and families and for the economy as a whole. Under the status-quo health insurance system, women are particularly vulnerable to being un- or under-insured.[65] Women are more vulnerable to high health care costs than men, both because women's health care needs differ from men's and because women are more economically vulnerable than men. The inability of the status-quo system to serve women's health care needs has come at great expense. Over half of all medical bankruptcies impact a woman. And the economy as a whole suffers, too – women's chronic disease costs hundreds of billions of dollars each year.

Poor health care has left millions of women in poor health, and unhealthy workers are less productive than healthy workers. The job-lock created by a health insurance system tied to employers means that many women remain in sub-optimal jobs in order to maintain health insurance for themselves and their families, despite the fact that their economic value would be far greater elsewhere. These inefficiencies are part of why the health care reforms passed into law last spring are so critical, and why they must not be rolled back in future legislative sessions.

Myriad elements of the reform will be of particular help to boosting women's economic wellbeing. A ban on gender rating will put an end to discriminatory practices that charge women substantially more than similarly-situated men for the same health benefits policies. The creation of health insurance "exchanges" will expand access to health insurance coverage for the millions of women who do not have employer-based insurance, including the millions of women who work part-time and are therefore less likely to have access to an employer-based health insurance plan. The ban on cost-sharing for well-visits and preventative medicine for all insurers participating in the exchanges will expand access to cost-effective and necessary preventative and screening services and treatments for all women. Combined, the health reform legislation provides both the economic security that comes with access to quality, affordable health insurance as well as the potential for an economic productivity boost that comes from a healthy workforce.

In order to achieve the full promise of the law's reforms, continued vigilance is necessary in order to insure that implementation goes smoothly. Policymakers would do well to monitor progress.

Work-Family Policies

The United States is a global laggard in providing adequate social supports for working families. Our nation's policies are rooted in a set of antiquated assumptions about the structure of the typical family where the father brings home the bacon and the mother cares for the home and the children. These days are long past, and it is high time that our policies catch up. The failure to do so is holding back the United States economy from fully reaching its potential, because women remain overburdened with both unremunerated care work and their critical participation in the labor market. A wide variety of policies could remedy this situation and unlock our nation's economic potential.

In a time of fragile economic recovery, and given the need for fiscal responsibility, is it appropriate to consider work-life balance policies? The answer is a resounding yes, because such policies are a proven boon to business, and therefore have the potential to grow the economy. During recessions and recoveries, the provision of flexible work arrangements provides a win-win solution for employers, as companies can cut back on labor costs, and workers looking for reduced hours are able to transition into new, more flexible work arrangements. Flexible work arrangements also boost employer productivity by improving morale, and potentially by increasing employee efficiency on the job as well.[66] Similarly, the business case for paid sick leave and paid parental leave is strong because both reduce costly turnover costs and "presenteeism." Moreover, most proposals for work-life policies are budget neutral, as they require either regulatory reforms or employer-employee contributory systems that require little from the government checkbook.

The Right to Request
a Flexible Schedule

The Working Families Flexibility Act would provide employees with the right to request a modification of work hours, schedule, or work location. It would make it illegal for employers to interfere or retaliate against employees who utilize the process. The bill is modeled on the very-successful "Work-Life Balance Campaign" begun by Tony Blair's government in the United Kingdom in 2000. The campaign provides parents with the right to request a flexible schedule, and, after just one year, about one-quarter of eligible employees –

about 800,000 parents – had successfully reduced or rearranged their work hours, with the majority of employers reporting no significant problems in complying with the legislation.[67]

The Working Families Flexibility Act would promote flexibility at a minimal cost. It simply requires that employers be open to exploring flexible work arrangements, without requiring that the employer accept the arrangements if the business will suffer. The bill would expand flexibility across a broad range of practices, including flexible work schedules, compressed workweeks, reduced-hours arrangements, and telecommuting. Enacting the legislation would be particularly useful during this period of high unemployment because it motivates both employers and employees to identify and implement win-win work arrangements that can help to save American jobs.

Paid Sick Days

The Healthy Families Act, which applies to businesses with 15 or more employees, would allow workers to earn up to 56 hours (7 days) of paid sick time – one hour for every 30 hours worked – to use to stay home and get well when they are ill, to care for a sick family member, to obtain preventative or diagnostic treatment, or to seek help if they are victims of domestic violence.

The bill would expand paid sick days to an estimated 46 million employees who currently do not earn paid sick days from their employer.[68] The ability of American employees to take time off without pay has been severely compromised by the recession because more families are now relying on a single income-earner due to rising unemployment. Most employers already provide paid sick days, so the cost of the legislation would be minimal, and it would serve to level the economic playing field across employers who currently do and do not provide paid sick days. It would be particularly valuable in the event of a pandemic, since it would reduce the spread of contagious diseases.

Stronger Parental Level Policies

The Federal Employees Paid Parental Leave Act would provide four weeks of paid leave for the birth or adoption of a child by a federal employee. Currently, the federal government provides no paid parental leave beyond the accrual of sick or vacation days. The act was recently passed by the House of Representatives. Like other flexibility initiatives, this act would be low-cost, with the Congressional Budget Office finding that it is budget-neutral, and would not affect direct spending or receipts. It also would improve morale and employee commitment to provide high levels of service at a juncture when increasing numbers of Americans need services that only the federal government provides. It will serve as an investment in our future, since parents who are provided with paid leave are more likely to make sure their children receive regular health check-ups and immunizations, and will have more time to bond with their children during a crucial stage of early childhood development. The act would make the federal government a model employer, helping to prod other employers to introduce paid leave.

The Family and Medical Leave Enhancement Act expands the Family and Medical Leave Act of 1993 (FMLA) to cover employees at establishments that employ fewer than 50 but not less than 25 employees. The bill also would extend unpaid employee leave for workers to go to parent-teacher conferences or to take their children, grandchildren or other family members to the doctor for regular medical appointments. This bill would provide FMLA coverage to 13 million employees who cannot currently take time off for their own illness or that of a family member without worrying about losing their jobs.[69] It would do so at minimal expense to either the federal government or to employers, and the absence of pay requirements would help employers to better weather the aftermath of the recession because slack demand is likely to reduce the need to hire temporary replacement labor. It would provide employees with the opportunity to better meet the needs of family members for routine or intermittent medical care – a critical need given the growing population of elderly Americans – and would promote parental involvement in their children's education, one of the surest methods for improving educational outcomes.

While the Federal Employees Paid Parental Leave Act and the FMLA Enhancement Act are important moderate steps toward providing greater access to paid leave for American families, the United States is badly in need of a comprehensive federal paid parental leave system. As the only OECD country without a national paid parental leave policy, the United States is in danger of losing its competitive edge, as other nations' working mothers are provided with far greater support and therefore are potentially in a position to pull ahead as global economic producers and consumers. The design of such a paid parental leave system could take any number for forms – for instance, creating a right to access Social Security benefits upon the birth or adoption of a child, or creating a new system modeled on the employer/worker contribution system of unemployment insurance.[70] The time has come for a serious conversation about how to move the United States forward on paid leave policies, and doing so is a necessity in order to keep pace with our global peers.

Financial Regulatory Reform

While women have made progress in joining the ranks of corporate leadership, the pace has been slow and women remain too few and far between in corporate board rooms and C-suites. The Dodd-Frank Wall Street Reform and Consumer Protection Act, signed into law earlier this year, will make a difference for women in business leadership, and it will boost women's power as consumers as well.

The establishment of Offices of Minority and Women Inclusion at each federal financial services agency has the potential to boost women's clout in the corporate world. These Offices will allow qualified minority- and women-owned securities, accounting, and legal businesses to more effectively access contracting opportunities. The promotion of diversity in financial services, including gender diversity, is powerful protection against the "too big to fail" policies that dragged the economy to the brink of collapse in 2008. Federal agencies' current contracting policies promote "too big to fail" by allowing government agencies to continue contracting with the same large firms who, in many cases, played a role in the recent financial crisis. Diversification among contractors is crucial if the government is to ensure that no one company continues to benefit from its largesse. The Dodd-Frank Act empowers these Offices to increase the participation of minority- and women-owned businesses by ensuring that they are included at all business levels. By doing so, these Offices have the potential to enhance women's power as business leaders.

The creation of the Consumer Financial Protection Bureau promises to provide a boost to women as consumers. An unregulated consumer credit industry preyed on customers by burying costly traps in the fine print, concealing true costs. These practices dragged down the economy as a whole,[71] but women have incurred particular injury. Women were 32 percent more likely than men to receive sub-prime loans, and 41 percent more likely to receive higher-cost sub-prime loans, regardless of income.[72] The Dodd-Frank Act's creation of the

Consumer Financial Protection Bureau, spearheaded by Elizabeth Warren, promises to be a watchdog on behalf of all consumers. Because of women's heightened vulnerability to predatory lending practices, this watchdog agency will be of particular utility to women. The increased transparency in lending practices has the potential to enhance women's financial savvy, thereby increasing women's potential as consumers and investors.[73]

While the Dodd-Frank Act provides the starting point for bolstering women's positions as both business leaders and smart consumers, continued vigilance is necessary in order to ensure that the full potential of these provisions is achieved. Policymakers should monitor the implementation of these provisions carefully, and insure public reporting on their progress and results.

Value the Care Economy

The undervalued care economy means that families struggle to find quality, affordable early education and child care, and this social failure places an enormous burden on the shoulders of working women. Similarly, women's unique role in providing elder care – both as paid caregivers and as unpaid family caretakers – creates economic stresses that impact both families and the nation as a whole. Investing in early education and child care programs – boosting funding for Early Head Start and Head Start, for instance, and funding universal pre-kindergarten programs – is one step toward creating a more secure set of caregiving institutions that will allow women to meet their full potential in the labor market.

Investing in the care sector of the economy is also a critical step toward women's economic empowerment. Child and elder care workers are a high-turnover, poorly paid group, and they are predominantly women.[74] High turnover means lower quality care. For children in particular, high-quality care yields phenomenal long-term economic rewards – and lower-quality care means that the United States' economy is missing out on those rewards. Boosting wages and improving job quality could serve to reduce turnover in the paid care economy, which would both improve the quality of care received and boost the economic fortunes of those employed in care professions.

The federal role in fostering improvements to the care economy could take various forms. For instance, the Department of Education (DOE) and the Department of Health and Human Services (HHS) could convene a national expert panel to address disparities in salaries between the birthto-five and the K-3 workforces with equivalent educational backgrounds, and these agencies could also use federal dollars to encourage states to address better compensation in their quality rating and improvement systems. DOE and HHS could invest federal dollars in professional development, and could incentivize states to include work environment practices that lead to effective performance and employee well-being as part of their quality rating and improvement systems.

The federal government could play a role in improving the prospects of the elder care workforce, as well. For instance, home care workers are exempted from federal overtime and minimum wage rules under the Fair Labor Standards Act (FLSA). In the recent *Coke v. Long Island Home Care* decision, the Supreme Court upheld this exemption, leaving 1.7 million home health aides without recourse.[75] Legislative action could amend the FLSA to better protect home health care workers, who provide a critical service to our nations' elderly and play a large and growing role in the American workforce, particularly in light of the aging Baby Boom cohort and projected elder care needs in the coming decades.

Consider the Impact of Tax and Entitlement
Reforms on Women

The flurry of reports from deficit-reduction commissions and chatter over reforms to the tax code have largely ignored the distributional impact of their recommendations. For instance, the President's Bi-Partisan Fiscal Commission has paid no attention to the gendered impact of cuts or changes to the Social Security program. Debates over extensions to the Bush tax cuts have not focused on this perspective, either. Yet, because of women's unique work histories and the continued double-duty they play as workers and caregivers in our economy, such a gendered perspective is imperative if we are to chart a course toward a prosperous and just future economy. Any efforts to reform Social Security or revise the tax code ought to take a careful and conscientious look at the impact on women, and should work to right the continued injustices that plague women and their families.

Conclusion

The Great Recession left a great deal of damage in its wake. Yet, as our nation works to rebuild and restore the promise of prosperity and growth, we have a tremendous opportunity to become a better version of our former selves. Doing so will require recognizing our greatest assets, understanding what's holding us back from capitalizing on those strengths, and putting in place the policies necessary to unlock our potential as a great economic power. Women's role in the economy is central to that economic renaissance, so the time has come for a focus on economic gender equity in the 21st century. Doing so means investing in women, and investing in women means an investment in the economy as a whole. The nation, and America's 156 million women and girls, deserve nothing less.

PART II – COMPENDIUM OF JEC REPORTS AND HEARINGS FROM THE 111TH CONGRESS:

A. Women in the Economy Today

Women and the Economy 2010:
25 Years of Progress but Challenges Remain

A Report by the Joint Economic Committee Representative
Carolyn B. Maloney,
Chair Senator

Charles E. Schumer,
Vice Chair

August 2010

Introduction

On August 26, 2010, Americans will celebrate the 90th anniversary of the ratification of the 19th amendment, which granted women the right to vote and led to their increased participation in our political system. In 1984, Geraldine Ferraro shattered the political glass ceiling by becoming the first woman nominated to a national ticket and ushered in a new era of political leadership for women. Over the last quarter century, women have become a powerful political force, both as voters and as elected leaders. Did that political benchmark have implications for women's economic well-being? Data compiled by the Joint Economic Committee suggest that the answer is yes.

Twenty-five years ago, America was recovering from the double-dip recession of the 1980s, and women's role in the labor force was beginning a multi-decade-long period of expansion. Today, as our nation's economy continues down the road to recovery from the Great Recession, women are poised to be the engine of future economic growth. Women comprise half of all U.S. workers, and well over half of all American women are in the labor force. Women's educational attainment outstrips that of men, and women's share of union membership is growing rapidly. Families are increasingly dependent on working wives' incomes in order to make ends meet.

Despite a quarter-century of progress, however, challenges remain. While the pay gap has narrowed over the last 25 years, the average full-time working woman earns only 80 cents for every dollar earned by the average full-time working man. Certain industries remain heavily gender-segregated. In addition, millions of women are struggling to juggle work outside the home with family care-giving responsibilities.

This report, which includes annual data from 1984 through 2009, provides a comprehensive overview of women's economic progress over the last twenty-five years and highlights the additional work left to be done. The role of women in the American economy is of indisputable importance. The future of the American economy depends on women's work, both inside and outside the home.

Women are a Critically Important Part of the Labor Force

o   In the last 25 years, women's labor force participation has grown sharply. In 1984, 53.6 percent of women were in the labor market. By 2009, that number had grown to 59.2 percent. All of the growth in women's labor force participation occurred prior to 2000. In contrast, over that same period, men's labor force participation rates were falling. Since the late 1990s, women's labor force participation rates have remained roughly flat while men's labor force participation has continued to decline. (See Figure 1.)

o   Women's share of payroll employment has grown over the last 25 years. In 1984, women comprised just 44 percent of payroll employment. In 2009, women comprised nearly half (49.8 percent) of payroll employment. The recent gender parity in payroll employment is most likely explained by the disparate impact of the Great Recession on industries, such as construction and manufacturing, which employ greater concentrations of men than women. (See Figures 2 and 3.)

o   The number of women in the workforce has grown by 44.2 percent over the last 25 years, from 46 million in 1984 to 66 million in 2009. Yet the distribution of those working women's work schedules has remained remarkably constant: about one-quarter work part-time, while the remaining three-quarters work full-time. (See Figure 4.)

o   Progress toward gender parity by industry has been varied over the last 25 years. In 1984, women made up 50 percent or more of the workforce in three industries: government, education and health services, and financial activities. By 2009, women made up 50 percent or more of the workforce in 5 industries: government, leisure and hospitality, education and health services, financial activities, and other services. In some industries, little progress has been made. For instance, women comprised just over 13 percent of those employed in construction in 2009, compared to 12 percent in 1984. And in some industries, women have lost ground.

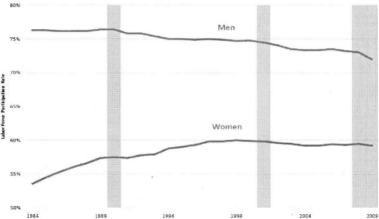

Sourse: Bureau of Labor Statistics, Current Population Survey. Recessions as dated by the National Bureau of Economic Research are shaded gray.

Figure 1. Labor Force Participation Rates, 1984-2009.

Sourse: Bureau of Labor Statistics, Current Employment Survey. Recessions as dated by the National Bureau of Economic Research are shaded gray.

Figure 2. Non-farm Payroll Employment, 1984-2009.

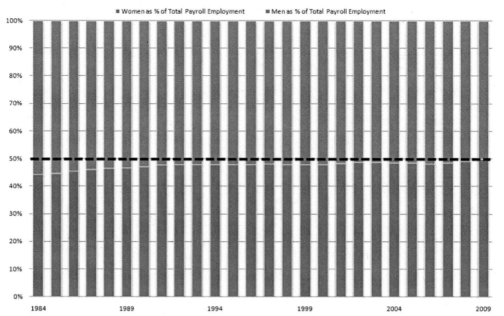

Source: Bureau of Labor Statistics, Current Employment Statistics. Payroll employment refers to non-farm payrolls.

Figure 3. Share of Payroll Employment by Gender, 1984-2009.

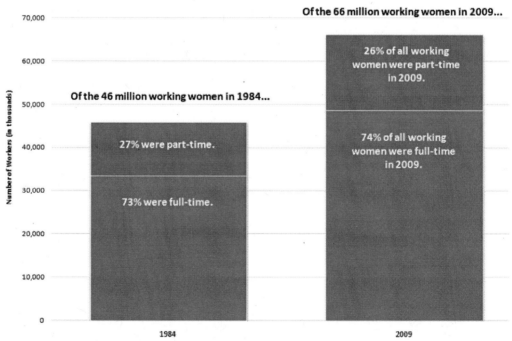

Source: Bureau of Labor Statistics, Current Population Survey.

Figrue 4. Women at work,1984-2009.

While women comprised 49 percent of those employed in the information industry in 1984, they made up just 42 percent of the industry in 2009. Similarly, in 1984 women comprised 32 percent of the manufacturing industry. In 2009, women were just 29 percent of the manufacturing workforce. (See Figure 5.)

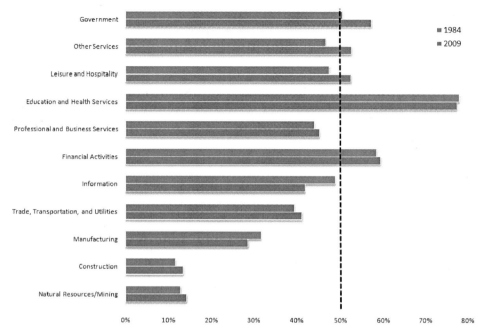

Sourse: Bureau of Labor Statistics, Current Employment Statistics.

Figure 5. Women's share of Total Employment, by Industry, 1984 and 2009.

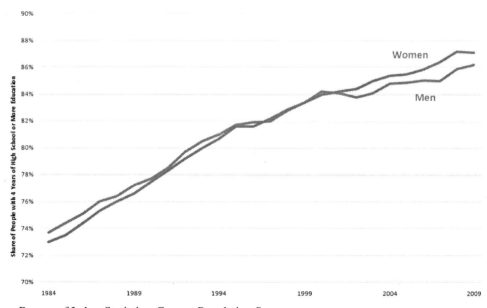

Sourse: Bureau of Labor Statistics, Current Population Survey.

Figure 6. Educational Attainment, 1984-2009.

o Women's educational attainment has edged out men's in the last twenty-five years. In 2009, 87 percent of women had at least four years of high school or more education, as compared to 86 percent of men. In contrast, in 1984, 74 percent of men and 73 percent of women had at least four years of high school or more education. (See Figure 6.)

o While total union membership has declined over the last twenty-five years, women's union membership has been on the rise. In 1984, women made up just over one-third (34 percent) of all union members. In 2008, women comprised 45 percent of all union members. The growing importance of women in the labor movement is likely due to the expansion of female-concentrated sectors such as health care, education, and the service sector combined with the contraction of male-concentrated sectors such as manufacturing. (See Figure 7.)

o While the pay gap between men's and women's wages has decreased sharply over the last 25 years, it remains remarkably high. In 1984, the average full-time weekly wage for women was just 68 percent of men's full-time weekly wage. In 2009, the average full-time weekly wage for women was 80 percent of men's full-time weekly wage. (See Figure 8.)

Families Depend on Women's Earnings
o Wives' earnings play an increasingly important role in families' incomes. In 1983, wives' incomes comprised just 29 percent of total family income. By 2008, wives' incomes comprised 36 percent of total family income. (See Figure 9.)

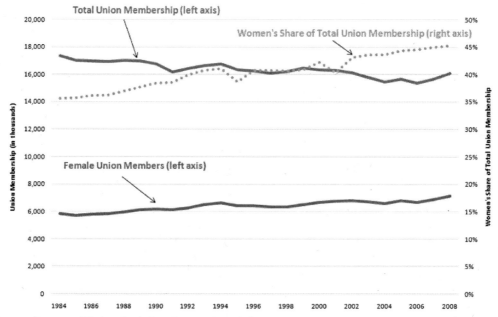

Sourse: Bureau of Labor Statistics, Current Population Survey.

Figure 7. Union Affiliation, 1983-2008.

Sourse: Bureau of Labor Statistics, Current Employment Statistics.

Figure 8. The Earnings Gap, 1984-2009.

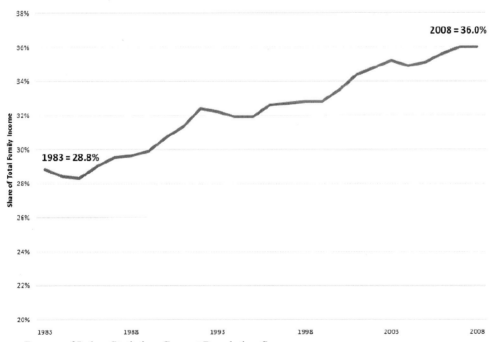

Sourse: Bureau of Labor Statistics, Current Population Survey.

Figure 9. Wives' Earnings as a Share of Total Family Income, 1983-2008.

o   Families need a working wife in order to see their incomes grow. Between 1983 and 2008, married couples with a working wife enjoyed average annual income growth of 1.12 percent per year. In contrast, married couples with a stay-at-home wife saw their average annual incomes decrease by 0.22 percent per year. (See Figure 10.)

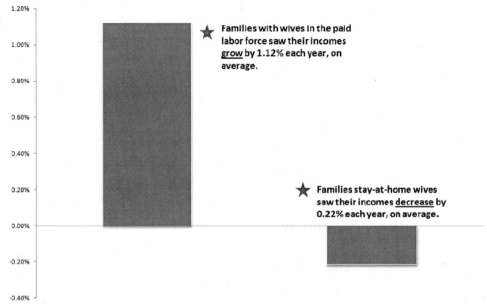

Source: Joint Economic Committee Majority Staff calculations based on the Current population Survey.

Figure 10. Avarage Annual Income Growth for Married Families, 1983-2008.

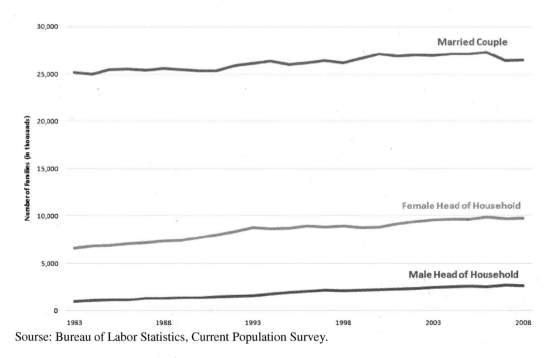

Sourse: Bureau of Labor Statistics, Current Population Survey.

Figure 11. Families with Dependent Children Age 18 or Less, 1983-2008.

Working Women Have Significant Care-Giving
Responsibilities at Home

   o   Female heads of household for families with children ages 18 and under comprise an increasing share of all families with children. In 1983, 20 percent of all families with children (or 6.6 million families) were female-headed households. By 2009, 25 percent of all families with children (9.8 million families) were female-headed households. The increase in female-headed households was sharpest during the second half of the 1980s and in the early 2000s. (See Figures 11 and 12.)

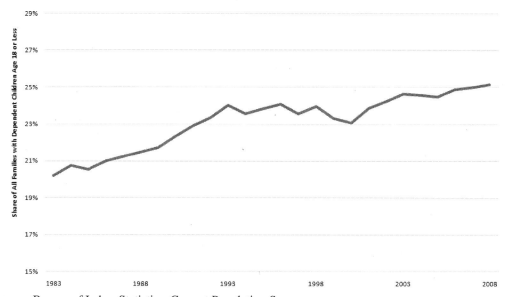

Sourse: Bureau of Labor Statistics, Current Population Survey.

Figure 12. Female Heads of household as Share of All Families with Children, 1983-2008.

   o   Mothers' labor force participation rose over the last 25 years. While mothers with young children are less likely to work than are mothers of older children, both groups' labor force participation rates have increased over time. In 1984, 52 percent of mothers with children under the age of 6 and 68 percent of mothers with children ages 6-17 were in the labor force. In 2008, 64 percent of mothers with children under the age of 6 and 78 percent of mothers with children ages 6-17 were in the labor force. (See Figure 13.)

   o   .Amongst employed mothers with children under the age of 18, over a third (34 percent) were their families' sole breadwinners in 2009. Two-thirds (66 percent) of working women with children were in dual-earner households. (See Figure 14.)

   o   Child care costs place a significant burden on families, particularly the working poor and the middle class. Child care for an infant costs a two-parent family living at the federal poverty line nearly 50 percent of their annual income, while a family living at 200 percent of the federal poverty line spends nearly 25 percent of their annual income on child care for an infant. While costs are somewhat lower for an older child, the burden on working families remains heavy. (See Figure 15.)

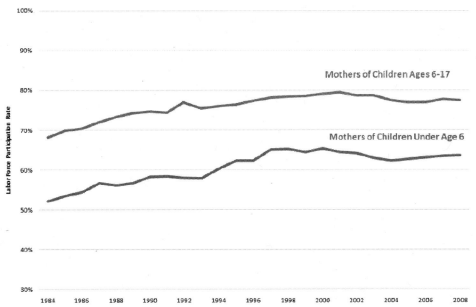

Sourse: Bureau of Labor Statistics, Current Population Survey March Supplement.

Figure 13. Mothers' Labor Force Participation Rates, 1984-2008.

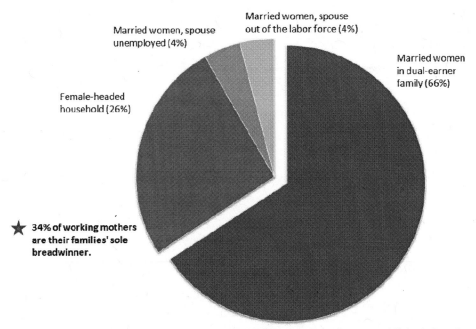

Source: Joint Economic Committee Majority Staff Calculations based on unpublished data from the bureau of Labor Statistics, Current Population Survey.

Figure 14. Employed Mothers with Children under 18 Years Old, 2009.

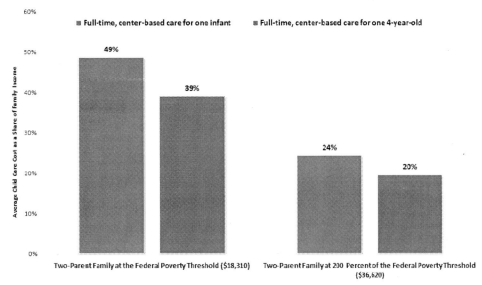

Source: National Association of Child Care Resource and Referral Agencies.

Figure 15. Child Care Costs as a Share of Family Income, 2009.

Easing the Squeeze on Women and their Families
A Report by the Joint Economic Committee Representative
Carolyn B. Maloney,
Chair

Senator Charles E. Schumer,
Vice Chair

May 21, 2009

Democrats inherited one of the worst economic crises in our nation's history, a crisis that is putting put extraordinary stress on millions of American families struggling to pay the bills and invest in their children's futures. The strain on women and their families is compounded by a continuing gender pay gap. The road to recovery will be long, but Congress has worked quickly with the Obama Administration to ease the pressure on working families by advancing an economic policy agenda aimed at restoring broad-based growth, reducing the high costs of health care, improving retirement security, and increasing prosperity for all Americans.

The Bush Legacy: The Squeeze
on Women and their Families

1. Falling Incomes, Rising Expenses.

- Median annual income for female-headed families fell $1,492 to $25,897 between 2000 and 2007, the most recent year for which data is available. For all families, median annual income in 2007 was $52,153.
- The average family health insurance premium increased by nearly 58 percent between 2000 and 2008, to $12,527.
- The average cost of college tuition at a four-year public university increased by 47 percent between 2000 and 2007.
- The average cost of full-time childcare for one child in 2008 was $6,094.

2. Disappearing Jobs.
- 1.5 million jobs held by women have vanished since the recession began in December 2007.
- Nearly 5 million women are unemployed, an increase of 70 percent since December 2007.
- The unemployment rate for women 20 years and older has increased to 7.1 percent, and to 10.0 percent for women maintaining families, which is 1.1 percentage points higher than the national average of 8.9 percent in April 2009.

3. One-Third of Single Mothers Living in Poverty.
- Nationwide, 3.6 million families headed by single mothers (33 percent of all female-headed households with children) lived below the poverty line in 2007.
- 43 percent of children living in female-headed households lived below the poverty line, compared to the national child poverty rate of 18 percent. 7.6 million children in female-headed households were poor in 2007, an increase of 20 percent since 2000.

4. Nearly 3 Million More Uninsured Women Since 2000.
- 21 million women (14 percent) had no health insurance in 2007, the most recent year of available data. 22 percent of single mothers had no health insurance.
- 14 percent of children under the age of 18 living in female-headed households had no health insurance in 2007.

5. Skyrocketing Debt.
- Women were forced to rely heavily on debt financing in order to pay their bills in the face of grim earnings and employment prospects since 2000. Average total debt amongst female headed-households shot up by 59 percent (from $28,000 to $44,300) between 2001 and 2007, the most recent year of available data.
- During the sub-prime boom – despite having higher credit scores on average – female home-buyers were 32 percent more likely than males to receive a high cost subprime mortgage loan. The Joint Economic Committee estimates that the number of subprime foreclosures for 2009 will be 830,000, with female homeowners bearing a disproportionate burden.
- Average credit card debt for female-headed households grew by 35 percent, from $1,523 to $2,058 between 2001 and 2007. Variable interest rates and other credit card practices mean that female-headed households are diverting an increasing share

of their incomes toward servicing their credit card debt, which puts a further strain on family finances.

- Average education-related debt for female-headed households doubled between 2001 and 2007, from $1,631 to $2,532, as families struggled to keep up with rising college tuition costs.

Easing the Squeeze on Women and their Families

While the problems are enormous, the 111th Congress and the Obama Administration have worked swiftly to chart a course toward a stronger economic future. The American Recovery and Reinvestment Act is designed to turn our economy around, and it includes many provisions that will put money in women's pockets today and help them invest in their futures. In addition, the FY2010 budget provides a blueprint for a policy agenda that invests in the economic well-being of women and their families.

1. Closing the wage gap.
- With the passage of the Lilly Ledbetter Fair Pay Act, Democrats restored the rights of women and other workers to challenge unfair pay—to help close the wage gap where women earn 78 cents for every $1 a man earns in America.

2. Putting money in the pockets of those who need it most.
- The Making Work Pay Tax Credit, an extended Child Tax Credit and an expanded Earned Income Tax Credit are already putting money in the wallets of working mothers and their families. A refundable Child Tax Credit and expanded saver's credit will provide a boost to millions saving for their families' futures.

3. Protecting the most vulnerable.
- The Recovery Act will help protect the health of low income families by helping states avoid cuts in Medicaid enrollment and services, and boosting funding for food stamps, WIC, and food bank programs that serve as critical sources of healthy food for struggling families across the country.

4. Investing in America's future through job training and education.
- Congress and the Administration have committed substantial funding towards job training in high-growth sectors, including "green jobs," expanded Trade Adjustment Assistance expansion to cover training programs for workers displaced from the service sector, and created a State Fiscal Stabilization Fund to help prevent teacher layoffs and cuts in other key service.

5. Making college affordable.
- The American Opportunity Tax Credit and increased Pell Grants are making college more affordable for millions more women, and the FY2010 Budget proposes an expansion of the Federal Perkins loan program and a new College Access and Completion Fund.

6. Helping families stay in their homes.

- Stabilizing the housing market is central to restoring the American economy, and Democrats have worked quickly to put in place policies that will ease the burden on working families. The Helping Families Save Their Homes Act of 2009 will provide lenders and homeowners with key tools and incentives to modify unfair loans and to avoid foreclosures. Coupled with the Administration's actions to help families refinance into lower interest rate loans if they have mortgages issued or guaranteed by Fannie Mae and Freddie Mac and owe more on their houses than their current value, this critical piece of legislation will halt the steep decline in home prices and keep the dream of homeownership alive for millions of American families.

7. Making child care affordable.

- The Recovery Act funded Child Care and Development Block Grants that support quality child care services for low-income families, additional funding for Head Start and Early Head Start over the next two years.

8. Making quality health care coverage affordable.

- With the reauthorization of the Children's Health Insurance Program, the Democrats expanded children's access to health insurance, and the FY2010 Budget includes a budget-neutral reserve fund that will facilitate the passage of health insurance reform that achieves America's shared goals of constraining costs, expanding access, and improving quality.

Sources: U.S. Census Bureau; Kaiser Family Foundation; National Association of Child Care Resource & Referral Agencies; College Board; Bureau of Labor Statistics; Consumer Federation of America; JEC calculations from the Survey of Consumer Finances, the Mortgage Bankers Association's National Delinquency Survey, the Bureau of Labor Statistics, and Global Insight.

Women in the Recession: Mothers and Families Hit Hard

A Report by the Joint Economic Committee Representative
Carolyn B. Maloney,
Chair

Senator Charles E. Schumer,
Vice Chair

May 28, 2009

Executive Summary

Working women have received pink slips in growing numbers over the course of the current recession, which began in December 2007. For the first 3 months of the recession, when job losses were relatively light, women actually gained rather than lost jobs. This uptick in women's employment is similar to what has happened in previous recessions. However, in August 2008, this recession began to look quite different from past downturns. Women's job losses picked up pace to become a significant fraction of the total monthly job losses.

As women's job losses have accelerated, so have the job losses for working mothers. A Joint Economic Committee analysis of published and unpublished data collected by the Bureau of Labor Statistics (BLS) finds that increases in unemployment during this recession have been especially steep for female heads of household – mothers who are solely responsible for maintaining their families' economic security. Key findings of the analysis include the following:

- In 2008, seven out of ten mothers with children under 18 years old were in the labor force. Over half of all mothers usually worked full time last year.
- As of April 2009, nearly one million working-age female heads of household wanted a job but could not find one.
- One out of every ten women maintaining a family is unemployed, which exceeds the highest rate (9.0 percent) experienced during the 2001 recession and the "jobless recovery" that followed.
- The ranks of female heads of household who are unemployed or "marginally attached" to the labor force has grown across all demographic groups, with women of color faring the worst. Black and Hispanic women in this group are currently experiencing unemployment at rates of 13.3 per-cent and 11.0 percent, respectively.

The American Recovery and Reinvestment Act (ARRA) will temper the effects of the current recession for these families right now and over time. Extended unemployment benefits, nutrition assistance programs, preserving Medicaid benefits and tax cuts will bring immediate relief for these families. In addition, ARRA invests in job creation in education, healthcare, and child care that tend to disproportionately employ women. This will help to ensure that female-headed households will not be left behind in the recovery.

Vast Majority of Mothers in the Labor Force,
Most Work Full-Time

Women's increased vulnerability to the business cycle has significant implications for family economic well-being.[1] Most children grow up in families with working parents, regardless of whether they live in dual- or single-parent families. Today, many families no longer have an additional worker to enter the labor force when times are tough, making rising unemployment among women a worrisome trend.

On average, in 2008, seven out of ten (71.4 percent) mothers with children under 18 years old were in the labor force.[2] The remaining 29 percent were not in the labor force and were usually not counted in official unemployment statistics. Over half of all mothers worked full time during 2008. An additional 16 percent worked part time, while 4 percent of all mothers were unemployed. (See Figure 1.) Of those employed mothers, about one-third were the sole breadwinners for the families – either because they were the head of the household or, for married women, be-cause their spouses were unemployed or out of the labor force. (See Figure 2.) Among those in the labor force, the unemployment rate for mothers with children under 18 years old averaged 5.6 percent in 2008, a full percentage point higher than in 2007.

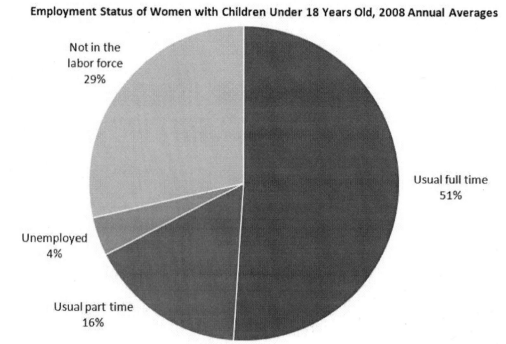

Source: JEC calculations based on data from the Bureau of Labor Statistics, Current Population Survey.

Figure 1. Over Half of All Mothers Worked Full Time Last Year.

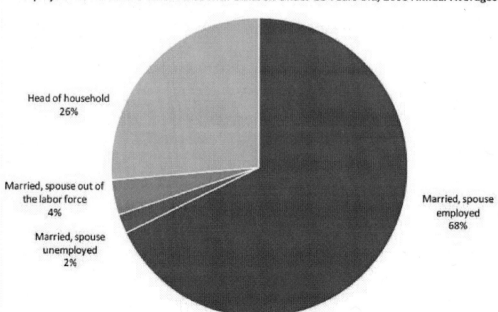

Source: JEC calculations based on data from the Bureau of Labor Statistics, Current Population Survey.

Figure 2. Nearly One-Third of Working Moms Are their Families' sole Earner.

As Recession Continues, Working Mothers Face
Rising Unemployment

Working women have received pink slips in growing numbers over the course of the current recession. For the first 3 months of the recession, when job losses were relatively light, unlike men, women actually gained jobs.[3] This uptick in women's employment is similar to what has happened in previous recessions. However, in August 2008, this recession began to look quite different from past downturns as women's job losses picked up pace to become a significant fraction of the total monthly job losses. On average, one-third of jobs lost were held by women during the past eight months.

Increases in unemployment during this recession have been especially steep for female heads of household, who are solely responsible for maintaining their families' economic security.[4] Among female heads of household, the unemployment rate rose 3.1 percentage points between December 2007 and April 2009, compared to an increase of 2.7 percentage points for all women 16 years and older (not seasonally adjusted).

During the current recession, the number of working-age (ages 25-54) female heads of household who are either unemployed or "marginally attached" to the labor force has increased dramatically. Marginally attached workers are those that are not counted as part of the labor force, even though they want a job, are available for work, and have searched for a job in the past 12 months.

Unlike those counted as unemployed, marginally attached workers have not searched for work in the preceding 4 weeks. (See Figure 3.) The increase in the number of marginally attached female heads of household has occurred across all demographic groups. Given that a female head of household is the sole breadwinner for her family, the growing rate of marginal labor force attachment among this group is particularly troublesome.

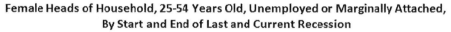

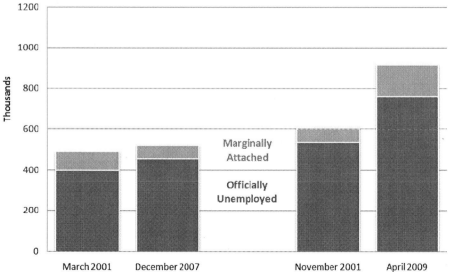

Source: JEC calculations based on unpublished tables from the Bureau of Labor Statistics, Current Population Survey.

Figure 3. Nearly 1 Million Women Maintaining Families Want a Job.

Nearly one million working age female heads of household wanted a job but could not find one as of April 2009, 16 months into the recession.[5] These included 761,000 unemployed working-age heads of household, 304,000 more than at the start of the recession, and an additional 154,000 "marginally attached," 92,000 more than at the start of the recession.[6]

The unemployment rate today for all female heads of households is 10.0 percent, which exceeds the highest rate (9.0 percent) experienced during the 2001 recession and the "jobless recovery" that followed. Because employment for female heads of household never regained strength during the jobless recovery of the 2000s, this group entered the current recession with a relatively high unemployment rate as compared to the rest of the population.[7] (See Figure 4.) In December 2007, the overall civilian unemployment rate was 4.9 percent[8] while the rate for female heads of household was 6.9 percent.[9]

Comparing the current recession to the 2001 recession shows how much more severe this recession is for female heads of household. While the unemployment rates were similar at the start of the recession, the duration of the current recession is taking a heavy toll. Over the past 12 months, the unemployment rate among all female heads of household has steadily climbed by 3.2 percentage points, to its current level of 10.0 percent. One out of every ten women maintaining a family is unemployed.[10] (See Figure 4.)

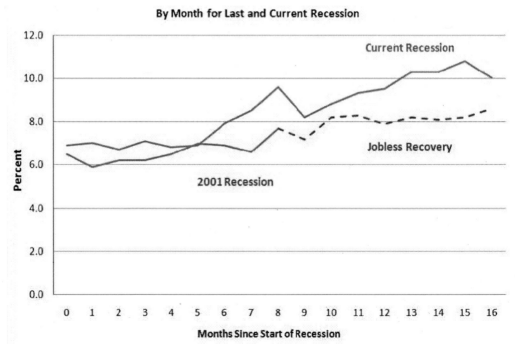

By Month for Last and Current Recession

Source: JEC calculations based on non-seasonally adjusted data from unpublished tables from the
Bureau of Labor Statistics, Current Population Survey.

Figure 4. Unemployment Rate among All Female Heads of Household.

Women of Color Are Faring the Worst in this Recession

White women, including white female heads of household, have fared somewhat better than women of color. In both recessions these households experienced a fairly steady, although high, rate of unemployment. (See Figure 5.) But the current recession now has this group facing an unemployment rate of 8.7 percent, 3.1 percentages points higher than one year ago and considerably higher than at any point during the 2001 recession.[11]

Black female heads of household started both recessions with an unemployment rate just under 10 percent, well above the average for all female heads of household.[12] (See Figure 6.) At first, their experience in the labor market during this recession was comparable to their experience in the 2001 recession. However, as the current recession intensified, the gap widened between the unemployment rates in the current recession and in the jobless recovery following the 2001 recession. The unemployment rate for black female heads of household is currently 3.7 percentage points higher than it was one year ago, suggesting that the employment situation for these women is quite difficult.

Hispanic female heads of household started this recession with a lower unemployment rate than in 2001. (See Figure 7.) Over the past 12 months, the unemployment rate for Hispanic female heads of household has increased 4.0 percentage points.[13]

Summary

The American Recovery and Reinvestment Act (ARRA) will temper the effects of the current recession for these families right now and over time. Extended unemployment benefits, nutrition assistance programs, preserving Medicaid benefits and tax cuts will bring immediate relief for these families. In addition, ARRA invests in job creation in education, healthcare, and child care that tend to disproportionately employ women. This will help to ensure that female-headed households will not be left behind in the recovery.

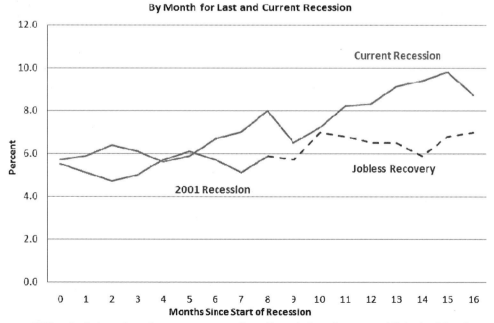

Source: JEC calculations based on non-seasonally adjusted data from unpublished tables from the Bureau of Labor Statistics, Current Population Survey.

Figure 5. Unemployment Rate among White Female Heads of Household.

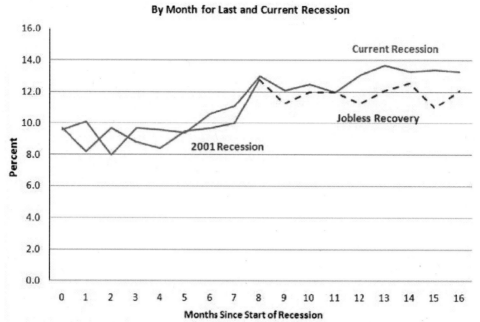

Source: JEC calculations based on non-seasonally adjusted data from unpublished tables from the
Bureau of Labor Statistics, Current Population Survey.

Figure 6. Unemployment Rate among Black Fermale Heads of Household.

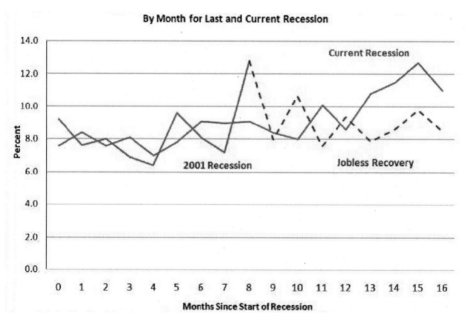

Source: JEC calculations based on non-seasonally adjusted data from unpublished tables from the
Bureau of Labor Statistics, Current Population Survey.

Figure 7. Unemployment Rate among Hispanic Female Heads of Household.

Understanding the Economy:
Working Mothers
in the Great Recession
A Report by the Joint Economic Committee Representative
Carolyn B. Maloney,
Chair

May 2010

An Update
on Working Moms

The Great Recession has taken a huge toll on working families. The vast majority of jobs lost were lost by men, but a substantial number of jobs were lost by women during this recession. From December 2007 to April 2010, women lost 46 jobs for every 100 jobs lost by men.[1] By comparison, during the 2001 recession, women lost 17 jobs for every 100 lost by men and women lost less than 2 jobs for every 100 jobs lost by men during the 1990s recession. Indeed, in recent months, women lost jobs while men gained jobs.[2] From October 2009 to March 2010, women lost 22,000 jobs while men gained 260,000.[3] Women's increased vulnerability to the business cycle has important repercussions for families' economic security. This report provides an updated look at the employment situation of working mothers[4] with children under 18 years old, and examines the impact of the recession on their participation in the labor market using unpublished data from the Bureau of Labor Statistics.[5]

Families Depend
on Mothers' Employment

Over the past several decades, women have played a role of growing importance in the labor force. It is clear that in the wake of the Great Recession, families continue to rely upon mothers' employment. Rather than opting out of the labor force, mothers increased their labor force participation over the recession. The share of mothers working or actively searching for work increased from 71.0 percent to 71.4 percent between 2007 and 2009.[6]

During that time, mothers' participation shifted away from full-time work to unemployment and part-time work, with the share of all mothers working full-time dropping to 48.3 percent in 2009 from 51.3 percent in 2007. (See Figure 1.) The share of all mothers working part-time rose almost a full percentage point to 17.2 percent, while the share of unemployed mothers increased 2.6 percentage points to 5.9 percent.

Of the 21.7 million mothers who were usually employed in 2009, two-thirds were in a dual-earner family. But the remaining one-third—7.5 million mothers—were the sole job-holders in their family, either because their spouse was unemployed or out of the labor force, or because they were heads of household. (See Figure 2.)

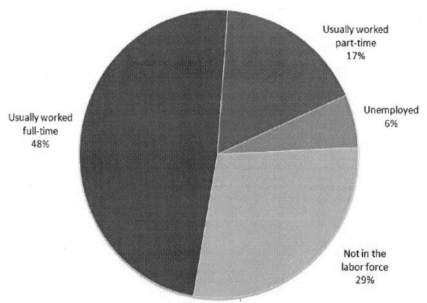

Source: Joint Economic Committee Majority Staff calculations based on unpublished data from the
    Bureau of Labor Statostocs, Current Population Survey.

Figure 1. Nearly Half of the All Mothers Worked Full Time Last Year.

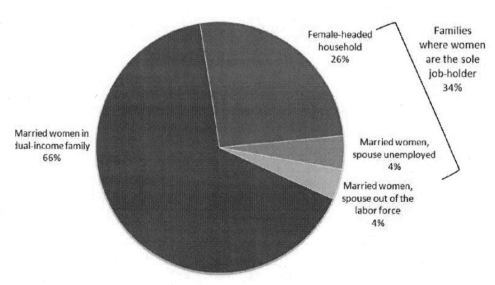

Source: Joint Economic Committee Majority Staff calculations based on unpublished data from the
    Bureau of Labor Statostocs, Current Population Survey.

Figure 2. One-in-Three Working Mothers Was the Only Jobholder in Her Family.

Married Mothers Search for Work to Improve their Families' Economic Security

Until recently, job losses were concentrated in male-dominated industries like construction and manufacturing, so fathers were more likely to lose a job and mothers were more likely to hold onto their employment or quickly find a new job. As job losses slowed in the final months of 2009, women continued to lose jobs as men found employment.

In order to cope with the widespread job losses during the recession, many parents who were previously out of the labor force entered the workforce, presumably to compensate for a spouse's lost wages. In general, mothers are far more likely than fathers to be out of the labor force, thus the movement of parents into the labor market largely reflects that of mothers. In 2007, 35.2 percent of two-parent families had only one employed parent, compared to 36.8 percent in 2009. That 1.6 percentage point net difference masks more dramatic changes in the share of families solely dependent on a mother's earnings. In fact, families where the mother was the only jobholder rose 2.5 percentage points from 4.9 percent of married-couple families to 7.4 percent. More than ever, families depend on mothers' work.

Many married mothers who looked for employment in order to bolster their families' economic security found it difficult to find work because of the severe shortage of jobs. The labor force participation rate rose for married mothers between 2007 and 2009, meaning that more married mothers were searching for a job. However, the employment-to-population ratio—the so called 'employment rate'—fell over the recession from 66.7 percent to 65.5 percent, indicating that fewer married mothers actually had a job. The unemployment rate nearly doubled to 5.8 percent during that time—a clear sign that mothers wanting work struggled to find a job.

Single Mothers Continue to Struggle with High Unemployment

Families headed by single mothers had no second parent to fall back on in the face of job loss or reduced hours and earnings. Labor force participation was already higher among these women, with over three-quarters (76.5 percent) of women maintaining families working or actively searching for work in 2007. Consequently, the recession did not boost their participation rate. Instead, the participation rate of mothers maintaining families dropped to 75.8 percent indicating that many single mothers dropped out of the labor force probably because they were unable to find work.

For single mothers in the labor force, unemployment increased dramatically during the recession. Between 2007 and 2009, the unemployment rate of single mothers increased from 8.0 percent to 13.6 percent. Single mothers of children under the age of 6 who are not yet in school had an unemployment rate of 17.5 percent in 2009. For these mothers, even searching for work can be a challenge because they may have to find child care in order to go on an interview, and high costs of child care eat away a substantial chunk of their earnings once they do find a job.

The Part-Time Penalty Can Be Even Greater for Mothers

Many women have been unable to find full-time employment because of the weak labor market. In 2009, 3.3 million women worked part-time for economic reasons, meaning that either their hours had been cut back or that they searched for full-time work but could only a part-time job.

Some of those part-time workers usually worked part-time but would have preferred to move to full-time work, likely because of economic hardship such as a spouse's job loss.

Part-time workers face a severe earnings penalty, with a wage equal to as little as 60 percent of the wage for full-time workers in the same occupation. (See Figure 3.) Part-time work also means lower earnings over time, and part-time jobs usually do not come with the same health benefits, paid time-off for vacation and sick leave, or pension benefits that full-time workers receive.[7]

Over one-third (35 percent, or 6.2 million) of all women working part-time in 2009 were mothers. For many of those, including 2.7 million mothers with children less than 6 years old and not yet in school, working a part-time job also means finding part-time child care. The part-time earnings penalty is even more devastating for those mothers because part-time child care can be just as costly as full-time care.[8]

Conclusion

Families depend on women's earnings. Mothers' work is vital not only for their families' economic security, but also for the strength of the American economy as a whole. Understanding and addressing the impact of the Great Recession on mothers is a crucial piece of the economic recovery.

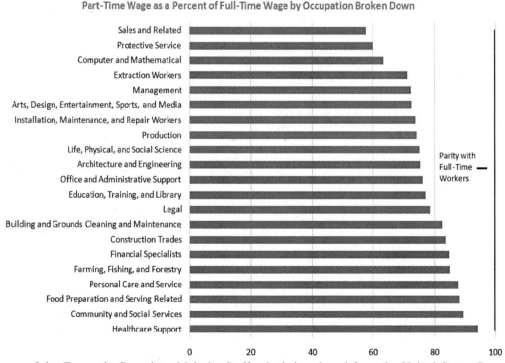

Source: Joint Economic Committee Majority Staff calculations based from the United States Census Bureau.

Figure 3. Part-Time Workers Are Subject to a Wage Penalty.

B. Equal Pay

Testimony of Lisa M. Maatz
Director Public Policy and Government Relations
American Association of University
Women before the United States

Joint Economic Committee Hearing on
"Equal Pay for Equal Work? New Evidence on the Persistence of the Gender Pay Gap"

April 28, 2009

"Chairwoman Maloney and members of the Committee, thank you for the opportunity to testify today on the critical issue of pay equity.

I am the Director of Public Policy and Government Relations at the American Association of University Women. Founded in 1881, AAUW has approximately 100,000 members and 1300 branches nationwide. AAUW has a proud 127-year history of breaking through barriers for women and girls, releasing its first report on pay equity in 1913. Today, AAUW continues its mission through education, research, and advocacy.

I am particularly pleased to be here to talk about pay equity, not simply because today is Equal Pay Day, but also because AAUW believes it's critical these tough economic times aren't used as an excuse to roll back the hard fought gains women have made. Instead, policy makers need to ensure that women workers – *all* workers – don't just survive the downturn but continue the march toward fair pay and workplace opportunity. Empowering women is one investment that always pays long-term dividends, not only for the women themselves but their families and the entire nation as well.

As the recession continues, women are increasingly becoming the sole breadwinners of their families – making pay equity not just a matter of fairness but the key to families making ends meet. The American Recovery and Reinvestment Act, signed into law in February, is intended to save or create 3.5 million jobs over the next two years. According to a White House report, an estimated 42 percent of the jobs created – nearly 1.5 million – are likely to go to women.[1] The recovery package clearly is counting on women to play a leading role in the nation's economic recovery, and their ability to do so is strengthened considerably when women's paychecks are a fair reflection of their work. In fact, this is just one of the reasons why new legislation strengthening pay equity laws is not only necessary but timely, amounting to an "equity" economic stimulus.

I am also pleased to share findings from AAUW's research report, *Behind the Pay Gap*. Our report provides reliable evidence that sex discrimination in the workplace continues to be a problem for women, including young college-educated women. I will also discuss pending legislation that we believe could make real progress in closing the pay gap between men and women, as well as how the wage gap generally affects women – especially mothers.

The Wage Gap Persists
According to the U.S. Census Bureau and Bureau of Labor Statistics, women who work full time earn about 78 cents for every dollar men earn.[2] Because of the wage gap, since 1960,

the real median earnings of women have fallen short by more than half a million dollars compared to men.[3] Minority women face a larger wage gap. Compared to white men, African American women make 67 cents on the dollar (African American men make 78 cents); Hispanic women make about 58 cents (Hispanic men make almost 66 cents).[4]

In addition, wage discrimination lowers total lifetime earnings, thereby reducing women's benefits from Social Security and pension plans and inhibiting their ability to save not only for retirement but for other lifetime goals such as buying a home and paying for a college education. New research calculates that the pay inequity shortfall in women's earnings is about $210,000 over a 35-year working life.[5]

Origins of the Wage Gap

One partial explanation for the wage gap is occupational segregation. According to AAUW research, women are still pigeonholed in "pink-collar" jobs that tend to depress their wages. AAUW's 2003 report, *Women at Work,* found that women are still concentrated in traditionally female-dominated professions, especially the health and education industries. The highest proportion of women with a college education work in traditionally female occupations: primary and secondary school teachers (8.7 percent) and registered nurses (6.9 percent).[6]

A 12-state analysis based on data from the Department of Education found that women tend to be overwhelmingly clustered in low-wage, low-skill fields. For example, women constitute 98 percent of students in the cosmetology industry, 87 percent in the child care industry, and 86 percent in the health aide industry. In high-wage, high-skill fields, women fall well below the 25 percent threshold to qualify as a "nontraditional field." For example, women account for 10 percent in the construction and repair industry, 9 percent of students in the automotive industry, 6 percent in the electrician industry, and 6 percent in the plumbing industry.[7]

Women's achievements in higher education during the past three decades are considered to be partly responsible for narrowing the wage gap.[8] But at every education level, women continue to earn less than similarly educated men. Educational gains have not yet translated into full equity for women in the workplace.

The AAUW Report:
Behind the Pay Gap

In our report, *Behind the Pay Gap,* AAUW found that just one year after college graduation, women earn only 80 percent of what their male counterparts earn. Even women who make the same choices as men in terms of major and occupation earn less than their male counterparts. Ten years after graduation, women fall further behind, earning only 69 percent of what men earn. After controlling for factors known to affect earnings, a portion of these pay gaps remains unexplained and is likely due to discrimination.

The study is based on nationally representative surveys conducted by the Department of Education. AAUW's research uses the Baccalaureate and Beyond Longitudinal Study, a nationally representative data set of college graduates produced by the Department of Education. This data set is unique because it is designed to follow bachelor's degree recipients as they navigate the workplace, graduate school and other life changes such as having a family. The research examines two sets of college graduates: men and women who graduated in 1999-2000, and men and women who graduated in 1992-93; we also limited our analysis to those who earned their first bachelor's degree at age 35 or younger.

The 1999-2000 graduates were chosen because they were the most recent graduates interviewed in the year after graduation. By looking at earnings just one year out of college, we believe you have as level a playing field as possible. These employees don't have a lot of work experience and, for the most part, don't have caregiving obligations, so you'd expect there to be very little difference in the wages of men and women. The 1992-1993 graduates were chosen so that we could analyze earnings ten years after graduation.

The pay gap can only be partially explained by differences in personal choices. Despite some gains, many majors remain strongly dominated by one gender. Female students are concentrated in majors that are associated with lower earnings, such as education, health, and psychology. Male students dominate the higher-paying majors: engineering, mathematics, physical sciences, and business. Both women and men who majored in "male-dominated" majors earn more than those who majored in "female-dominated" or "mixed-gender" majors.

The choice of major is not the full story, however, as a pay gap between recently graduated women and men is found in nearly every field and in every occupation. Women full-time workers earn less than men full-time workers in nearly every major, although the size of the gap varies. In education, a female-dominated major and occupation, women earn 95 percent as much as their male colleagues earn. In biology, a mixed-gender field, women earn only 75 percent as much as men earn, just one year after graduation.

The kinds of jobs that women and men accept also account for a portion of the pay gap. While the choice of major is related to occupation, the relationship is not strict. For example, some mathematics majors teach, while others work in business or computer science. It is important to bear in mind that such choices themselves can be constrained in part by biased assumptions regarding appropriate career paths for men and women. Other differences in type of jobs also affect earnings. For example, women are more likely than men to work in the nonprofit and public sectors, where wages are typically lower than in the for-profit sector.

AAUW's analysis showed that men and women's different choices can explain only some of the pay gap. After controlling for factors like major, occupation, industry, sector, hours worked, workplace flexibility, experience, educational attainment, enrollment status, GPA, institution selectivity, age, race/ethnicity, region, marital status and children, a five percent difference in the earnings of male and female college graduates is unexplained. It is reasonable to assume that this difference is the product of discrimination.

Discrimination is difficult to measure directly. It is illegal, and furthermore, most people don't recognize discriminatory behavior in themselves or others. This research asked a basic but important question: If a woman made the same choices as a man, would she earn the same pay? The answer is no.

Ten years after graduation, the pay gap widens. AAUW's analysis found that, ten years after graduation, the pay gap widened – so much so that female full-time workers earned only 69 percent of what their male peers earned.

Ten years out, the pay gap within occupations also increased. For example, in engineering and architecture, where wages were at parity one year out of college, we now see that women earn only 93 percent of what their male counterparts earn. In business and management, the pay gap widens, with women earning 69 percent of men's wages, compared to 81 percent one year out. Strikingly, women did not make gains in any fields compared to their male counterparts.

Similar to what we saw one year out of college, this pay gap can only partially be explained as a result of women's characteristics and choices. In terms of occupation, women and men remained segregated in the workforce over time, and the difference in earnings among occupations grew over this time period. Women also continued to be much more likely to work in the lower-paying non-profit sector. Among full-time workers, women reported working fewer hours than men, and their employment and experience continuity also differed from men. These choices were associated with wage penalties.

It is important to note that what we are calling women's "choices" are often constrained and need to be looked at in context. When women earn less most couples are likely to prioritize the higher-earning husband's well-being and career path in relation to child care, choice of residence, and other household decisions. When women are married, this trade-off may be worthwhile; however, nearly one half of women did not live with a husband in 2005.[9] While most women marry at some point, most also spend a large part of their lives on their own. Women are also much more likely than men to be single parents.[10] Therefore the presumption of the presence of a higher earning mate is often a false one. It is important for us to remember that lower pay for women means fewer resources for their children today and women's retirement tomorrow.

Women are investing in higher education, but not receiving the same salaries as men. Choices made in college affect earnings ten years later. College selectivity matters for men and women, but gender differences were more pronounced. Strikingly, a woman who earned a degree from a highly selective institution had lower earnings than men with degrees from highly selective institutions or moderately selective schools, and about the same pay as a man who attended a minimally selective college. Both women and men invest a great deal of financial resources in their college educations, and often graduate with substantial student loans. AAUW's research suggests that a woman's investment in attending a highly selective school – which is typically more expensive – does not pay off for her in the same way it does for her male counterparts.[11] Further, because of the pay gap, women often have a harder time paying off their student loans.

Ten years out, the unexplained portion of the pay gap widens. AAUW's analysis showed that while choices mattered, they explained even less of the pay gap ten years after graduation. Controlling for a similar set of factors, we found that ten years after graduation, a 12 percent difference in the earnings of male and female college graduates is unexplained and attributable only to gender.

The pay gap among full-time workers understates the lifetime difference in the earnings of women and men. The impact of personal choices such as parenting has profoundly different effects on men and women. Ten years after graduation, 23 percent of mothers in this sample were out of the work force, and 17 percent worked part-time. Among fathers, only 1 percent were out of the work force, and only 2 percent worked part-time. Stay-at home dads in this study appear to be a rare breed. We know that most mothers return to the workforce, and hence it is reasonable to assume that the pay gap between men and women will widen as mothers return to full-time employment, driving down average earnings for women.

Interestingly, motherhood is not the driving factor behind the wage gap among women working full-time ten years after graduation.[12] That is, mothers who were in the workforce full-time did not earn less than other women also working full-time, controlling for other factors such as occupation and major.

The Search for Solutions to the Pay Gap

First, it must be publicly recognized as a serious problem. Too often, both women and men dismiss the pay gap as simply a matter of differing personal choices. While choices about college major and jobs can make a difference, individuals cannot simply avoid the pay gap by making different choices. Even women who make the same occupational choices as men will not end up with the same earnings. If "too many" women make the same occupational choice, resulting in job segregation, earnings can be expected to decline.

Women's progress throughout the past 30 years attests to the possibility of change. Before the Equal Pay Act of 1963, Title IX of the Education Amendments of 1972, Title VII of the Civil Rights Act of 1964, and the Pregnancy Discrimination Act of 1978, employers could – and did – refuse to hire women for occupations deemed "unsuitable," fire women when they became pregnant, openly pay differently based on sex, or limit women's work schedules simply because they were female. Schools could – and did – set quotas for the number of women admitted or refuse women admission altogether. In the decades since these civil rights laws were enacted, women have made remarkable progress in fields such as law, medicine, and business. Thirty years ago the pay gap was attributed to the notion that women's education and skills just didn't "measure up." If that was ever the case, it certainly isn't true now.

Unfortunately, women's educational gains – ironically likely motivated in part by women's desire for economic security[13] – have *not* translated into equal pay for women in the workforce. In fact, while a college degree does absolutely increase women's earnings, the pay gap remains larger for college graduates than the population as a whole.[14]

AAUW's research report provides strong evidence that sex discrimination still exists in the workplace and that this discrimination is not disappearing on its own. It's clear that existing laws have failed to end the inequities that women face in the workplace. AAUW believes we must take stronger steps to address this critical issue. While enactment of the Lilly Ledbetter Fair Pay Act was a critical first step, restoring the ability of working women to have their day in court to combat wage discrimination, additional legislation is needed to truly make real progress on pay equity.

The Paycheck Fairness Act

AAUW applauds Congress and the Obama Administration for moving quickly to pass the Ledbetter Fair Pay Act. However, the Ledbetter bill is only a down payment on the real change needed to close the pay gap. The next critical step is for the Senate to pass the Paycheck Fairness Act (S. 182/H.R. 12); the House already passed the measure in January 2009 by an even stronger vote (256-163) than the Ledbetter bill (247-171).

Passing both bills is critical to the overall goal of achieving pay equity for all. The Lilly Ledbetter Fair Pay Act amended Title VII of the Civil Rights Act of 1964 and righted the wrongs done by the Supreme Court, regaining ground we'd lost. Ledbetter was a narrow fix that simply returned legal practices and EEOC policies to what they were the day before the *Ledbetter* decision was issued in 2007 – nothing more, nothing less. The Paycheck Fairness Act is a much needed update of the 45-year-old Equal Pay Act, closing longstanding loopholes and strengthening incentives to prevent pay discrimination. Together, these bills can help to create a climate where wage discrimination is not tolerated, and give the administration the enforcement tools it needs to make real progress on pay equity.

Background on the Equal
Pay Act of 1963

This law requires that men and women be given equal pay for equal work in the same place of business or establishment. The jobs do not have to be identical, but they must be substantially equal. It is job content – *not* job titles – that determines whether jobs are substantially equal. Pay differentials are permitted only when they are based on seniority, merit, quantity or quality of production, or a factor other than sex. It is important to note that when correcting a pay differential, no employee's pay may be reduced. Instead, the pay of the lower paid employee(s) must be increased. While laudable in its goals, the Equal Pay Act of 1963 has never lived up to its promise to provide "equal pay for equal work."

What Will the Paycheck
Fairness Act Do?

The Paycheck Fairness Act is a comprehensive bill that strengthens the Equal Pay Act by taking meaningful steps to create incentives for employers to follow the law, empower women to negotiate for equal pay, and strengthen federal outreach and enforcement efforts. The bill would also deter wage discrimination by strengthening penalties for equal pay violations, and by prohibiting retaliation against workers who inquire about employers' wage practices or disclose their own wages. The Paycheck Fairness Act would:

- *Close a loophole in affirmative defenses for employers*: The legislation clarifies acceptable reasons for differences in pay by requiring employers to demonstrate that wage gaps between men and women doing the same work have a business justification and are truly a result of factors other than sex.
- *Fix the "Establishment" Requirement:* The bill would clarify the establishment provision under the Equal Pay Act, which would allow for reasonable comparisons between employees within clearly defined geographical areas to determine fair wages. This provision is based on a similar plan successfully used in the state of Illinois.
- *Prohibit Employer Retaliation:* The legislation would deter wage discrimination by prohibiting retaliation against workers who inquire about employers' wage practices or disclose their own wages (NOTE: employees with access to colleagues' wage information in the course of their work, such as human resources employees, may still be prohibited from sharing that information.) This non-retaliation provision would have been particularly helpful to Lilly Ledbetter, because Goodyear prohibited employees from discussing or sharing their wages. This policy delayed her discovery of the discrimination against her by more than a decade.
- *Improve Equal Pay Remedies:* The bill would deter wage discrimination by strengthening penalties for equal pay violations by providing women with a fair option to proceed in an opt-out class action suit under the Equal Pay Act, and allowing women to receive punitive and compensatory damages for pay discrimination. The bill's measured approach levels the playing field by ensuring that women can obtain the same remedies as those subject to discrimination on the basis of race or national origin.

Increase Training, Research and Education: The legislation would authorize additional training for Equal Employment Opportunity Commission staff to better identify and handle wage disputes. It would also aid in the efficient and effective enforcement of federal anti-pay discrimination laws by requiring the EEOC to develop regulations directing employers to collect wage data, reported by the race, sex, and national origin of employees. The bill would also require the U.S. Department of Labor to reinstate activities that promote equal pay, such as: directing educational programs, providing technical assistance to employers, recognizing businesses that address the wage gap, and conducting and promoting research about pay disparities between men and women.

- Establish Salary Negotiation Skills Training: The bill would create a competitive grant program to develop salary negotiation training for women and girls.
- Improve Collection of Pay Information: The bill would also reinstate the Equal Opportunity Survey, to enable targeting of the Labor Department's enforcement efforts by requiring all federal contractors to submit data on employment practices such as hiring, promotions, terminations and pay. This survey was developed over two decades and three presidential administrations, was first used in 2000, but was rescinded by the Department of Labor in 2006.

The Paycheck Fairness Act maintains the protections currently provided to small businesses under the Equal Pay Act, and updates its remedies and protections using familiar principles and concepts from other civil rights laws. These new provisions are not onerous and are well-known to employers, the legal community, and the courts. As a result, the legislation will enhance women's civil rights protections while simultaneously protecting the job-creating capacity of small businesses. That's why – in addition to AAUW and almost 300 other organizations – groups such as Business and Professional Women/USA and the U.S. Women's Chamber of Commerce support the Paycheck Fairness Act.

Despite Progress, the Pay Gap Remains

Despite the progress that women have made, pay equity still remains out of reach and partly unexplained. Even government economists say that a portion of the pay gap remains a mystery even after adjusting for women's life choices. Skeptics like to claim that there is no real pay gap – that somehow it's all a product of our imaginations. Worse, these critics prefer to blame women for any pay disparities, saying that the pay gap is due to the "choices" that women make. But excuses are excuses, and facts are facts.

Women are working harder than ever to balance the roles of work and family. They've developed and supported successful legislation that has opened doors and helped to keep them in the workforce while they raise their children. When women don't earn equal pay, they're not the only ones to suffer – their families do, too. In these days when two incomes are needed to make ends meet, and where female-headed households are so much more likely to be poor, it is disturbing how maternal profiling is used to undercut women's wages because of their caregiving roles. It is also ironic and short sighted in a nation that needs women's labor to be competitive in a global economy.

One popular argument is that motherhood (and the choices it engenders) – rather than discrimination – is the real culprit behind the pay gap. If that's the case, than we have much larger problems than the pay gap to deal with. If that's true, than this country – including its policy makers – needs to take a long, hard look at why the marketplace punishes women for being mothers – or as AAUW's research has showed, for simply their potential to be mothers – while fatherhood carries no financial risk when it comes to wages and may in fact carry financial benefits.

Here's the bottom line: There's a pay gap that most economists agree can't be explained away completely by women's choices – no matter how convenient, no matter how comfortable, no matter how much easier it would be for the critics if they could do so. And we ignore it at our peril.

AAUW plans to continue to take an active role in challenging the persistent inequity in women's paychecks, by unmasking the real root causes of the issue, relying on facts over inflated rhetoric, and by urging the creation of more workplaces that are supportive of all employees with family responsibilities, regardless of gender. We also, quite strongly, urge the Senate to join the House and pass the Paycheck Fairness Act.

Collectively, women have demonstrated that they have the skills and the intelligence to do any job. Women have also shown they can do these jobs while minding the home front and raising the next generation. No one is disputing that women have made significant gains in education and labor force participation. In fact, AAUW revels in them and our role in making them happen. But our work is not done, and pay equity remains a pernicious problem with both daily and long term consequences. It's past time for women's paychecks to catch up with our achievements."

Testimony of Randy Albelda
Professor of Economics and Senior Research Associate,
Center for Social Policy
University of Massachusetts
Boston Boston, MA 02125 Randy.albelda@umb.edu
before the United States Joint Economic Committee Hearing
on "Equal Pay for Equal Work? New Evidence on the Persistence
of the Gender Pay Gap"

April 28, 2009

"Madam Chairwoman and members of the committee: Thank you for this opportunity to testify about the persistent wage gap between men and women. My name is Randy Albelda and I am a professor of economics and senior research associate at the Center for Social Policy at the University of Massachusetts Boston. I am a labor economist and my expertise is on women's economic status.

While there has been progress is reducing the pay gap between men and women over the last several decades, it is still the case that women, on average, make less than men. While there are some differences in what men and women "bring" to the workplace that influence levels of pay, these differences account for only a small part of the gender wage gap – the difference in men's and women's pay. Further, the differences in skill levels and experience have been narrowing over the last three decades and doing so at a faster pace than the wage gap is narrowing. *There are three enduring and intersecting reasons why women's pay is less than men's: workplace discrimination; occupational sorting; and family responsibilities.*

The Wage Gap

In the mid-1970s, the National Organization for Women issued "59¢" buttons, calling attention to the fact that year-round, full-time women workers earned 59 cents to every man's dollar. Today we could replace those with a "78¢" buttons.[1]

This graph on the following page comes from the most recent US Census Bureau's *Income, Poverty, and Health Insurance Coverage in the United States* report. It provides a nice illustration of the median annual earnings of year-round, full-time men and women workers from 1960 through 2007, adjusted for inflation. The most substantial gains were made in the 1980s, with the wage ratio of women's earnings to men's earnings narrowing from .60 in 1980 to .72 in 1990. In the 1990s, there was very little change in this ratio – moving from .72 in 1990 to .74 in 2000.[2]

Different work, different pay? No. The gender pay gap persists even after taking into account hours worked, skill levels and occupations.

As noted above, looking only at full-time year-round workers, women's *annual* median earnings are 78 percent of men's. Similarly, the median *weekly* earnings of full-time wage and salary women workers was 80 percent of men's in 2007.[3]

Women have somewhat less work time experience than men, which would explain some of the pay gap. However, it explains less and less of that gap over time and several studies have found that each year of men's experience pays off at a higher rate than an additional year of women's work experience. [4]

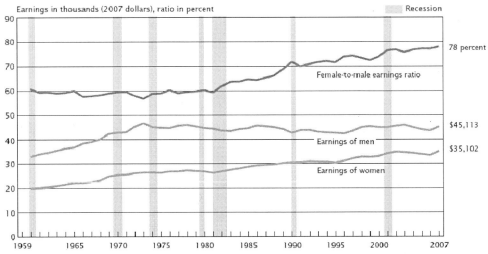

Note: Data on earings of full-time, year-round workers are not readily available before 1960. For information on recessions, see Appendix A.

Source: U.S. Census Bureau, Current population Survey, 1961 to 2008 Annual Social and Economic Supplement.

Figure 2. Female-to Male Earnings Ratio and Median Earnings of full-Time, Year-Round Workers 15 Years and older by Sex: 1960 to 2007.

Different work, different pay? No. The gender pay gap persists even after taking into account hours worked, skill levels and occupations.

As noted above, looking only at full-time year-round workers, women's *annual* median earnings are 78 percent of men's. Similarly, the median *weekly* earnings of full-time wage and salary women workers was 80 percent of men's in 2007.[3]

Women have somewhat less work time experience than men, which would explain some of the pay gap. However, it explains less and less of that gap over time and several studies have found that each year of men's experience pays off at a higher rate than an additional year of women's work experience. [4]

Women workers bring higher educational levels to the workplace than do men[5], which is one reason why "human capital" endowments explain less of the pay gap now than they did in the 1980s.[6] Still, female college graduates working full-time earned 80 percent less than male college graduates just one year out of school in 2001.[7]

Women tend to work in different types of jobs than do men. But, even when men and women work in the same fields or even the same occupations, women typically earn less than men.

- The starting salaries for women college graduates were $1,443 less than they were for men in the same fields.[8]

- Across the occupational landscape, women make less than men. The table below depicts the wage gap (using median usual weekly earnings of full-time wage and salary workers) for some detailed occupations. Of the over 100 detailed occupations with median earnings listed, there are only six in which women's earnings are higher than those of men.[9]

The Gender Wage Gap in Selected Detailed Occupations, 2006
Managerial Occupations:

Chief executives .	.72
Human resource specialists.	.81
Professional Occupations	
Lawyers	.70
Elementary and middle school teachers	.90
Service Occupations	
Security guards	.84
Home health care aides	.89
Sales and Office Occupations	
Retail salesperson	.68
Secretaries/administrative asst.	1.04
Construction occupations.	.86
Production and transportation Occupations	
Electronic assemblers	.76
Bus drivers	.80

Source: Table 18 of U.S. Department of Labor, U.S. Bureau of Labor Statistics, Women in the Labor Force: A Databook (2008 Edition).

- Francine Blau and Lawrence Kahn show that in 2004 after controlling for education, experience, occupation and industry, women earned 83.5 percent of what men did, compared to 81.6 percent without any of those adjustments. That means these factors explain less than 2 percentage points (10 percent) of the entire wage gap between men and women, leaving most of it unexplained by measurable differences between men's and women's attributes.[10]

Economists have explored the gender pay gap for many decades and produced hundreds (if not 1000s) of articles and reports to explain the reasons for the gender pay gap. No matter how sophisticated and complex their models, they *always* find that some portion of the wage gap is unexplained by the sets of variables for which they can measure differences between men's and women's education levels, work experiences, ages, occupation or industry in which they work, or region of the country they reside. Because the wage differences cannot be explained by any of the differences in workers' traits, this unexplained portion of the wage gap is attributed to gender discrimination.

- A recent meta-regression analysis that compiled the results of 49 econometric studies of the gender wage gap over the last decade found that on average, there was still a substantial gap – women earned 70 percent of what men did, after adjusting for all the various factors that help explain wage difference.[11]
- In a forthcoming study of college professors in one specific college of a large public university, researchers controlled for years experience, mobility, teaching and research productivity, and department and found that even in the identical job in the same institution women made three percent less than men.[12]

Progress toward pay equity has stalled over the last decade.

- The unexplained portion of gender gap (the part attributable to discrimination) got considerably smaller in the 1980s and hardly fell at all in the 1990s.[13]

There are three intersecting reasons why women's pay is less than men's: workplace discrimination; occupational sorting; and family responsibilities.

- *Lilly Ledbetter's experience reminds us that workplace discrimination still exists.* Routinely women are not hired at all, hired at lower wages and not promoted over equally qualified men. This shows up in economists' studies as the part of the earnings gaps that can't be attributed to anything else. In addition, using experimental approaches, economists find considerable evidence of hiring discrimination as well.[14]
- *Women are in different occupations than men.* Men are much more likely to be in construction and manufacturing jobs which pay more than female dominated jobs with comparable skill levels such as administrative assistants and retail salespersons.[15] While about one-third of all women are in professional and managerial jobs, these too are often sex segregated, with women predominating in teaching, nursing and social work jobs and men predominating in architecture,

engineering and computer occupations. Finally, women predominate in both high and low paying jobs in the "care sector" – the industries which educate our children, provide us with health services, and take care of young children, disabled adults and the elderly. There is a care work wage penalty. Careful research has shown that care workers, in part because they compete with unpaid workers at home, are not rewarded commensurately with their skills and experience.[16] This sector is large. About 20 percent of all workers work in the care sector and women comprise 75 percent of all workers.[17]

- Family responsibilities squeeze women's work time and preclude them from taking and keeping jobs that make few or no accommodations for these responsibilities. Jobs that require long hours, often pay well and provide a strong set of employer benefits, but employers also usually assume the workers in those jobs are unencumbered by household and family responsibilities. This "ideal" worker can (and often does) work overtime or just about any time an employer wants.[18] Workers with family responsibilities do not have that flexibility. Regardless of their skill levels, these workers often must work fewer hours or trade off wages for more time flexibility. Research clearly demonstrates a mothers' wage penalty. Mothers' earn less than women with the same sets of skills and are rewarded less for experience than are men or women who are not mothers. Some of this is a result of time demands and less job flexibility, but some is attributable to discrimination against workers with family responsibilities.[19]

The recession makes addressing this issue especially important because women's earnings are a vital, if not main component, of family well-being.

- One third of all households are headed by women. Of these households, one-quarter are families with children.[20] Women are almost always the only support of these households.
- One half of households have married couples.[21] If these households, 64 percent of wives are employed, compared to 48 percent in 1970. Further, wives' earnings comprise 35 percent of family income, up from 27 percent in 1970.[22]
- In this recession, more men have lost jobs than women have, since men – so far -- are disproportionately found in the hardest hit sectors.[23] As a result, even more households are more dependent on women's earnings. Unequal pay hurts these households.
- The stimulus package will help both men and women, but differently.
  o Increased funds for physical infrastructure, improved medical record keeping, and green energy investments will likely create many more jobs for men than women. Assuring access to these jobs and trade apprenticeship programs would be useful for women's employment in these male-dominated and often well-paying jobs.
  o Increased funding to the states, especially for health care and education, will help reduce the number of layoffs for more women, since they are more heavily employed in these sectors than are men. However, state budget deficits are deep and even with stimulus funds there will be large cuts to the care sector, which

will increase women's unemployment. The cuts will also put more pressure on women's unpaid work time, as their families lose needed care.

Reducing the Pay Gap

There are several things that would boost women's wages and reduce the pay gap.

Addressing Workplace Discrimination

- Ensure that our current anti-discrimination laws are enforced.
- Pass the Paycheck Fairness Act. This will strengthen penalties for discrimination and prohibit employer retaliation for workers who inquiry about wage practices.
- Pass the Employee Free Choice Act. Unions boost women's wages and improve the likelihood they will have health insurance at work.[24] Unions also provide workers structured mechanisms to pursue employer discrimination claims.

Addressing Occupational Sorting

- Increase the minimum wage since women predominate in low-wage jobs.
- Support improved wages for care workers. Care work is heavily supported by federal, state and local government funds. This is because care work has many positive spillover effects, making it a vital public good. Government funds for child care and elder care can assure that workers in these fields are compensated appropriately and have opportunities for professional development.
- Target stimulus money to assure that women are included in physical infrastructure projects.

Addressing Family Responsibility Discrimination

- Make sure that current laws that protect workers with caregiving responsibilities, such as the Family and Medical Leave Act, are enforced.
- Extend the Family and Medical Leave Act to cover more workers.
- Support the Family Leave Insurance Act of 2009 which would provide workers with 12 weeks of paid family and medical leave.
- Develop legislation that encourages employers to negotiate with employees over flexible work arrangements.

Testimony of Andrew Sherrill
Director, Education, Workforce,
and Income Security Issues
Government Accountability Office

before the United States Joint Economic Committee
Hearing on "Equal Pay for Equal Work?
New Evidence on the Persistence of the Gender Pay Gap"

April 28, 2009

Women's Pay

Converging Characteristics of Men and Women in the Federal Workforce Help Explain the Narrowing Pay Gap (GAO-09-621T)

GAO Highlights

Why GAO Did this Study

Previous research has found that, despite improvements over time, women generally earned less than men in both the general and federal workforces, even after controlling for factors that might explain differences in pay. To determine the extent to which the pay gap exists in the federal workforce, GAO addressed the following question: To what extent has the pay gap between men and women in the federal workforce changed over the past 20 years and what factors account for the gap? This testimony is based on a report that GAO is releasing today (GAO-09-279).

To answer this question, GAO used data from the Office of Personnel Management's (OPM) Central Personnel Data File (CPDF)—a database that contains salary and employment data for the majority of employees in the executive branch. GAO used these data to analyze (1) "snapshots" of the workforce as a whole at three points in time (1988, 1998, and 2007) to show changes over a 20- year period, and (2) the group, or cohort, of employees who began their federal careers in 1988 to track their pay over a 20-year period and examine the effects of breaks in service and use of unpaid leave. GAO is not making any recommendations.

OPM and the Equal Employment Opportunity Commission reviewed the report on which this statement is based. They generally agreed with our methods and findings and provided technical comments that we incorporated as appropriate.

What GAO Found

The gender pay gap—the difference between men's and women's average salaries— declined significantly in the federal workforce between 1988 and 2007. Specifically, the gap declined from 28 cents on the dollar in 1988 to 19 cents in 1998 and further to 11 cents in 2007. For the 3 years we examined, all but about 7 cents of the gap can be explained by differences in measurable factors such as the occupations of men and women and, to a lesser extent, other factors such as education levels and years of federal experience. The pay gap narrowed as men and women in the federal workforce increasingly shared similar characteristics in terms of the jobs they held, their educational attainment, and their levels of experience. For example, the professional, administrative, and clerical occupations—which accounted for 68 percent of all federal jobs in 2007—have become more integrated by gender since 1988. Some or all of the remaining 7 cent gap might be explained by factors for which we lacked data or are difficult to measure, such as work experience outside the federal government. Finally, it is important to note that this analysis neither confirms nor refutes the presence of discriminatory practices.

GAO's case study analysis of workers who entered the workforce in 1988 found that the pay gap between men and women in this group grew overall from 22 to 25 cents on the dollar between 1988 and 2007. As with the overall federal workforce, differences between men and women that can affect pay explained a significant portion of the pay gap over the 20-year period. In particular, differences in occupations explained from 11 to 19 cents of the gap over this period. In contrast, differences in breaks in federal service and use of unpaid leave explained little of the pay gap. However, the results of this analysis are not necessarily representative of other cohorts.

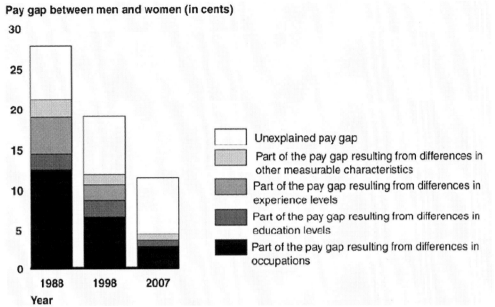

Source: GAO analysis of CPDF data.

"Chair Maloney and Members of the Committee:

I am pleased to be here today to discuss the gender pay gap in the federal workforce. Previous research shows that despite improvements over time, a pay gap remains between men and women in both the U.S. workforce as a whole and within the federal government. For example, in 2003, GAO found that women in the general workforce earned, on average, 80 cents for every dollar earned by men in 2000 when differences in work patterns, industry, occupation, marital status, and other factors were taken into account. [1] Our prior work has also made recommendations to strengthen federal agencies' enforcement of laws addressing gender pay disparities in the private sector and among federal contractors. [2] My statement is based on our report that is being released today, titled Women's Pay: Gender Pay Gap in the Federal Workforce Narrows as Differences in Occupation, Education, and Experience Diminish.[3] To prepare the report, we used data from the Office of Personnel Management's (OPM) Central Personnel Data File (CPDF)—a database that contains salary and employment-related information for the majority of civilian employees in the executive branch. [4] We used CPDF data to analyze (1) "snapshots" of the federal workforce in 1988, 1998, and 2007 to show changes in the workforce as a whole over a 20-year period; and (2) the cohort (or group) of employees who entered the federal workforce in 1988 to track differences in pay between men and women and the effects of breaks in service and unpaid leave over a 20-year period. The report includes a detailed description of our scope and methodology. We conducted our work in accordance with GAO's Quality Assurance Framework.

My statement today focuses on the following question: To what extent has the pay gap between men and women in the federal workforce changed over the past 20 years and what factors account for the gap?

In summary, we found that the pay gap—the difference between men's and women's average pay—in the federal workforce declined from 28 cents on the dollar in 1988 to 19 cents in 1998 and further to 11 cents in 2007. For each of the 3 years we examined, all but about 7 cents of the gap could be explained by differences in measurable factors between men and women, including their occupations, and, to a lesser extent, their educational levels and years of federal experience.[5] The gap diminished over time largely because men and women in the federal workforce are more alike in these characteristics than they were in past years. For the cohort of employees who entered in 1988, we found that their pay gap grew from 22 to 25 cents on the dollar by the end of the 20-year period. Again, differences between men's and women's characteristics that can affect pay, especially occupation, explained a significant portion of the pay gap. Specifically, differences in the occupations held by men and women in this group explained between 11 and 19 cents of the pay gap over the 20-year period. On the other hand, differences in breaks in federal service and use of unpaid leave explained little of the pay gap. For both analyses, factors for which we lacked data or are difficult to measure, such as experience outside the federal government, may account for some or all of the remaining pay gap that we could not explain, and this analysis neither confirms nor refutes the presence of discriminatory practices.

Background

The federal government has experienced significant changes over the past 20 years, particularly in the people it employs and the type of work its employees perform. Since 1988, the federal workforce has become increasingly concentrated in the professional and administrative fields, which typically require a college education. Conversely, the past 20 years have seen significant decreases in clerical and blue-collar occupations. While we are not certain what accounts for the decline in these occupations, possible reasons include the phasing out of many defense-related jobs after the end of the Cold War, increased use of automation, and contracting out to the private sector. Overall, the federal workforce has more education and experience than it did 20 years ago. The proportion of federal employees with a bachelor's degree or higher increased from 33 percent in 1988 to 44 percent in 2007. Similarly, the average years of federal service increased from 13 to 15 years over this period, and the proportion of employees with over 20 years of experience increased from 21 to 34 percent.

Converging Characteristics Explain Substantial
Decline in the Federal Pay
Gap between 1988 and 2007

Before accounting for differences in measurable factors, we found that the pay gap between men and women in the federal workforce declined significantly between 1988 and 2007. Specifically, for every dollar earned by men in 1988, women earned 28 cents less. This gap closed to 19 cents by 1998 and closed further to 11 cents by 2007. Using a statistical model we developed, we were able to estimate the extent to which different measurable factors contributed to the pay gap.

Besides gender, these measurable factors included work characteristics, such as occupational category, agency, and state; worker characteristics, such as education level, years of federal experience, bargaining unit status, part-time work status, and veteran status; and demographic characteristics such as age, race and ethnicity, and disability status. Our statistical results show that differences in measurable factors account for much of the gap in the years we examined. As shown in figure 1, the individual factors that contributed most to the pay gap were differences between men and women in the occupations they held, their educational levels, and their years of federal experience.

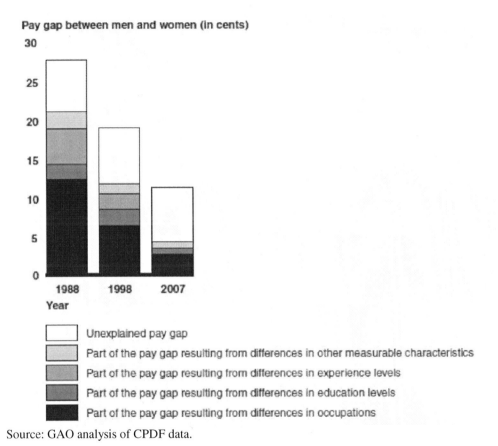

Source: GAO analysis of CPDF data.

Figure 1. Federal Workers: Proportion of the Pay Gap Explained by Differences in Measurable Factors between Men and Women and Remaining Unexplained Gap.

While occupation, education, and federal experience accounted for much of the pay gap, the convergence between men and women with respect to these factors largely explains why the gap diminished over time.

- *Occupation:* We found that the pay gap decreased in part because clerical, professional, and administrative occupational categories—which together accounted for 68 percent of federal jobs in 2007—became more integrated by gender between 1988 and 2007. In particular, changes in the government's clerical workforce explain a large reduction in the pay gap. In 1988, the clerical workforce—which accounted for 38 percent of all female federal workers—was among the lowest paid. From 1988 to 2007, the clerical workforce shrank in size by about 61 percent, and also became more integrated—i.e., the proportion of women decreased from 85 percent to 69 percent. In addition, the proportion of women in professional positions rose from 30 percent to 43 percent, and those in administrative positions rose from 38 percent to 45 percent.

- *Education:* The pay gap also decreased as men and women in the federal workforce became increasingly similar in their levels of education. In 1988, only 23 percent of women held a bachelor's degree or higher compared with 40 percent of men. By 2007, 41 percent of women held a bachelor's degree or higher, compared with 47 percent of men.

- *Federal experience:* Finally, men and women in the federal government became increasingly similar in their levels of experience. On average, men in 1988 had 14.4 years of federal experience, compared with 10.8 for women—nearly a 4-year difference. By 2007, women had slightly more experience on average with 15.5 years of federal experience compared with 15.2 for men.

In each of the 3 years we examined, our model could not account for about 7 cents of the pay gap. While we cannot be sure what accounts for this portion of the gap, it is possible that other factors for which we lacked data or are difficult to measure, such as work experience outside the federal government, could account for some of the unexplained gap. In addition, it is important to note that this analysis neither confirms nor refutes the presence of discriminatory practices.

The Pay Gap for Employees Who Joined the Federal Workforce in 1988 Grew Overall, but Breaks in Service and Unpaid Leave Contributed Little to the Gap.

The gender pay gap for workers who entered the federal workforce in 1988 grew between 1988 and 2007. Specifically, it grew from 22 cents in 1988 to a maximum of 28 cents in 1993 through 1996 and then declined to 25 cents in 2007. As with our analysis of the workforce, differences in measurable factors—especially in occupation—explained much of the pay gap in each year. For example, occupational differences explained between 11 and 19 cents of the gap over this period, due in part to more women than men holding clerical jobs, which were among the lowest paid in the federal workforce. The unexplained portion of the pay gap also grew over time, increasing from 2 cents in 1988 to 9 cents in 2007, as shown in figure 2. However, other factors not captured by our data could account for some of the unexplained pay gap.

We also found that differences in the use of unpaid leave or breaks in service did not contribute significantly to the pay gap. As shown in table 1, women in this cohort were more likely to take unpaid leave or have a break in service than men. Nonetheless, differences in the use of unpaid leave and breaks in service consistently explained less than 1 cent of the pay gap for this cohort over our study period. However, our analysis of unpaid leave was limited by the fact that we could not accurately measure the duration of the unpaid leave or determine why it was taken.

Table 1. Use of unpaid leave and breaks in service by employees in the 1988 cohort

	Women	Men
Took unpaid leave at least once between 1988 and 2007	18%	11%
Had a break in service at least once between 1988 and 2007	17%	15%

Source: GAO analysis of CPDF data.

Finally, it is important to note that this group is different from those in our analysis of the entire federal workforce in two important ways. First, this cohort includes only employees who started working for the government in 1988, so by definition, new workers did not enter this group. Therefore, any changes in the relative characteristics of men and women in the overall federal workforce resulting from an influx of new workers would not have occurred in the cohort. Additionally, because we examined only this cohort, we cannot say with any certainty whether this group is representative of other cohorts, so the findings pertaining to the cohort are not generalizable.

OPM and the Equal Employment Opportunity Commission (EEOC) reviewed our work and generally agreed with our methods and findings. OPM reviewed our methodology and found our use of the CPDF data to be appropriate. EEOC stated that our study has a solid research design and modeling analysis and will serve as an important source of information to the federal sector. They provided suggestions for clarification of our analyses and technical comments, which we incorporated as appropriate.

Madam Chair, this concludes my remarks. I would be happy to answer any questions you or other members of the committee may have."

Testimony of Andrew Sherrill, Director
Education, Workforce, and Income Security Issues
Government Accountability Office

Before the United States Joint Economic Committee
Hearing on "New Evidence on the Gender Pay Gap
for Women and Mothers in Management"

September 28, 2010

Women in Management

Female Managers' Representation, Characteristics, and Pay (GAO-10-1064T) "Chair Maloney and Members of the Committee:

I am pleased to be here today as you examine issues related to women in management. Although women's representation across the general workforce is growing, there remains a need for information about the challenges women face in advancing their careers. In 2001, using 1995 and 2000 data from the Current Population Survey, we found women were less represented in management than in the overall workforce in 4 of the 10 industries reviewed.[1] We also found differences in the characteristics and pay of male and female managers, which we explored using statistical modeling techniques. To respond to your request that we update this information to 2007, we addressed the following three questions: (1) What is the representation of women in management positions compared to their representation in nonmanagement positions by industry? (2) What are the key characteristics of women and men in management positions by industry? and (3) What is the difference in pay between women and men in full-time management positions by industry? My remarks today are based on our report, released at this hearing, *Women in Management: Analysis of Female Managers' Representation, Characteristics, and Pay.*[2]

To examine these questions, we analyzed data from the U.S. Census Bureau's American Community Survey (ACS) for the years 2000 through 2007.[3] We selected ACS rather than the Current Population Survey due to the greater number of observations in ACS. We analyzed managers across all of the broad industry categories used in ACS, representing the entire workforce, except for the agriculture and mining sectors, individuals living in group quarters, and those who were not living in a U.S. state or the District of Columbia.[4] We defined "managers" as all individuals classified under the "manager occupation" category in ACS, which includes a wide range of more than 1,000 job titles. In our multivariate analysis of the differences in pay between male and female managers working full time and year round by industry,[5] we used annual earnings as our dependent variable, adjusting for certain characteristics that were available in the dataset and are commonly used to estimate adjusted pay differences. These include age, hours worked beyond full time, race and ethnicity, state, veteran status, education level, citizenship, marital status, and presence of children in the household.[6] We assessed the reliability of the ACS generally and of critical data elements and determined that they were sufficiently reliable for our analyses. We conducted our work from February 2010 to September 2010 in accordance with all sections of GAO's Quality Assurance Framework that are relevant to our objectives. The framework requires that we plan and perform the engagement to obtain sufficient and appropriate evidence to meet our stated objectives and to discuss any limitations in our work. We believe that the information and data obtained, and the analysis conducted, provide a reasonable basis for any findings and conclusions in this product.

In summary, when looking across all industries combined from 2000 to 2007, female managers' representation and differences between female and male managers' characteristics remained largely similar. However, differences narrowed substantially in level of education and slightly in pay.

In 2007, women comprised an estimated 40 percent of managers and 49 percent of nonmanagers on average for the 13 industry sectors we analyzed—industries that comprised almost all of the nation's workforce—compared to 39 percent of managers and 49 percent of nonmanagers in 2000. In all but three industry sectors women were less than proportionately represented in management positions than in nonmanagement positions in 2007. Women were more than proportionately represented in management positions in construction and public administration, and there was no statistically significant difference between women's representation in management and nonmanagement positions for the transportation and utilities sector (see figure 1). On average for the 13 industry sectors, an estimated 14 percent of managers in 2007 were mothers—with their own children under age 18 living in the household—compared to 17 percent of nonmanagers.

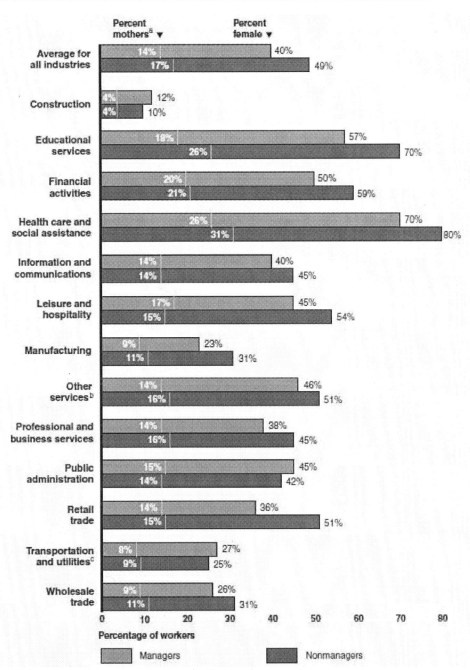

Source: GAO analysis of American Community Survey data.
[a] Mothers refers to women with their own children under age 18 living in the household.
[b] Positions included, for example, auto repair shop managers and parking lot managers.
[c] The difference in proportions of female managers and nonmanagers was not statistically significant.

Figure 1. Estimated female Representation by Industry, 2007.

According to our estimates, female managers in 2007 had less education, were younger on average, were more likely to work part-time,7 and were less likely to be married or have children, than male managers (see figure 2). While the average female married manager earned the majority of her own household's wages, her share of household wages was smaller than the share contributed by the average male married manager to his household's wages. These findings were generally similar to findings for 2000. While both male and female managers experienced increases in attainment of bachelor's degrees or higher, women's gains surpassed men's. According to our estimates, male managers with a bachelor's degree or higher increased three percentage points from 53 percent in 2000 to 56 percent in 2007, while female managers with a bachelor's degree or higher increased 6 percentage points from 45 percent in 2000 to 51 percent in 2007. Similarly, while the share of male managers with a master's degree or higher went up less than 1 percentage point from 2000 to 2007, the share of female managers with a master's degree or higher rose nearly 4 percentage points.

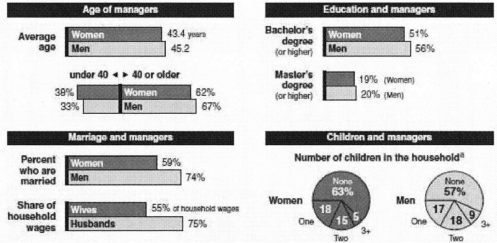

Source: GAO analysis of American Community Survey data.
[a] This refers to the number of children under age 18 living in a household with a manager.

Figure 2. Estimates for Characteristics of Managers by Gender, 2007.

The estimated difference in pay between female managers working full time and male managers working full time narrowed slightly between 2000 and 2007 after adjusting for selected factors that were available and are commonly used in examining salary levels, such as age, hours worked beyond full time, and education (see figure 3). When looking at all industry sectors together and adjusting for these factors, we estimated that female managers earned 81 cents for every dollar earned by male managers in 2007, compared to 79 cents in 2000. The estimated adjusted pay difference varied by industry sector, with female managers' earnings ranging from 78 cents to 87 cents for every dollar earned by male managers in 2007, depending on the industry sector.

Our analysis is descriptive in nature and neither confirms nor refutes the presence of discriminatory practices. Some of the unexplained differences in pay seen here could be explained by factors for which we lacked data or are difficult to measure, such as level of managerial responsibility, field of study, years of experience, or discriminatory practices, all of which are cited in the research literature as affecting earnings.

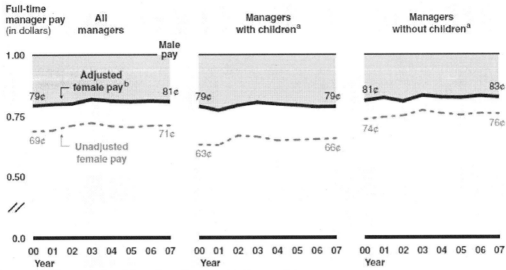

Source: GAO ananlysis of American Community Survey data.

Note: The narrowing of the gap between 2000 and 2007 for all managers and managers without children in the household was statistically significant at the 95 percent confidence level. For 2001-2007, the margins of error for pay gaps differed for any single year by no greater than plus or minus 2 cents.

[a] Children refer to children under age 18 living in a household with a manager.

[b] For this analysis, we adjusted for age, hours worked beyond full time, race and ethnicity, state, veteran status, education, industry sector, citizenship, marital status, and presence of children in the household. We adjusted for industry sector to control for the possibility that pay differences could occur because female managers tender to be employed in industries that had lower rates of pay. However, we acknowledge that the distribution of female managers by industry sector itself might reflect some level of discrimination associated with hiring, promotion, or other employer practices. For the subsequent industry-specific analysis, we adjusted for the same variables, except we excluded industry sector.

Figure 3. Estimated Pay Differences for Full-Time Managers, 2000-2007.

More detailed information on the characteristics of women in management in specific industries could help policymakers to identify possible actions to help women advance to management positions. For example, starting in 2009, the ACS included a question on field of study, a variable recognized as important in examining differences in pay and advancement. Improvements to the type of data available, such as this one, could help researchers to better understand the determinants of salary and advancement.

The Departments of Commerce and Labor provided technical comments on a draft of our report, which we incorporated as appropriate.

Madam Chair, this concludes my prepared remarks. I would be happy to answer any questions that you or the other members of the committee may have."

For further information on this testimony, please contact Andrew Sherrill at (202) 512-7215 or sherrilla@gao.gov. Contact points for our Offices of Congressional Relations and Public Affairs may be found on the last page of this statement. Individuals making key contributions to this testimony include Gretta Goodwin (Assistant Director), Kate Blumenreich, Lindsay Read, James Bennett, Susan Bernstein, Ben Bolitzer, Russ Burnett,

Heather Hahn, Anna Maria Ortiz, and Shana Wallace. Also contributing to this work were Ron Fecso, James Rebbe, and Patrina Clark. Andrew Sherrill, Director Education, Workforce, and Income Security Issues.

Testimony of Ilene H. Lang
President and Chief Executive
Officer, Catalyst, Inc.

Before the United States Joint Economic Committee Hearing on
"New Evidence on the Gender Pay Gap for Women and Mothers in Management"
September 28, 2010
Targeting Inequity: The Gender Gap in U.S. Corporate Leadership

Introduction

> "He has monopolized nearly all the profitable employments, and from those she is permitted to follow, she receives but a scanty remuneration. – The Declaration of Sentiments, Seneca Falls, NY, July 20, 1848

Generations have passed since this nation's first women's summit issued the Declaration of Sentiments, yet stark gender gaps in business leadership and pay persist. The latest data reveals leadership gaps across all *Fortune* 500 industries and a glacial rate of progress for women in business. Women constitute nearly half the total work force,[1] earn 57 percent of Bachelor's degrees, 60 percent of Master's degrees,[2] and control or influence 73 percent of the consumer decisions[3] in America. Yet among *Fortune* 500 companies, women make up less than three percent of CEOs[4] and hold roughly 15 percent of board seats.[5] And in 2009, women made up only 6.3 percent of Executive Officer top earning positions within the *Fortune* 500.[6] These inequities don't just hurt women. They harm families, employers, and the U.S. economy.

Catalyst believes that until women achieve parity in pay and business leadership, they will be marginalized in every other arena.

Founded in 1962, Catalyst is the leading nonprofit organization working globally to advance women and business. With offices in New York, Silicon Valley, Toronto, and Zug, Switzerland, we count as members more than 400 companies, firms, business schools, and associations from around the world. Our Advisory Services assesses global and regional challenges to support our members and policy makers as they build, sustain and leverage female talent in the markets in which they operate. And our research—widely considered the "gold standard" on women in corporate leadership—identifies major barriers to women's advancement and predicts the most effective strategies for creating sustainable change.

When looking at inequity in the United States, Catalyst focuses on the *Fortune* 500 because these corporations are a barometer of American corporate culture. If inequities persist in America's most powerful and influential companies, they are present in smaller businesses too. Because our Census includes the entire population of *Fortune* 500 companies, we know this is a precise count of women leaders in our nations' top 500 businesses. Our findings, cited in media around the world, reveal the challenges and opportunities for working women and their employers.

In this report, we document that the number of women in *Fortune* 500 leadership positions decreases the further up the corporate ladder one goes and how women's representation in leadership has remained flat over time, regardless of industry. We show how the *Fortune* 500 leadership gap persists even though women comprise nearly half of the U.S. labor force[1] and earn more advanced degrees than men.[8] We discuss how the low representation of women top earners underscores that women continue to be underrepresented in the highest paying positions in corporate America and how the pay gap for women begins with their very first job.

Finally, we present the correlation between women's representation in corporate leadership and corporate financial performance, the vital role women play in the United States economy, and the necessary steps to end gender inequity.

Women Lag Men in Leadership Positions
Despite Being Nearly 50 Percent
of the Labor Force.

Women are a critical part of the U.S. labor force, but according to our data, they are stuck in lower levels of management with little, if any, movement upward. If corporate America were a true meritocracy, there would be equal representation of women and men in every job level. Instead, it looks like a pyramid where women are clustered in the lower ranks and lower paying positions, and where few ascend to senior management, CEO or board positions.

Women in Fortune 500 Companies[9]

- 2.6% CEOs
- 15.2% Board Seats
- 6.3% Top Earners
- 13.5% Executive Officers
- 25.9% Senior Officers & Managers
- 39.8% Low-Mid Officers & Managers & Professionals
- 46.4% Total Employees

Women's Representation in Fortune 500 Leadership
Is Stagnant Over Time.

Progress for women in leadership has moved at a glacial pace. The percentage of women CEOs in the Fortune 500 increased by less than two-and-half percentage points over the past 14 years:

Fortune 500 Women CEOs[10]

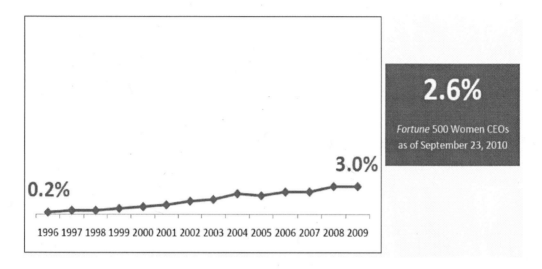

Over the past 13 years, the share of women Corporate Officers increased by less than six percentage points and has remained flat for the past four years:

Fortune 500 Corporate Officer Positions Held by Women[11]

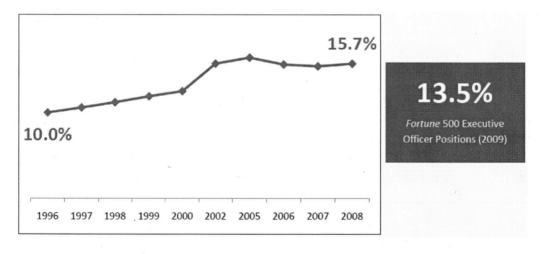

The trend line for corporate board positions has remained stagnant over the past six years, increasing only five percentage points over the past decade:

Fortune 500 Board Seats Held by Women[12]

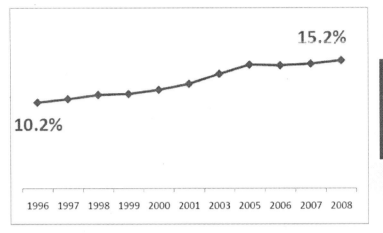

Women's Leadership Representation Has Failed to Grow Appreciably—Regardless of Industry.

Women are severely underrepresented in leadership positions across industry sectors. The percentage of women Executive Officers and board directors in *Fortune* 500 companies is stuck in the teens and single digits, while only about 26% of Senior Officers and Managers are women.

Fortune 500 Catalyst Data and EEOC Data by NAICS Industry

	Companies[23]	Employees[24]	Women						
			CEOs[25]	Directors[26]	Executive Officers[27]	Senior Officers & Managers[28]	Low-Mid Officers & Managers[28]	Professionals[30]	Total Employees[31]
Retail Trade	11.9%	38.6%	6.8%	18.2%	17.9%	29.7%	42.7%	53.0%	55.6%
Finance & Insurance	16.1%	11.8%	2.5%	16.8%	18.1%	33.3%	47.4%	50.7%	58.2%
Manufacturing-Durable Goods	19.6%	11.6%	1.0%	12.7%	9.4%	16.8%	21.0%	26.5%	26.2%
Manufacturing-Nondurable Goods	16.3%	8.9%	8.6%	16.6%	13.7%	23.5%	31.0%	42.8%	33.9%
Information	5.4%	6.6%	3.7%	14.5%	12.4%	31.9%	36.8%	36.0%	40.1%
Transportation & Warehousing	5.4%	6.0%	0.0%	10.8%	12.6%	18.8%	27.3%	18.4%	24.2%
Accommodations & Food Services	2.0%	5.3%	0.0%	18.1%	15.5%	32.4%	46.8%	50.6%	54.0%
Professional & Business Services	3.4%	2.4%	0.0%	17.6%	13.0%	28.9%	33.3%	39.6%	38.8%
Utilities	8.5%	2.2%	0.0%	16.9%	11.7%	18.5%	17.3%	30.5%	23.4%
Wholesale Trade	5.0%	1.7%	0.0%	15.7%	11.1%	22.4%	34.4%	49.1%	42.6%
Mining, Quarrying, and Oil & Gas Extraction	3.2%	0.6%	0.0%	9.0%	10.7%	12.3%	15.3%	26.7%	20.9%
Overall			3.0%	15.2%	13.5%	25.9%	37.0%	41.8%	46.4%

Women Lag Men in Fortune 500 Leadership— Including in Female-Prevalent Industries

One might expect female-prevalent industries would have high representations of women in leadership, but they do not. In fact, in the industries displayed below, the percentage of women-held board seats and corporate officer positions is not substantially different from those of other industries, except in Utilities, Mining, Quarrying, and Oil & Gas Extraction, where women's representation is much lower.

Fortune 500 Women Leaders in Female-Prevalent Industries[22]

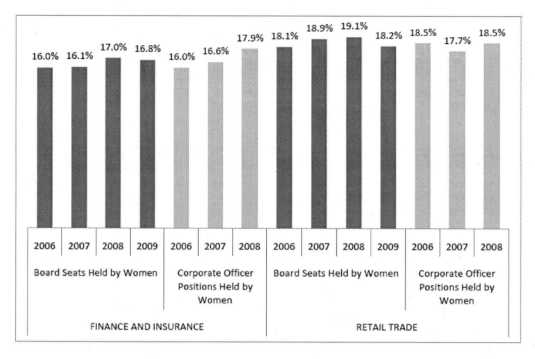

Fortune 500 Women Leaders in Male-Dominated Industries[23]

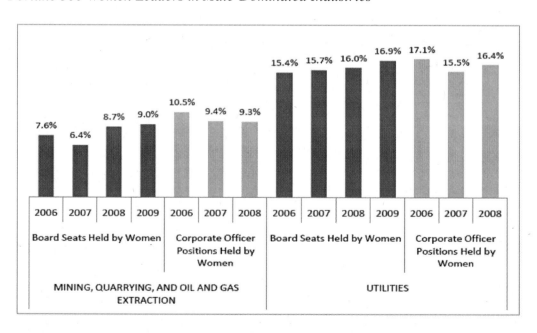

Fortune 500 Women Leaders in the Largest Industry[24]

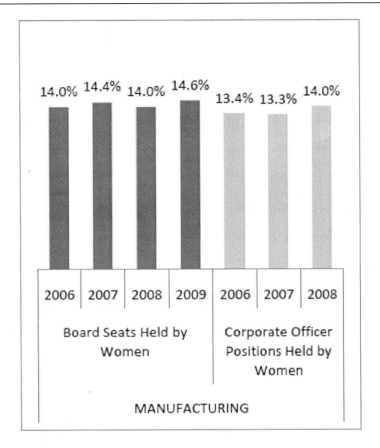

The Fortune 500 Leadership Gap Persists Despite
High Female Workforce Representation and Women
Outpace Men in Advanced Degrees

"Give it more time" is often suggested as a solution to the lack of women in business leadership. But women have been near 50% of the workforce for many years and have not advanced to leadership positions.

Women in Labor Force[25]

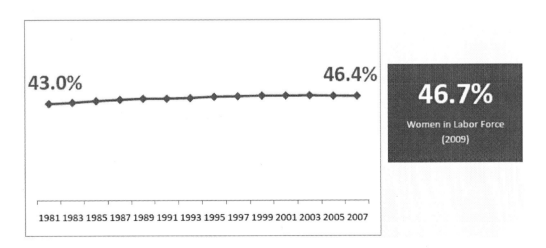

Women are not ascending into business leadership despite the fact that women have been outpacing men in earning advanced and professional degrees for many years. Women earned more B.A.s than men starting in 1981-1982:

Bachelor's Degrees Earned by Women[26]

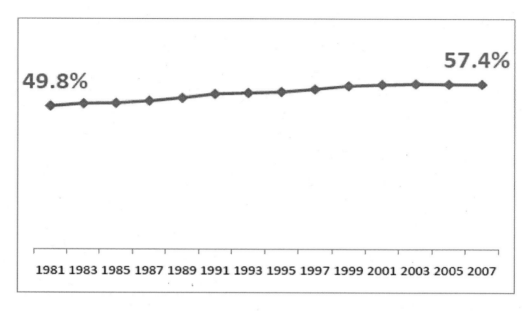

For Master's degrees, women first became the majority in 1980-1981, the figure dropped below 50 percent soon after, then passed 50 percent again in 1985-1986. It has very slowly risen since then:

Master's Degrees Earned by Women[27]

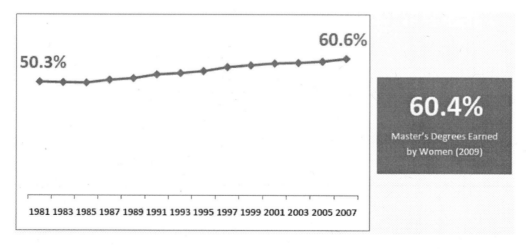

The chart below shows a snap-shot of the percent of advanced degrees earned by women. Women earn as many or more degrees than men in all categories:

Degrees Earned by Women, 2006-2007[28]

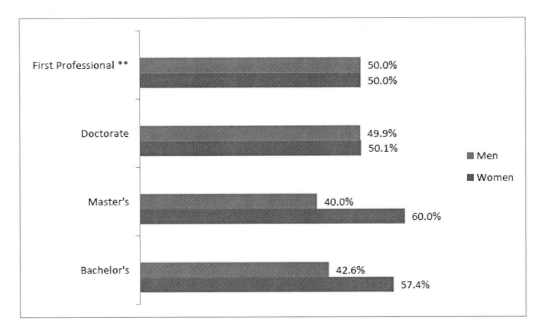

The pay gap for women at the top reflects a system that continues to perpetuate pay inequity for women in the workplace.

The low representation of women top earners underscores how women continue to be underrepresented in the highest paying positions in corporate America. Women constitute only 6.3 percent of *Fortune* 500 top earners:

Fortune 500 Top Earner Positions Held by Women[29]

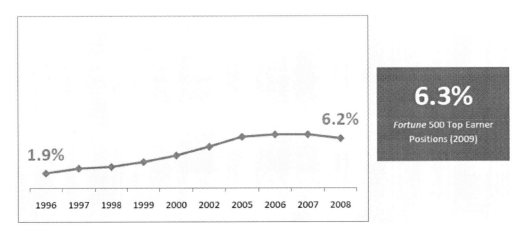

The pay gap for women begins with their very first job—and increases over time.

Women start behind, and stay behind, equally qualified men. Catalyst's report, *Pipeline's Broken Promise,* surveyed more than 4,100 women and men who earned their MBA degrees between 1996 and 2007 at 26 leading business schools, including 12 in the United States. The results accounted for, among other factors, time elapsed since earning the MBA, years of experience, industry, and region. These factors being equal, the survey found that after business school:[30]

- Women averaged $4,600 less in their initial jobs, after controlling for their job level.
- Women started at lower levels than men, even after controlling for career aspirations and parenthood status.
- Women were outpaced by men in salary growth. In fact, the gap in pay intensified as time went on, and can't be explained by career aspirations or parenthood status.
- Even if they both started at entry level, men progressed more quickly than women up the corporate ladder.
- Although women and men step off the corporate track at equal rates, women paid a greater penalty than men in position and compensation when they return.
- Men reported greater career satisfaction than women—37 percent of men said they were "very satisfied" with their overall advancement versus 30 percent of women.

Level of First Position[31]

Women in business leadership are essential to a healthy economy and to business performance.

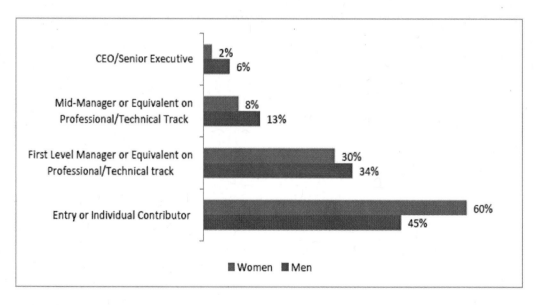

Our *Bottom Line* studies discovered that women are a critical factor in company profitability. *The Bottom Line: Connecting Corporate Performance and Gender Diversity* (2004) found that companies with the highest representation of women on their top management teams, on average, experienced better financial performance than companies with the lowest women's representation. This finding holds for both financial measures analyzed: Return on Equity (ROE), which was 35 percent higher, and Total Return to Shareholders (TRS), which was 34 percent higher.[32]

Corporate Performance and Women's Representation in Corporate Officer Positions[33]

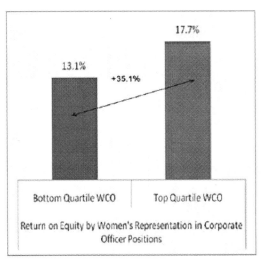 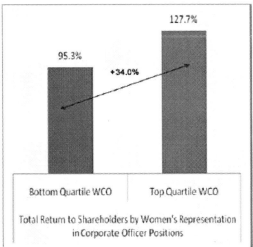

The Bottom Line: Corporate Performance and Women's Representation on Boards further linked profitability to women in leadership. We found that companies with more women board members, on average, significantly outperform those with fewer women, by 53 percent on Return on Equity, 42 percent on Return on Sales, and a whopping 66 percent of Return on Invested Capital:[34]

Corporate Performance and Women's Representation on Boards[35]

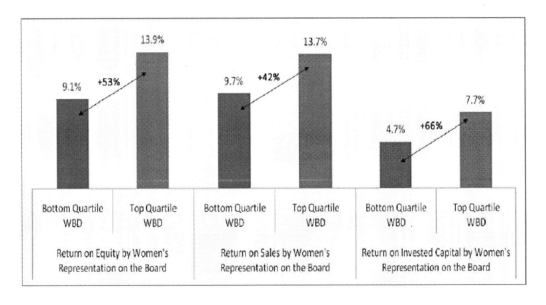

Financial Performance at Companies with Three or More Women Directors[36]

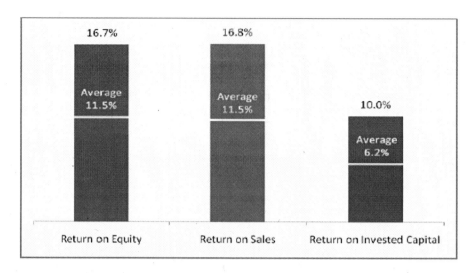

The percent of women board directors is a predictor of more women Corporate Officers.

Our report, *Advancing Women Leaders*, revealed that the percent of women in the boardroom predicts the percent of women in senior positions. This report showed that the percent of women in the boardroom impacts women in line roles more than women in staff roles.[37] As Catalyst's *Bottom Line* research has shown, high numbers of women board directors and corporate officers are correlated with increased financial performance. So increasing women's representation in the boardroom and subsequently in corporate leadership holds great promise for companies' financial results.

Percent of Women Directors Predicts Future Percent of Women Corporate Officers[38]

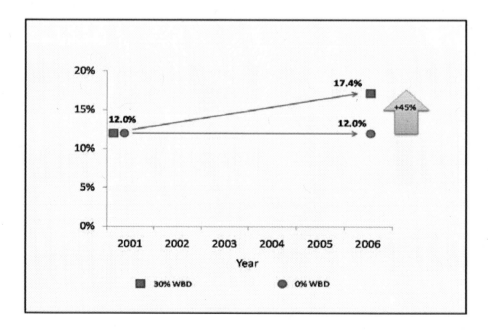

Women Directors Predict More Women Officers in Line Positions[39]

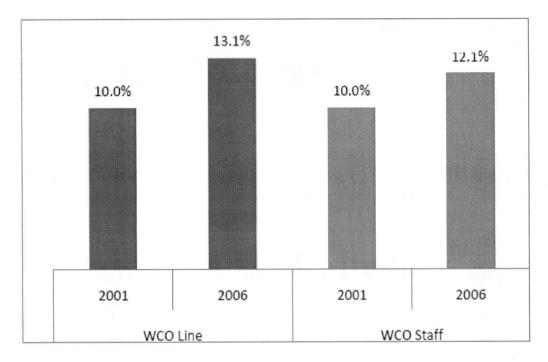

Conclusion

The gender leadership and pay gaps are alive and well.

Women lag men in *Fortune* 500 leadership positions[40]—and the rate of change per year remains flat across industries, including female-dominated sectors.[41] Women are underrepresented in the highest earning positions in *Fortune* 500 companies.[42] And the glass ceiling starts at the very first job for our most talented young women.[43]

"Giving it more time" is not the answer. These inequities persist despite the fact that for many years women have both earned more advanced degrees than men[44] and have comprised nearly 50 percent of the U.S. labor force.[45] Aggressive efforts are required to ensure that the talent pipeline fueling our nation's most powerful companies—and in effect, our economy—remains full of diverse talent. Companies that exclude women from leadership lose out on half of the talent pool. This is like playing cards with half a deck.

The Solutions Are Clear.

When top leadership understands the clear financial case for advancing women to leadership, it sets the tone throughout the organization. Yet the very systems that are put in place to develop the best talent are often fraught with unintended biases that promote only those whose leadership skills match the mostly male leadership currently in place.[46] This problem reinforces assumptions about what a successful leader looks and acts like and produces "more of the same."

Meritocracy and representation should go hand-in-hand. When an organization values women and men equally, the gender balance should be the same at the bottom, in the middle, and at the top. The fact that it isn't indicates systemic barriers that interfere with progress for half of the talent pool. This is a waste of human capital. Companies must make sure that top and middle management is held accountable for results in attaining an inclusive workplace. Companies must seek to advance women to leadership and pay equity throughout the system.

Research indicates that inclusive workplaces enhance results because independent thought leads to more innovation.[47] A business where women and men are equally represented at all levels better reflects stakeholders and the marketplace it serves. Only through our focused efforts can we address the challenges first spelled out in The Declaration of Sentiments more than 160 years ago. The pay and leadership gaps don't just harm women. Men, families, businesses, and the U.S. economy all pay a steep price. It is a price that we cannot afford.

Appendix

Testimony Data

For the purposes of this testimony, Catalyst utilized data from the following sources. To examine trends about women board directors, Catalyst analyzed data from the years 1996 – 1999; 2003; and 2005-2009. To examine trends about women Corporate Officers, Catalyst analyzed data from the years 1996-2000; 2002; and 2005-2008. To examine the current representation of women Executive Officers, Catalyst analyzed data from 2009. To investigate the current status of women in the pipeline to senior leadership positions, Catalyst obtained from the Equal Opportunity Employment Commission (EEOC) unpublished aggregate data from the 2009 EEO-1 survey for the 496 companies included in the 2009 Catalyst Census reports.[1] For each company, the EEOC data comprises all full-time and part-time employees[2] at the time the company submitted the consolidated EEO-1 form.[3]

To examine trends in women's representation by industry, Catalyst explored the historical status of women in male-dominated and female-prevalent industries, as well as the largest industry on the *Fortune* 500 list. Male-dominated industries are those in which women account for 25% or less of all individuals employed in the field.[4] Because there are very few female-dominated industries,[5] Catalyst examined female-prevalent industries, or those in which women account for more than 40% of all those employed in the field. The manufacturing industry, which accounts for about one-third of *Fortune* 500 companies, has been the largest industry for many years.

To examine the current pipeline of women leaders by industry sector, Catalyst excluded any industry sector with fewer than 10 companies represented in the 2009 *Fortune* 500 list: Agriculture, Forestry, Fishing and Hunting (3 companies); Arts, Entertainment, and Recreation (0); Construction (9); Educational Services (0); Health Care and Social Assistance (6); Real Estate and Rental and Leasing (7); Other Services Except Public Administration (0); and Public Administration (0).

Catalyst Census Objectives
and Methodology

Catalyst designed the annual Census report series to establish an accurate gauge of women's representation at the highest levels of corporate America, both in the boardroom and in senior leadership positions. The purpose of this research is to provide points of comparison across time with the goal of promoting women's advancement in business and garnering attention for this issue.

Catalyst's research methodology is a true census that counts all elements of the population. This research design differentiates our research from studies that utilize survey methodologies because it removes the need for a sample, thereby producing a more precise picture of women's status and progress. Catalyst studies *Fortune* 500 companies as the population for the Census report series because not only are these the largest companies by revenue in the United States each year, but they are also widely recognized as the most powerful and influential businesses.

Historical Methodology of Catalyst Census: Fortune 500[06]

General Report

From 1996–2005, the Catalyst *Fortune* 500 Census used a consistent two-part methodology to study women in corporate leadership, both on boards and in management positions. First, Catalyst gathered data from publicly available sources, including annual reports, proxy statements, and company websites. Catalyst then authenticated the public source data through a verification process. Catalyst sent a letter to contacts at each of the *Fortune* 500 companies to verify or correct the public source data by letter, fax, or telephone. In any instance where a company failed to respond to multiple requests for verification, Catalyst utilized publicly available information for analysis. While Catalyst outlined guidelines for companies to identify Corporate Officers through the verification process, companies ultimately self-defined their Corporate Officers.

In 2005, Catalyst compared the data gathered from public sources to the verified data and found no statistical difference. From 2006-2008, Catalyst gathered data from publicly available annual reports, proxy statements, and company websites. Because companies choose the individuals listed in public sources, companies were still involved in the process of defining their Corporate Officers.

In 2009, Catalyst implemented a change in methodology to facilitate a focus on top leadership and provide a more reliable comparison across companies and industries. Catalyst gathered data from publicly available Securities and Exchange Commission (SEC) annual filings submitted by June 30, 2009. For insurance companies that do not file with the SEC, Catalyst obtained data from the National Association of Insurance Commissioners' (NAIC) regulatory database of key annual statements submitted by June 30, 2009. Data collected by the SEC and NAIC comply with federal or state requirements governing the content and timing of the filings, resulting in more equivalent comparisons across companies. Although companies ultimately determine which individuals qualify to be listed in the filings, the decision is based on common definitions and regulations.

As a result of the change in data collection method, the population counted in the *2009 Catalyst Census:* Fortune *500 Women Board Directors* report is composed of those listed in SEC filings as serving on the board up to the annual meeting of shareholders and those listed in NAIC filings as Directors. The population of directors was not significantly altered by the methodology change, permitting comparisons to data from previous Catalyst Censuses of Board Directors.

The population counted in the *2009 Catalyst Census: Fortune 500 Women Executive Officers and Top Earners* report is composed of those listed as Executive Officers[7] in SEC filings and those listed as Officers in NAIC filings. Executive Officers are generally a subset of the Corporate Officer population as defined in previous Catalyst Census reports. The population change makes comparisons to data from previous Catalyst Censuses of Corporate Officers inappropriate. In practice, the typical differences between Executive and Corporate Officers are:

Executive Officers	**Corporate Officers**
Appointed or elected by the board of directors	Selected by CEO
Includes CEO and up to two reporting levels below	Includes CEO and up to four reporting levels below
Defined by SEC	Defined by company

Industry Data Collection and Analysis

From 1996–2005, industry classifications were based on the fifty or more industry groups from each year's *Fortune* list. The exact number and name of the industry groups varied with each list.

From 2006–2008, industry classifications were coded by Catalyst into the 20 two-digit sector codes of the North American Industrial Classification System (NAICS). Not all 20 sector codes are represented on the *Fortune* list every year.

In 2009, industry classifications were coded by Catalyst into the 20 two-digit NAICS sectors with two modifications adopted from the NAICS Supersectors for the Current Employment Statistics Program. Manufacturing (Sectors 31–33) was reclassified into two sectors: Durable Goods and Nondurable Goods. Three sectors, Professional, Scientific, and Technical Services (Sector 54); Management of Companies and Enterprises (Sector 55); and Administrative and Support and Waste Management and Remediation Services (Sector 56) were aggregated into one sector, Professional and Business Services. As a result of these changes, there were 19 industries.

Race/Ethnicity Data Collection and Analysis

From 2001–2009, Catalyst utilized many sources to gather data about the race/ethnicity of women board directors, including previous Catalyst Census data, people of color associations' publications, and biographies. Catalyst also emailed and telephoned contacts at *Fortune* 500 companies to request the verification of the collected race/ethnicity data. Additionally, Catalyst wrote to women board directors for self-verification through email and mail. Each year, data analysis is based on a sample of companies that either a) have complete race/ethnicity data for each woman board director or b) have no women board directors.[8]

Catalyst Bottom Line Objectives
and Methodology

Catalyst designed the Bottom Line report series to investigate the hypothetical link between gender diversity in corporate leadership, both in senior management and in the boardroom, and financial performance. These are correlational studies that do not prove or imply causation.

For each report, Catalyst compiled a list of all companies that appeared in the *Fortune* 500 for a specific time period, after accounting for name changes and merger and acquisitions activity. Financial data for the companies examined were obtained from the Standard & Poor's Compustat database. Gender diversity data for senior leadership teams and boards of directors were compiled from Catalyst's *Fortune* 500 Census report series.

To analyze the data, Catalyst divided companies into quartiles based on the average percentage of women leaders across the specific time period. The top quartile included the companies with the highest average percentage of women leaders, while the bottom quartile included the companies with the lowest average percentage of women leaders.

The Bottom Line: Connecting Corporate
Performance and Gender Diversity

Data and Analysis

Catalyst compiled a list of all companies appearing in the *Fortune* 500 from 1996 to 2000. The sample was narrowed by excluding companies with fewer than four years of data on financial performance and gender diversity of the top management team, resulting in a sample of 353 companies. The top quartile contained 88 companies, while the bottom quartile contained 89 companies.

The Return on Equity (ROE) measure for each company is the average of annual ROEs from 1996 to 2000. An average of the annual ROEs for the period shows the returns for the long-term, reducing the impact of any unusual year-to-year fluctuations. The Total Return to Shareholders (TRS) measure is the cumulative total shareholder return over the period 1996 to 2000 for which data are available. This measure adjusts for both stock splits and stock dividends. Gender diversity of top management teams was determined by averaging the annual percentages of women Corporate Officers over the period between 1996 and 2000.

The Bottom Line: Corporate Performance
and Women's Representation on Boards

Data and Analysis

Catalyst compiled a list of all companies that appeared in the *Fortune* 500 in 2001 and 2003, resulting in a sample of 520 companies. The top quartile contained 132 companies, while the bottom quartile contained 129 companies.

The ROE, the Return on Sales (ROS), and the Return on Invested Capital (ROIC) measures for each company are the average of each from 2001 to 2004. Gender diversity of the board of directors was determined by averaging the annual percentages of women board directors in 2001 and 2003.

Catalyst Advancing Women
Leaders Methodology

Catalyst designed the Advancing Women Leaders report to investigate the hypothetical link between the representation of women on boards in the past and the future representation of women in Corporate Officer ranks. Catalyst also sought to expand research in this area by investigating the potential connection between women on boards and women in line positions. This is a correlational study that does not prove or imply causation.

Data and Analysis

Catalyst compiled a list of all companies that appeared in the *Fortune* 500 in 2000, 2001, and 2006, resulting in a matched sample of 359 companies. For these companies, Catalyst utilized women Corporate Officer data from the 2000 and 2006 Catalyst Census reports, as well as women board director data from the 2001 Catalyst Census report.

Using regression analysis, Catalyst examined the relationship between the percentage of women board directors that a Fortune 500 company had in 2001 and the percentage of women Corporate Officers the same company had in 2006. The analysis controlled for the effects of industry, revenue, and the percentage of corporate officer positions held by women in 2000.

Definitions

Corporate Officers. Corporate Officers are recognized as the leaders of a company. They have day-to-day responsibilities for operations, policymaking responsibility, and the power to legally bind their corporations. In practice, Corporate Officers typically are within four reporting levels of the CEO and are defined by the company. Nomenclature used by companies includes groups such as: company officers, corporate management, executive management, senior officers, senior management, and senior leadership team. Common titles of corporate officers include: "Chief" titles, Executive Vice President, Senior Vice President, and Vice President. Catalyst ceased studying the *Fortune* 500 Corporate Officer population in 2008.

Executive Officers. Executive Officers are a specific group of individuals, legally defined by the Securities and Exchange Commission (SEC) in the United States as: "a company's president, any vice-president of the registrant in charge of a principal business unit, division or function (such as sales, administration or finance), any other officer who performs similar policy making functions for company. Executive officers of subsidiaries may be deemed executive officers of the registrant if they perform such policy making functions for the registrant."[9] In practice, Executive Officers represent the highest level of senior leadership, typically within two reporting levels of the CEO and generally appointed by the board of directors. Executive Officers represent a segment of the Corporate Officer population as defined in previous Catalyst Census reports. Catalyst has been studying the Executive Officer population since 2009.

Fortune 500. Fortune magazine's ranking of the top 500 U.S. incorporated companies filing financial statements with the government is based on each company's gross annual revenue. Included in the list are public companies, private companies, and cooperatives that file a 10-K with the Securities and Exchange Commission (SEC), and mutual insurance companies that file with state regulators.[10]

Line Officers. Line officers are responsible for a company's profits and losses. Examples include positions within functions such as supply chain, marketing, or sales.

Low-Mid Level Officials & Managers and Professionals. Catalyst combined two categories to create the Low-Mid Level Officials & Managers and Professionals level of the "Women in *Fortune* 500 Companies" chart. Please refer to EEOC definitions for more information.[11]

Quartile analysis. Catalyst divided the sample of companies into four sections based on women's representation. The top quartile included the companies with the highest average percentage of women leaders, while the bottom quartile included the companies with the lowest average percentage of women leaders.

Race/Ethnicity. The race/ethnicity category definitions used by Catalyst were established by the U.S. Census Bureau. Catalyst uses 6 categories to report information about race/ethnicity.[12]

Return on Equity (ROE). The ratio of after-tax net profit to stockholders' equity.

Return on Invested Capital (ROIC). The ratio of after-tax net operating profit to invested capital.

Return on Sales (ROS). The pre-tax net profit divided by revenue.

Senior Level Officials & Managers. Please refer to EEOC definitions for more information.[13]

Staff Officers. Staff officers are responsible for the auxiliary functioning of the business. Examples include positions within functions such as human resources, corporate affairs, legal, and finance.

Top Earner. As per Item 402 of Regulation S-K (§ 229.402), paragraph (a)(3), federal securities laws require the disclosure of the total compensation of at least five individuals: the principal executive officer (CEO), the principal financial officer (CFO), and the company's three most highly compensated executive officers (excluding the CEO/CFO) as of the company's fiscal year end. Furthermore, companies must disclose the total compensation of up to two additional individuals who would have been top earners except for the fact that these individuals were not employed as Named Executive Officers as of the company's fiscal year end.[14]

Catalyst reports on top earners for *Fortune* 500 companies that file annual 10-K reports and Proxy statements with the Securities and Exchange Commission (SEC). In 2009, Catalyst defined top earners as those current Executive Officers whose total compensation is among the top five amounts disclosed; prior to 2009 Catalyst defined top earners as those current Corporate Officers whose total compensation is among the top five amounts disclosed. A company can thus have five or fewer top earners. Because Catalyst views the representation of women top earners as a proxy for status in the organization rather than a method to measure pay inequity, Catalyst does not track the compensation amounts of top earners.

Total Return to Shareholders (TRS). The sum of stock price appreciation plus reinvestment of dividends declared over a calendar year.

Testimony of Michelle J. Budig
Associate Professor of Sociology Faculty Associate,
Center for Public Policy Administration
W33cd Machmer Hall University of Massachusetts
Amherst, MA 01003-9278 budig@soc.umass.edu 413-545-5972

Before the United States Joint Economic Committee Hearing on "New Evidence on the Gender Pay Gap for Women and Mothers in Management"

September 28, 2010

Introduction

"Chairwoman Maloney and members of the committee, I thank you for the opportunity to speak. My name is Michelle Budig, and I am an Associate Professor of Sociology and Faculty Associate at the Center for Public Policy Administration at the University of Massachusetts. My expertise is in gender, work, and family issues, and most relevant to today, the wage penalty for motherhood and work-family policy.

Today I will testify that a significant portion of the persistent gender gap in earnings, among workers with equivalent qualifications and in similar jobs, is attributable to parenthood. Specifically, to the systematically lower earnings of mothers and higher earnings of fathers, among comparable workers. Thus, *public policies that target the difficulties families face in balancing work and family responsibilities, as well as discrimination by employers by workers' parental status, may be the most effective at reducing the gender pay gap.*

My testimony today will address 4 points. *First,* I will discuss the relative absence of wives and mothers among managers and leaders of organizations. *Second,* I will compare gender pay gaps among young childless workers and among parents. *Third,* I will summarize statistical evidence of unaccountably lower wages for mothers and higher wages for fathers. *Finally,* I will present research on work-family policies and their impact on the wage penalty for motherhood, with an eye to drawing policy implications for the United States.

The report presented by the GAO demonstrated that, relative to men, women in management are younger and less educated. This begs the question, where are the older, more educated and experienced, female mangers? And why are they under-represented? A generation ago we might have hypothesized this relative absence of more senior women was simply due to the lack of qualified and experienced women in potential pool of women managers. However, since the 1980s, these qualifications and experience differences between women and men have eroded, so much so that women now earn college degrees at higher rates than men.[1] If a lack of qualified candidates cannot explain the absence of experienced female managers, what can?

My research and others demonstrates that *a significant portion of gender-based differences in employment, earnings, and experiences of discrimination are increasingly related to parenthood, and the greater struggles of mothers to balance careers and family demands.*

Point One: Parenthood, Gender, and Employment

Let us first step back from the pay gap to look at gender differences in the family structures of managers in the GAO report.

Wives and mothers are relatively more absent among managers, compared with the representation of husbands and fathers.

If we subtract the rates of marriage among men from those among women, we might compute a *Managerial Gender Marriage Gap:* Women managers are far less likely to be married overall, compared with male managers. This gap in marital rates ranges from 8 to 19 percentage points across industries, with an average gap of 15 percentage points.

Second, if we subtract the rates of parenthood among men from those among women, we would compute a *Managerial Gender Parenthood Gap:* Women managers are less likely to be mothers, and have smaller family sizes, relative to male managers. The parenthood gap ranges from 0 to 9 percentage points across industries, with an average gap of 6 percentage points.

The absence of mothers and the rise in childlessness among highly skilled women is also found in national data. Table 1 in your handout shows that, controlling for differences in age, marital status, education, and other household income, the gender employment gap among the childless is minimal whereas the gender employment gap among parents is quite large.

Table 1. Likelihood of Being Employed by Parenthood and Gender

Childless Men	Childless Women	Fathers	Mothers
88.5%	82.2%	93.0%	73.4%

Note: Currrent Population Survey data, from statistical models controlling for age, marital status, education, and other household income), Non-institutionalized Civilians, Aged 25-492 Childlessness has risen among American women since the 1970s, and particularly among highly educated women. In 2004, among college educated white women in their 40s, fully 27% were childless.3 Researchers estimate about 44% of this childlessness is voluntary, while 56% is due to age-related infertility.4 A major reason why women delay or forego motherhood is due to the perceived and experienced incompatibility between careers and motherhood.[5]

Thus, *high-achieving women are forgoing families at rates not observed among high-achieving men.*

Before we move on to considering the link between the persistent gender pay gap and parenthood among the employed, we need to recognize that we are missing the mothers from these statistics. Thus, the mothers who persist are a qualitatively select group, or potentially the cream of the crop, if you will. This implies that our current estimates of the gender pay gap may be much smaller than they would be if mothers were not disproportionately absent from the work force.

Point Two: Gender Pay Gaps
among the Childless and among Parents

In the GAO report, among the mothers who persist in management, their gender pay gap relative to fathers is far larger (ranging from 21% to 34%) than the gender pay gap among childless managers (17% to 24%).

The shrinking gender gap among young childless workers has captured national attention this month with the highly publicized study by James Chung of Reach Advisors, on the lack of a gender gap among childless workers. Chung, who analyzes data from the American Community Survey, shows that among 20-something unmarried, childless workers in urban areas, there is no gender pay gap.[6] Moreover, in multiple instances in this unencumbered group, women out-earn men. Chung notes that these women are also largely unmarried.

Estimates from my research of the gender pay gaps among full-time workers are presented in table 2 in your handout. *Whereas childless women earn 94 cents of a childless man's dollar, mothers earn only 60 cents of a father's dollar.*

Table 2. Unadjusted Gender Pay Gap for Full-time Employed Civilians, Aged 25 to 49[7]

Women's Pay per $1 Male Dollar	Mother's Pay per $1 Father Dollar	Childless Woman's Pay per $1 Childless Man's Dollar
79¢	60¢	94¢

Note: Author's calculations from Current Population Survey data.

While causality is complex, there is a strong empirical association between the gender gap (pay differences between women and men) and the family gap (pay differences between households with and without children) .[8, 9, 10] Economist Jane Waldfogel's research (1998a) shows that *40% to 50% of the gender gap can be explained by the impact of parental and marital status on men's and women's earnings.* Moreover, Waldfogel (1998b) shows that while the gender pay gap has been decreasing, the pay gap related to parenthood is increasing.

This greater gender inequality found among parents brings me to my next point, the wage penalty for motherhood.

Point Three, Part A: The Wage Penalty for Motherhood

The finding that having children reduces women's earnings, even among workers with comparable qualifications, experience, work hours, and jobs, is now well established in the social science literature. [11, 12, 13, 14, 15, 16, 17] In your handout, Table 3 shows the effect of children on earnings from my published research. *All women experience reduced earnings for each additional child they have.* This penalty ranges in size from -15% per child among low-wage workers to about 4% per child among high-wage workers.

That mothers work less and may accept lower earnings for more family-friendly jobs explains part of the penalty experienced by low wage workers, and that mothers have less experience, due to interruptions for childbearing, explains a part of the penalty for high-wage workers.

But a significant motherhood penalty persists even in estimates that account for these differences, such that the size of the wage penalty after all factors are controlled is roughly 3% per child. This means we would expect the typical full-time female worker in 2009[18] to earn roughly $1,100 less per child in annual wages, all else equal.

What lies behind this motherhood penalty that is unexplained by measurable characteristics of workers and jobs? One factor may be employer discrimination against mothers. It is difficult to obtain data on discrimination and virtually impossible to match it to outcomes in large-scale national surveys. However, *evidence from experimental and audit studies support arguments of employer discrimination against mothers in callbacks for job applications, hiring decisions, wage offers, and promotions.*[20] Stanford sociologist Shelley Correll's experimental research shows that, after reviewing resumes that differed only in noting parental status, subjects in an experiment systematically rated childless women and fathers significantly higher than mothers on competency, work commitment, promotability, and recommendations for hire. Most telling, Correll and colleagues found that raters gave mothers the lowest wage offers, averaging $13,000 lower than wage offers for fathers.

This privileging of fathers brings me to my next point.

Table 3. Effect Each Additional Child on Women's Hourly Wage[19]

	Low-Wage Women (5th Percentile)	Average Earner (50th Percentile)	High-Wage Women (95th Percentile)
Baseline Model [a]	–15.1%	–5.7%	–3.9%
+ Controls for Work Hours [b]	–10.6%	–4.0%	–5.0%
+ Controls for Education, experience, seniority [c]	–11.1%	–2.4%	–2.3%
+ Controls for Job Characteristics [d]	–4.4%	–1.4%	–2.5%
Controlling for all differences, averaging across all women	-3.0% = $1,100		

Notes: [a] Model controls for number of children, age of respondent, region of country, population density, marital status, spouse's annual earnings, and spouse's work hours.

[b] Model also controls for usual weekly hours and annual weeks worked.

[c] Model also controls for education, experience, seniority, and employer changes.

[d] Model also controls for level of job gender segregation, professional/managerial status, public sector, irregular shift work, self-employed status, employer-sponsored health insurance, employer-sponsored life insurance, labor union membership, and 12 dummies for industrial sector.

Point Three, Part B: The Wage Bonus for Fatherhood

The motherhood penalty compares women against women to see how children depress their wages. While it is well known that fathers earn more than mothers, new research is highlighting the importance of fatherhood among men in enhancing their wages.21, 22A portion of fathers' higher earnings can be explained by the facts fathers tend to work more hours, have more experience, and have higher ranking occupations, relative to childless men. But after we adjust for these differences, we still find a wage bonus for fatherhood, and one that increases with educational attainment. Figure 1 in your handout shows that, *controlling for an array of labor market characteristics, men of all racial/ethnic groups receive a fatherhood bonus in annual earnings, and this bonus is greatest among white and Latino college graduates, whose wages, all else equal, are $4,000 to $5,000 higher than childless men.*

Putting these sets of findings together, we see that parenthood exacerbates gender inequality in American workplaces. Mothers lose while fathers gain from parenthood, and these penalties and bonuses are found beyond the differences between parents and childless persons in terms of hours worked, job experience, seniority, and a wide host of other relevant labor market characteristics.

Point Four: Policy Implications

What kinds of policies might enable mothers to maintain employment, workplaces assist parents in balancing work and family demands, and reducing the gender gap in pay attributable to wage bonuses for fatherhood and wage penalties for motherhood?

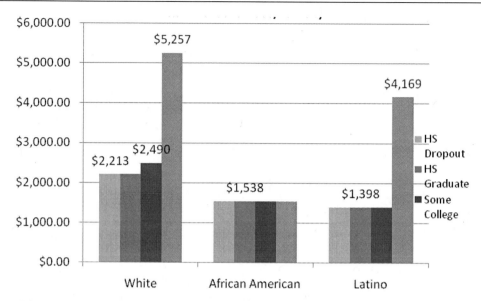

Note: figure taken from Hodges, Melissa J. and Michelle J. Budig. 2010. "Who Gets the Daddy Bonus? Organizational Hegemonic Masculinity and the Impact of Fatherhood on Men's Earnings." Gender & Society 24(6): December Issue.

Figure 1. The Effect of Fatherhood (in Dollars) by Educational attainment and Race/Ethnicity.

In an NSF-funded cross-national study of 22 nations I've been conducting with colleague Joya Misra and student collaborator Irene Boeckmann, we've identified three key policies that are linked to smaller motherhood penalties:

Universal Early Childhood Education for preschool children and increased availability of affordable, high-quality care for very young children reduces the motherhood wage penalty.

Figure 2 in your handout shows *the wage penalty for motherhood dramatically declines with the availability of publicly funded childcare for infants under 2 years old.* Whereas we observe motherhood penalties of over 6% per child in countries lacking such care, the motherhood penalty declines toward zero as the enrollment of children in publicly funded infant care approaches 40%.

Universal moderate length job-protected leave
following the birth/adoption of a child

In the US, FMLA was designed to provide short-term unpaid leave to new parents, as well as other family caregivers. But less than a majority of gainfully employed American workers are covered by this act, due to exemptions of employer types from the law. Of those employers covered by FMLA, researchers estimate only 54% to 77% are in compliance with the law.[23, 24]

FMLA needs to be extended to all workplaces and workers, and ideally should be longer than 12 weeks.

Cross-nationally, job-protected leaves range up to 3 years, as can be seen on figure 3 in your hand out. Our research shows that countries with very short and countries with very long leaves have the highest motherhood penalties.

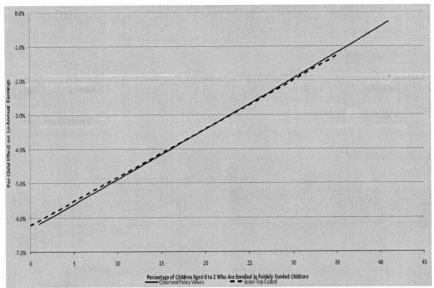

Note: figure taken from Budig, Michelle J., Joya Misra, and Irene Boeckmann. 2010. "The Cross-National Effects of Work-Family Policies on the Motherhood Wage Penalty: Findings from Multilevel Analyses." Paper presented at the 2010 Annual Meetings of the Population Association of America (Dallas, TX).

Figure 2. Net Per Child Effect on Ln Annual Earnings, by the Percentage of Children Age 0 to 2 Who are Enrolled in Publicly Funded Childcare.

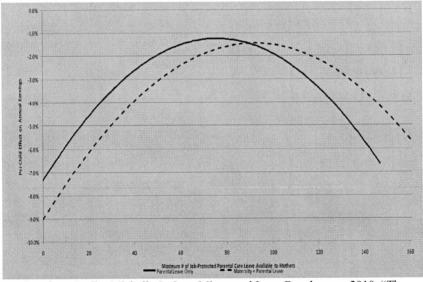

Note: figure taken from Budig, Michelle J., Joya Misra, and Irene Boeckmann. 2010. "The Cross-National Effects of Work-Family Policies on the Motherhood Wage Penalty: Findings from Multilevel Analyses." Paper presented at the 2010 Annual Meetings of the Population Association of America (Dallas, TX).

Figure 3. Net Per Child Effect on Ln Annual Earnings by Maximum Number of Weeks of Parental Care Leave Available to Mothers.

Job-protected leaves of roughly one year do the best at minimizing the wage penalty for motherhood. Obviously, this is far beyond what is currently offered by FMLA, but emphasizes the importance of such leave in minimizing gender inequality.

Short-Term Paid Maternity
and Paternity Leave

Short-term paid maternity leave (6 to 12 weeks) reduces the likelihood that women will have to exit jobs to recover from childbirth, and increases their ability to return to the same employer upon re-entry. The ability to return to work with the same employer following the birth of a child greatly reduces the wage penalty for motherhood.[25] The effects of paid leave reserved for fathers on the wage penalty for motherhood, cross-nationally are also dramatic. Our research shows that countries that offer non-transferable paid leave to fathers evidence significantly lower wage penalties to mothers.

Addressing workplace discrimination against mothers and those making use of family benefits.

Some American workplaces offer various work-family benefits designed to help parents manage work and family responsibilities, such as *paid leave, flexible scheduling, flexible work location, part-time options, and childcare assistance,* these benefits vary in availability and usage across workplaces. Research finds that many employees are unaware of the benefits available, and many employees fear negative impacts on their careers for making use of such policies.[26] Moreover, some research indicates that usage of these policies can exacerbate the motherhood wage penalty. [27] *Federal-level work-family policies could eliminate many of these problems with uneven access across workplaces to work-family assistance, and discrimination against those workers who make use of legally sanctioned work-family benefits.*

Conclusion

A significant portion of the persistent gender gap in earnings is attributable to parenthood, specifically, the systematically lower earnings of mothers and higher earnings of fathers, among comparable workers. *To reduce the gender pay gap, public policies should target the difficulties families face in balancing work and family responsibilities, as well as discrimination by employers based on workers' parental status.*

I thank you for your time, I hope my testimony is of use to this committee.

Handout

Table 1. Likelihood of Being Employed
by Parenthood and Gender

Childless Men	Childless Women	Fathers	Mothers
88.5%	82.2%	93.0%	73.4%

Note: From statistical models controlling for age, marital status, education, and other household income), Non-institutionalized Civilians, Aged 25-49.

Tables 1 and 2 calculated from data presented in Misra, Joya, Michelle J. Budig and Irene S. Boeckmann. 2010. "Cross-National Patterns in Individual and Household Employment and Work Hours by Gender and Parenthood." Forthcoming at *Research in the Sociology of Work*. Presented at the 2010 annual meetings of the American Sociological Association (Atlanta, GA).

Table 2. Unadjusted Gender Pay Gap for Non-institutionalized, Full-time Employed Adults, Aged 25 to 49

Women's Pay per $1 Male Dollar	Mother's Pay per $1 Father Dollar	Childless Woman's Pay per $1 Childless Man's Dollar
79¢	60¢	94¢

Table 3. Effect Each Additional Child on Women's Hourly Wage

	Low-Wage Women (5th Percentile)	Average Earner (50th Percentile)	High-Wage Women (95th Percentile)
Baseline Model [a]	–15.1%	–5.7%	–3.9%
+ Controls for Work Hours [b]	–10.6%	–4.0%	–5.0%
+ Controls for Education, experience, seniority [c]	–11.1%	–2.4%	–2.3%
+ Controls for Job Characteristics [d]	–4.4%	–1.4%	–2.5%
Controlling for all differences, averaging across all women	-3.0% = $1,100		

Budig, Michelle J. and Melissa J. Hodges. 2010. "Differences in Disadvantage: Variation in the Motherhood Penalty Across White Women's Earnings Distribution." *American Sociological Review* 75(5): October Issue.

Notes:

[a] Model controls for number of children, age of respondent, region of country, population density, marital status, spouse's annual earnings, and spouse's work hours.

[b] Model also controls for usual weekly hours and annual weeks worked.

[c] Model also controls for education, experience, seniority, and employer changes.

[d] Model also controls for level of job gender segregation, professional/managerial status, public sector, irregular shift work, self-employed status, employer-sponsored health insurance, employer-sponsored life insurance, labor union membership, and 12 dummies for industrial sector.

Figures 2 and 3 from: Budig, Michelle J., Joya Misra, and Irene Boeckmann. 2010. "The Cross-National Effects of Work-Family Policies on the Motherhood Wage Penalty: Findings from Multilevel Analyses." Paper presented at the 2010 Annual Meetings of the Population Association of America (Dallas, TX).

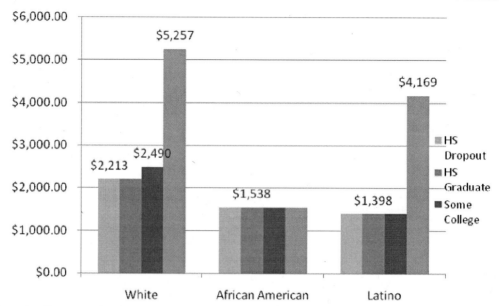

Hodges, Melissa J. and Michelle J. Budig. 2010. "Who Gets the Daddy Bonus? Organizational Hegemonic Masculinity and the Impact of Fatherhood on Men's Earnings." *Gender & Society* 24(6):December Issue.

Figure 1. The Effect of Fatherhood (in Dollars) by Educational Attainment and Race/Ethnicity.

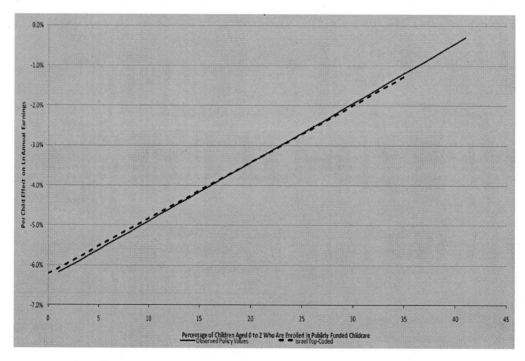

Figure 2. Net Per Child Effect on Ln Annual Earnings, by the Percentage of Children Age) to 2 Who Are Enrolled in Publicly Funded Childcare.

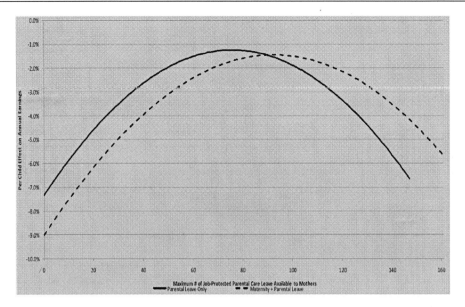

Figure 3. Net Per Child Effect on Ln Annual Earnings by Maximum Number of Weeks of Parental Care.

The Earnings Penalty for Part-Time Work:
An Obstacle to Equal Pay

A Report by the Joint Economic Committee
Representative Carolyn B. Maloney,
Chair

April 20, 2010 (Equal Pay Day)

Introduction

Equal Pay Day highlights an issue of social and policy significance: the gap between the earnings of men and women. Estimates of the gender pay gap vary, but it is clear that women earn less than men.[1] This gap has arisen for a variety of reasons, but one dimension of the problem involves the earnings penalty for part-time work. Closing the pay gap between full-time and part-time workers will contribute significantly to closing the pay gap between men and women. The part-time earnings penalty has had a particularly large impact on the economic wellbeing of families during the Great Recession since the number of part-time workers who would like full-time employment has risen by 4.4 million workers since December 2007.

Part-Time Workers
are Disproportionately Female

In 2009, over 17 million women worked part time. Out of the pool of individuals who work part time, nearly two-thirds are women. (See Figure 1.)

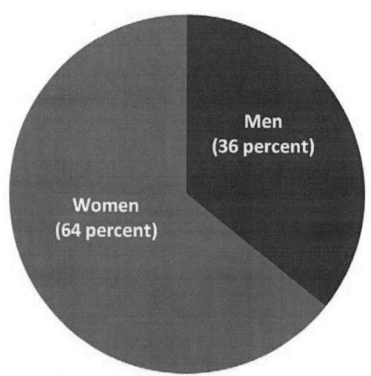

Source: JEC Majority Staff calculations from Bureau of Labor Statistics, Current Population Survey 2009.

Note: Employed persons are classified as full-or part-time workers based pn their usual weekly hours at all jobs regardless of the number of hours they are at work during the reference week. Persons absent from work also classified according to their usual status.

Figure 1. Nearly Two-Thirds of Part-time Workers are Women.

While most working women work full time, one-quarter (26 percent) of all employed women work part time, compared to 13 percent of employed men. (See Figure 2.) In many of the occupations with large shares of part-time workers, employment is dominated by women. Women make up over half (56 percent) of the employees working in food preparation and serving related jobs, where 49 percent of workers are employed part time. Over three-quarters (77 percent) of personal care and service positions are held by women – an occupation where 43 percent of employees work part time.

Part-Time Workers Face
an Earnings Penalty

Part-time workers across a spectrum of occupations earn hourly wages below those of full-time workers, which contributes to the wage gap between men and women. For example, for every dollar of earnings a full-time worker receives in a sales or related occupation, a part-time worker receives 58 cents. A similar story is true for workers in computer and mathematical occupations: a part-time worker receives about 63 cents for every dollar of earnings a full-time worker receives. (See Figure 3.)

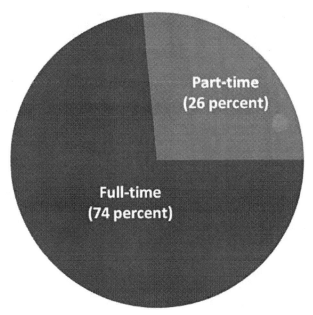

Source: Source: JEC Majority Staff calculations from Bureau of Labor Statistics, Current Population
    Survey 2009.
Note: Employed persons are classified as full-or part-time workers based on their usual weekly hours at
    all jobs regardless of the number of hours they are at work during the reference week. Persons
    absent from work also are classified according to their usual status.

Figure 2. One-inFour Employed Women Usually Work Part Time.

Source: JEC majority staff calculations vased on data from the United States Sensus Bureau.

Figure 3. Part-time Workers Are Subject to a Large Wage Penalty.

Part-Time Work Can Lead to Lower
Long-Run Earnings

Evidence shows that part of the long-run earnings gap between men and women may be explained by the longer time that women, relative to men, spend working part time.[2]

Conclusion

Not only do part-time workers earn lower hourly wages than full-time workers, but longer durations of part-time work can contribute to lower earnings. These are just two of the ways that part-time work can drive the wage gap between men and women.

The part-time wage penalty also affects men. While men represent a smaller fraction of the pool of part-time workers, men who work part time suffer from some of the same problems in the labor market that women do.

Finally, wage gaps between part-time and full-time workers understate the difference in total compensation. Many part-time workers do not receive the same health benefits, paid time-off for vacation or sick leave, or pension benefits that full-time workers receive.

Large Gender Pay Gap for Older Workers
Threatens Economic Security of Older Women

A Report by the Joint Economic Committee Representative
Carolyn B. Maloney,
Chair

December 2010

Much is often made about the significant narrowing of the gender pay gap over the past three decades. However, in 2009, full-time working women 50 and older earned only three-fourths of what full-time working men the same age earned. The wage penalty paid by older women is often overlooked because of the improvement in the overall gender wage gap. This sizable gender pay gap for older workers threatens the retirement security of our country's older women and families that depend on their earnings for their well-being.

The wage gap is larger for older workers than for younger workers. In 2009, women 50 and older working full-time earned only 75 percent of their male counterparts' earnings, leaving a 25 percent gap (see chart and table). For full-time workers 16 and older, women's median weekly earnings were 80 percent of their male counterparts', leaving a 20 percent gap between women's and men's earnings. According to the Bureau of Labor Statistics, the gender wage gap for workers ages 45-54 years narrowed between 1979 and 2009. For workers 65 and older the gap was essentially flat over that period, despite some fluctuations.[1]

Employment patterns, including industry, occupation and career interruptions, affect the gender pay gap. Researchers have documented several sources of the greater earnings disparity for older men and women. First, women have historically been more likely to be employed in lower-paying industries such as the health care and education industries.[2] Second, across industries, women tend to be employed in lower-paying occupations. For example, 23 percent of women working full-time in 2009 were employed in office and administrative support occupations, compared to only 7 percent of men working full-time.[3] Occupational segregation has repercussions for women's economic security. Jobs traditionally held by women have long been undervalued by society and are therefore paid less than jobs typically held by men. Third, women are more likely than men to work part-time or temporarily exit the labor force at some point during their careers, often to raise children. Such interruptions over one's career can result in lower earnings growth over time.[4]

Persistent discrimination over the course of women's careers would exacerbate the gender wage gap in older workers. Across myriad studies, a portion of the wage gap remains unexplained and could be caused by persistent gender-based discrimination.[5] Discrimination-based wage differences early in women's careers would be compounded over time and could explain the larger pay gap for older women. A lifetime of lower earnings leaves older women more likely to live in poverty than men.

The size of the gender pay gap for older workers varies by state. State-by-state analysis conducted by the Joint Economic Committee reveals that there is a wide range in the gender pay gap for older workers across states, ranging from a gap of 13 percent in Arkansas to a gap of 37 percent in Kentucky (see table). In nearly all states, the gender pay gap for older workers is larger than the overall gender pay gap within the state. States where the gender pay gap for older workers is substantially larger (more than nine percentage points greater) than the overall gender pay gap include Colorado, Kentucky, Maryland, Massachusetts, Mississippi, Nevada, North Carolina, Oklahoma, and Wisconsin. The difference is less than two percentage points in Arkansas, Connecticut, Georgia, Louisiana, New Mexico, Nebraska, Oregon, and Utah. Individual state data was not available on the median weekly earnings of older workers in states with smaller populations.

Addressing the gender wage gap for older workers is critical for women's retirement security. Families depend on women's earnings for economic security, including during retirement. The gap between women's and men's earnings translates into lower income for women in retirement. Lower earnings over a woman's career would result in smaller private savings to draw upon in retirement, smaller contributions to employer-sponsored retirement plans, smaller Social Security benefits, and smaller paychecks for those women who continue to work later in life. Furthermore, a steep increase in the number of female-headed households in the late 1980s means that a larger number of women are preparing to enter retirement without a spouse's income to rely on.[6] In 2009, 5.7 million older women without a spouse were in the labor force.[7]

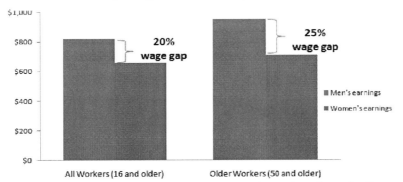

Gender Pay Gap Is Larger For Older Workers
Median Weekly Earnings of Full-Time Working Men and Women, 2009

Source: Joint Economic Committee Staff calculations based on data from the Bureau of Labor Statistics.

Table. Median Weekly Earnings by Age and Sex, 2009

State	Full-Time Workers 16 Years and Older				Full-Time Workers 50 Years and Older			
	Women's Median Weekly Earnings (Dollars)	Men's Median Weekly Earnings (Dollars)	Ratio, Women's Earnings to Men's Earnings	Gender Wage Gap for Workers 16 and older	Women's Median Weekly Earnings (Dollars)	Men's Median Weekly Earnings (Dollars)	Ratio, Women's Earnings to Men's Earnings	Gender Wage Gap for Workers 50 and older
Alabama	596	800	74.5%	25.5%	610	909	67.1%	32.9%
Alaska	729	1009	72.2%	27.8%	n.a.	n.a.	n.a.	n.a.
Arizona	654	860	76.0%	24.0%	667	919	72.6%	27.4%
Arkansas	547	620	88.2%	11.8%	654	752	87.0%	13.0%
California	753	849	88.7%	11.3%	856	1007	85.0%	15.0%
Colorado	723	873	82.8%	17.2%	773	1060	72.9%	27.1%
Connecticut	824	1099	75.0%	25.0%	891	1198	74.4%	25.6%
Delaware	699	825	84.7%	15.3%	n.a.	n.a.	n.a.	n.a.
District of Columbia	938	972	96.5%	3.5%	n.a.	n.a.	n.a.	n.a.
Florida	626	772	81.1%	18.9%	692	899	77.0%	23.0%
Georgia	664	789	84.2%	15.8%	727	870	83.6%	16.4%
Hawaii	620	761	81.5%	18.5%	673	890	75.6%	24.4%
Idaho	578	724	79.8%	20.2%	612	805	76.0%	24.0%
Illinois	636	851	74.7%	25.3%	673	963	69.9%	30.1%
Indiana	627	796	78.8%	21.2%	644	893	72.1%	27.9%
Iowa	625	777	80.4%	19.6%	656	861	76.2%	23.8%
Kansas	591	786	75.2%	24.8%	624	898	69.5%	30.5%
Kentucky	567	728	77.9%	22.1%	568	904	62.8%	37.2%
Louisiana	518	797	65.0%	35.0%	605	919	65.8%	34.2%
Maine	623	798	78.1%	21.9%	676	914	74.0%	26.0%
Maryland	797	913	87.3%	12.7%	843	1142	73.8%	26.2%
Massachusetts	797	1044	76.3%	23.7%	791	1234	64.1%	35.9%
Michigan	658	895	73.5%	26.5%	707	1041	67.9%	32.1%
Minnesota	733	877	83.6%	16.4%	758	1008	75.2%	24.8%
Mississippi	521	655	79.5%	20.5%	573	848	67.6%	32.4%
Missouri	596	773	77.1%	22.9%	614	893	68.8%	31.2%
Montana	549	710	77.3%	22.7%	n.a.	n.a.	n.a.	n.a.
Nebraska	607	752	80.7%	19.3%	692	879	78.7%	21.3%
Nevada	635	787	80.7%	19.3%	645	905	71.3%	28.7%
New Hampshire	716	966	74.1%	25.9%	746	1067	69.9%	30.1%
New Jersey	761	994	76.6%	23.4%	868	1214	71.5%	28.5%
New Mexico	618	793	77.9%	22.1%	701	921	76.1%	23.9%
New York	720	858	83.9%	16.1%	738	949	77.8%	22.2%

	Full-Time Workers 16 Years and Older				Full-Time Workers 50 Years and Older			
State	Women's Median Weekly Earnings (Dollars)	Men's Median Weekly Earnings (Dollars)	Ratio, Women's Earnings to Men's Earnings	Gender Wage Gap for Workers 16 and older	Women's Median Weekly Earnings (Dollars)	Men's Median Weekly Earnings (Dollars)	Ratio, Women's Earnings to Men's Earnings	Gender Wage Gap for Workers 50 and older
North Carolina	617	698	88.4%	11.6%	625	864	72.3%	27.7%
North Dakota	570	757	75.3%	24.7%	n.a.	n.a.	n.a.	n.a.
Ohio	623	784	79.5%	20.5%	656	902	72.7%	27.3%
Oklahoma	591	678	87.2%	12.8%	635	858	74.0%	26.0%
Oregon	652	849	76.8%	23.2%	727	956	76.0%	24.0%
Pennsylvania	654	825	79.3%	20.7%	689	923	74.6%	25.4%
Rhode Island	701	901	77.8%	22.2%	n.a.	1025	n.a.	n.a.
South Carolina	581	724	80.2%	19.8%	595	795	74.8%	25.2%
South Dakota	567	698	81.2%	18.8%	n.a.	n.a.	n.a.	n.a.
Tennessee	580	735	78.9%	21.1%	636	854	74.5%	25.5%
Texas	596	732	81.4%	18.6%	671	896	74.9%	25.1%
Utah	608	809	75.2%	24.8%	696	888	78.4%	21.6%
Vermont	668	816	81.9%	18.1%	n.a.	n.a.	n.a.	n.a.
Virginia	705	877	80.4%	19.6%	782	1083	72.2%	27.8%
Washington	726	959	75.7%	24.3%	831	1151	72.2%	27.8%
West Virginia	603	753	80.1%	19.9%	660	894	73.8%	26.2%
Wisconsin	660	831	79.4%	20.6%	675	965	69.9%	30.1%
Wyoming	616	917	67.2%	32.8%	n.a.	n.a.	n.a.	n.a.
United States	657	819	80.2%	19.8%	713	953	74.8%	25.2%

n.a. = Data is not available due to a small sample size.

Source: Joint Economic Committee Majority Staff based on data from the Bureau of Labor Statistics (BLS). Data for full-time workers 16 and older was published in BLS Report 1025, Highlights of Women's Earnings in 2009, Table 3 (June 2010). Data for full-time workers 50 and older has not been previously published.

C. Access to Benefits

Comprehensive Health Care Reform: An Essential Prescription for Women

A Report by the Joint Economic Committee Representative
Carolyn B. Maloney,
Chair

Senator Charles E. Schumer,
Vice Chair

October 8, 2009

Executive Summary

The status-quo health insurance system is serving women poorly. An estimated 64 million women lack adequate health insurance.[1] Over half of all medical bankruptcies impact a woman.[2] For too many women and their families today, quality, affordable health care is out of reach. Women are more vulnerable to high health care costs than men. Several factors explain why.

First, women's health needs differ from men's, so women are obliged to interact more regularly with the health care system – regardless of whether they have adequate insurance coverage or not. Second, women are more likely to be economically vulnerable and therefore face devastating consequences when faced with a mounting pile of medical bills. The inability of the current system to adequately serve women's health care needs has come at great expense. One recent study estimates that women's chronic disease conditions cost hundreds of billions of dollars every year.[3]

The following brief provides an overview of the basic facts regarding women's insurance coverage, and the consequences of our broken health insurance system on women's health – both physical and financial. Specifically:

- *Over one million women have lost their health insurance due to a spouse's job loss during the current economic downturn.* Women have lost 1.9 million jobs since the recession began in December 2007, and many of those women saw their health insurance benefits disappear along with their paychecks.[4] Second, women whose spouses lose their jobs are also vulnerable to losing their health benefits, be-cause so many women receive coverage through a spouse's job-based plan. The Joint Economic Committee estimates that *1.7 million women* have lost health insurance benefits because of the contraction in the labor market since December 2007. 68 percent (1,153,166) lost their insurance due to a spouse's job loss. 32 percent (547,285) of those women lost their insurance due to their own job loss.

- *As a consequence of single mothers' job loss, the Joint Economic Committee estimates that at least 276,000 children have lost health insurance coverage.*[5] The weak job market has been rough on single mothers; the number of unemployed female heads of household has increased 40 percent over the past twelve months.[6] For many of these women, the loss of a job means not only a disappearing paycheck, but also the disappearance of employer-sponsored health insurance coverage for their families.

- *Women between the ages of 55 and 64 are particularly vulnerable to losing their health insurance benefits because of their husbands' transition from employer-sponsored coverage to Medicare.* One recent study concludes that a husband's transition from employer-sponsored coverage to Medicare at age 65 can be problematic

- for his younger wife. Many of these wives depended on their spouse's employer-based coverage and are not yet age-eligible for Medicare. As a result, 75 percent of these women reported delaying filling prescriptions or taking fewer medications than prescribed because of cost.[7]

- *Younger women are particularly vulnerable to lacking adequate health insurance coverage.* Over one-quarter (26 percent) of all young women (ages 19-24) do not have health insurance coverage. The weak job market has hit young workers particularly hard, with the unemployment rate amongst young women at 15.5 percent in September 2009, substantially higher than the national unemployment rate of 9.8 per-cent.[8] The dismal job market means that young women are less likely than ever to have access to job-based coverage, and many women who once received coverage through a parent's health insurance plan have seen this coverage evaporate with their parents' jobs.

- *39 percent of all low-income women lack health insurance coverage.* Because of wide variability in state Medicaid eligibility rules, millions of American women fall through the safety net every day. The devastating impact of the recession on state budgets has forced some states to further tighten Medicaid eligibility rules at precisely the time when need is growing fastest.

- *The health consequences of inadequate coverage are more severe for women than for men.* Women are more likely than men to run into problems receiving adequate medical care. Over a quarter (27 percent) of women had health problems requiring medical attention but were not able to see a doctor, compared to 21 percent of men. Similarly, nearly a quarter (22 percent) of women reported that they were un-able to fill a needed prescription, as compared to 15 percent of men.

- *While the financial burden of inadequate health insurance coverage weighs heavily on all Americans, uninsured and under-insured women suffer more severe economic consequences than do men.* Women are more likely than men to deplete their savings accounts in order to pay medical bills. One-third of under-insured women deplete their savings to pay medical bills, as compared to a quarter of under-insured men. The disparity is comparable amongst the uninsured (34 percent of uninsured women as compared to 29 percent of uninsured men).

The comprehensive health care reform proposals offered by the Obama Administration and currently taking shape under the leadership of Democrats in the House and Senate include numerous provisions that are critical to providing quality, affordable health care for *all* Americans, both women and men. Many of these solutions are a key part of the prescription for easing the burden on America's women, for whom the status quo health care system is a failure.

Comprehensive Health Care Reform:
An Essential Prescription for Women

The status-quo health insurance system poorly serves women. An estimated 64 million women lack adequate health insurance.[9] Over half of all medical bankruptcies impact a woman.[10] For too many women and their families today, quality, affordable health care is out of reach. Women are more vulnerable to high health care costs than men. Several factors explain why. First, women's health needs differ from men's, so women are obliged to interact more regularly with the health care system – regardless of whether they have adequate insurance coverage or not. Women's reproductive health concerns, including pregnancy and childbirth, contraception, and the consequences of sexually-transmitted diseases, require more contact with medical providers.[11] Women are more likely than men to have one or more chronic diseases, including diabetes, asthma, and hypertension, all of which require ongoing coordinated care.[12] Second, women are more likely to be economically vulnerable and therefore face devastating consequences when faced with a mounting pile of medical bills. Women comprise more than half of America's poor, and millions of working women continue to earn less than their male counter-parts.[13] Regardless of marital status, women are more likely to be responsible for their children's health and well-being.[14]

The inability of the current system to adequately serve women's health care needs has come at great expense. One recent study estimates that women's chronic disease conditions cost hundreds of billions of dollars every year.[15] The direct costs of women's cardiovascular disease, which impacts 43 million American women, are estimated at $162 billion annually. The direct medical costs of diabetes on women total over $58 billion. The direct medical costs of osteoporosis, which impacts 8 million women, are estimated at nearly $14 billion annually. The direct medical costs of breast cancer are estimated at $9 billion.

The following brief provides an overview of the basic facts regarding women's insurance coverage, and the consequences of our broken health insurance system on women's health – both physical and financial.

Women are no more likely than men to be uninsured, but the sources of women's health insurance policies are quite different from men's. As a result, women are especially vulnerable to losing their health insurance coverage.

Because women are less likely than men to be employed full-time, they are less likely to be eligible for employer-provided health benefits. 27 percent of employed women work part-time, and are therefore excluded from their employers' health insurance benefit plans. In contrast, just 13 percent of working men are part-time employees.[16]

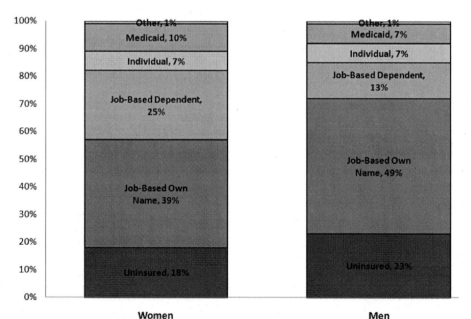

Non-elderly adults are ages 18-64. Numbers may not sum to 100% due to rounding.
Source: Joint Ecomomic Committee calculations from the 2009 ASEC Supplement to the CPS.

Figure 1. Health Insurance Status of Non-Elderly Adults.

Women are nearly twice as likely as men to depend on a family member (typically a spouse) for health insurance benefits. 25 percent of non-elderly women receive health insurance coverage as a dependent on a family members' job-based health insurance plan, as compared to just 13 percent of men. Women are particularly vulnerable to losing health insurance coverage when they are dependent on someone else for their benefits.

First, the weak job market means that a woman is vulnerable to losing employer-based coverage because of loss of her own job or her spouse's job loss. Women have lost 1.9 million jobs since the recession began in December 2007, and many of those women saw their health insurance benefits disappear along with their paychecks.17 Many more women have lost their employer-provided health insurance benefits as businesses have cut back on employees' hours. 3.3 million women who usually work full-time are currently working part-time because full-time work is not available, more than twice as many than when the recession began in December 2007. Many of these women are no longer eligible for employer-sponsored coverage.18 As noted above, women's health insurance coverage is impacted not only by their own employment, but also by their spouse's employment. Women whose spouses lose their jobs are also vulnerable to losing their health benefits, because so many women receive coverage through their spouses' job-based plans. Men have lost 5 million jobs since the recession began, resulting in over one million wives losing their health insurance coverage and joining the ranks of the uninsured. The combination of women's job loss and their spouse's job loss means that women are doubly vulnerable to losing their health insurance coverage in today's weak economy.

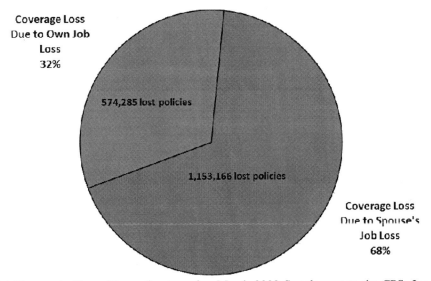

Source: Joint Ecomomic Committee estimates using March 2008 Supplement to the CPS, June 2009 CPS, and BLS Establishment Syrvey data. "Recession-driven job loss" refers to jobs lost between December 2007 and August 2009. A methodological appendix is available from the JEC upon request.

Figure 2. Womens' Health Insurance Coverage lost Due to Recession-Driven Job Loss, (total=1,700,451 women have lost coverage).

Using these job loss statistics and the share of men and women receiving health insurance benefits through employer-sponsored plans, we estimate that 1.7 million women have lost health insurance benefits because of the contraction in the labor market since December 2007. 32 percent (547,285) of those women lost their insurance due to their own job loss. 68 percent (1,153,166) lost their insurance due to a spouse's job loss. In contrast, 3.1 million men have lost health benefits due to job loss since the recession began. Nearly all (96 percent) of those losses are due to men's own job loss.[19]

Health insurance losses due to the economic contraction are likely substantially larger than the Joint Economic Committee's estimates of job-loss related health insurance losses. The rising cost of providing employees with health insurance coverage combined with the economic slow-down means that some employers have dropped health insurance benefits for their employees. Therefore, many Americans who remain employed may no longer have health insurance coverage.[20]

Second, women between the ages of 55 and 64 are particularly vulnerable to losing their health insurance benefits because of their husbands' transition from employer-sponsored coverage to Medicare. One recent study concludes that a husband's transition from employer-sponsored coverage to Medicare at age 65 can be problematic for his younger wife. Many of these wives depended on their spouse's employer-based coverage and are not yet age-eligible for Medicare. As a result, many of these women experience disruptions in medical care. For example, 75 percent of women who experienced an insurance disruption due to husbands' transitions to Medicare reported delaying filling prescriptions or taking fewer medications than prescribed due to cost. These numbers were substantially smaller for similar women who did not experience this insurance disruption.[21]

Women without access to employer-based health insurance benefits – either from their own job or a family members' job – are left to find insurance on their own. 10 percent of all women are insured through Medicaid. 7 percent purchase insurance on the individual market, which can come at an enormous cost. For instance, in many states, a 25 year-old woman purchasing health insurance on the individual market pays 45 percent more in monthly premiums for the exact same plan purchased by a 25 year-old male.[22]

Adult women comprise 38 percent of the uninsured. Certain groups of women are far more likely to be uninsured or under-insured than others. While just 18 percent of all women are uninsured, much larger shares of certain groups of women are left without coverage today.

Roughly one quarter (24 percent) of all single mothers do not have health insurance coverage. 37 percent of all children without health insurance live in single-parent families, the vast majority of which are headed by a working single mother.[23] The weak job market has been rough on single mothers; the number of unemployed female heads of household has increased 40 percent over the past twelve months.[24] For many of these women, the loss of a job means not only a disappearing paycheck, but also the disappearance of employer-sponsored health insurance coverage.

As a consequence of single mothers' job loss, the Joint Economic Committee estimates that *at least 276,000 children* have lost health insurance coverage that they received through their mother's employer-based plans.[25] The recovery package included subsidies to make COBRA coverage more affordable, allowing some of these families to purchase an extension of their existing health insurance coverage for a limited time. But COBRA coverage remains prohibitively expensive for many Americans, particularly working single parents, and many women work for businesses that are too small to be bound by COBRA regulations.[26]

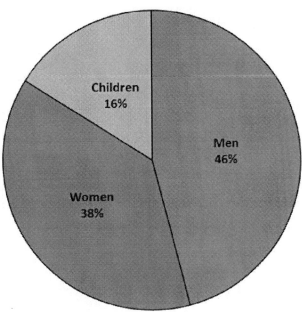

Children are under 18 years old.
Source: Joint Economic Committee calculations from the 2009 ASEC Supplement to the CPS.

Figure 3. Distribution of the Uninsured, (Total=46.3 million)

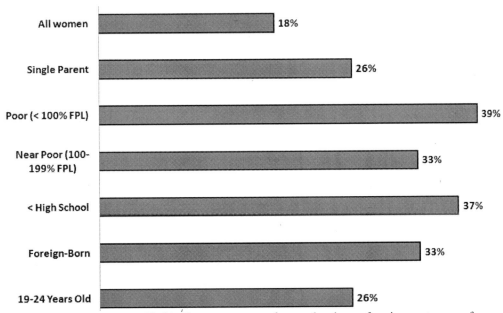

Non-elderly women are ages 18-64. The percentage refers to the share of a given category of women
that are uninsured , e.g. 33% of all foreign-born women were uninsured. FPL regers to the federal
poverty line.
Sources: Data are joint Economic Committee calculations from the 2009 ASEC Supplement to the
CPS.

Figure 4. Characteristics of Uninsured Non-Elderly Women.

Over one-quarter (26 percent) of all young women (ages 19-24) do not have health insurance coverage. The weak job market has hit young workers particularly hard, with the unemployment rate amongst young women at 15.5 percent in September 2009, substantially higher than the national unemployment rate of 9.8 percent.[27] The dismal job market means that young women are less likely than ever to have access to job-based coverage, and many women who once received coverage through a parent's health insurance plan have seen this coverage evaporate with their parents' jobs. Moreover, over half (60 percent) of employer-sponsored health plans do not cover dependents after age 19 if they are not enrolled in school. The vast majority of students covered through their parents' employer-based policies lose their health insurance benefits upon college graduation.[28]

Millions of poor and near-poor women lack health insurance. 39 percent of women living at or below the federal poverty line ($22,050 for a family of four in 2009) do not have health insurance coverage. One-third (33 percent) of near-poor women living between 100-199 percent of the federal poverty line lack coverage. Medicaid eligibility rules vary substantially across states.

The safety net program covers just 45 percent of low-income Americans, leaving millions of low-income women without access to affordable health insurance coverage.[29] Facing serious budgetary pressures due to the recession, some states have further pared back Medicaid eligibility and/or benefits at precisely the time when increasing numbers of families desperately need access to public benefits.[30]

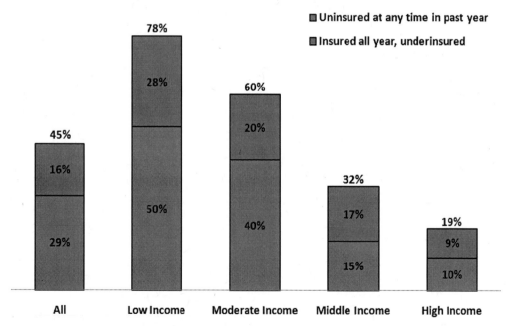

Underinsured is defined as insured all year but experienced one of the following: medical expenses equaled 10% or more of income; medical expenses equaled 5% or more of income if low income (<200%FPL); or deductibles equaled 5% or more of income. Subgroups may not sum total because of rounding. Low income is < $20k, moderate income is $20k-$39.9k, middle income is $40k-$59.9k, high income is $60k or greater.

Source: The Commonwealth Fund Biennial Health Insurance Survey, 2007.

Figure 5. Un-and Underinsured Women, by Income.

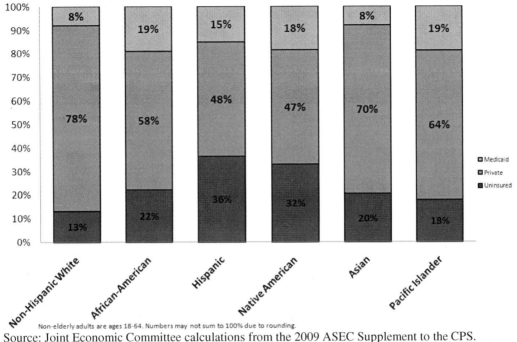

Source: Joint Economic Committee calculations from the 2009 ASEC Supplement to the CPS.

Figure 6. Health Insurance Status of Non-Elderly Women, by Race/Ethnicity.

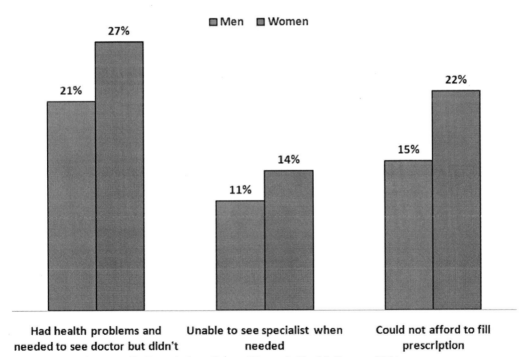

Source: The Kaiser Family Foundation, *Kaiser Women's Health Survey, 2004.*

Figure 7. Difficulty Obtaining Necessary Medical Care, by Gender.

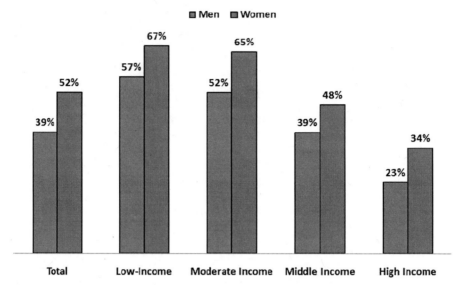

Source: The Commonwealth Fund Biennial Health Insurance Survey, 2007.

Figure 8. Share of Non-Elderly Adults Reporting Difficulty Obtaining Health Care, by Income.

While millions of women lack access to health insurance, millions more women are "underinsured," or covered by health insurance benefits that leave them vulnerable to significant financial hardship. Under an expanded definition of lack of access to health insurance coverage that includes both the uninsured and underinsured, the percentage of women lacking adequate health coverage rises to 45 percent. Over three-quarters (78 percent) of low-income women lack adequate coverage. 60 percent of moderate-income women lack adequate coverage. Even amongst relatively well-off Americans, access to adequate coverage remains tenu-ous.[31]

Health insurance coverage also varies substantially by race. Minority women, especially Hispanics and Native Americans, have the greatest rates of non-insurance – 36 percent of Hispanic women lack health coverage, as do 32 percent of Native American women.

Women are More Likely than Men
to Report Problems with Access to Medical Care

Women are more likely than men to run into problems receiving adequate medical care. Over a quarter (27 percent) of women had health problems requiring medical attention but were not able to see a doctor, compared to 21 percent of men. Similarly, nearly a quarter (22 percent) of women reported that they were unable to fill a needed prescription, as compared to 15 percent of men.

While the percent of men and women reporting difficulty obtaining needed care is inversely related to income, the gender gap in obtaining care is relatively constant regardless of income.[32] While 39 percent of all men reported difficulty, over half (52 percent) of all women reported trouble obtaining needed medical care. Amongst the lowest-income individuals, 57 percent of men report difficult as compared to 67 percent of women – a 10 percentage point gap. Amongst higher income individuals (those with incomes of $60,000 or more), the percentage of both men and women reporting difficulty obtaining needed care is lower, but the gender gap remains, at about 11 percentage points.

Even when compared to men with similar insurance coverage, women are more likely to report difficulty obtaining needed medical care due to cost. The gender disparity in cost-barriers to care is particularly stark for the underinsured. While nearly half (49 percent) of all underinsured men report forgoing needed medical care due to cost, 69 percent of underinsured women report foregoing needed care because they could not afford it. The persistent pay gap between men and women may explain part of this – women earn 77 cents for every dollar earned by their male colleagues, leaving them with a smaller paycheck to cover needed medical expenses.[33] Women are also more likely than men to be the custodial parent and therefore bear responsibility for children and their accompanying expenses, which leaves less money at the end of each month to cover necessities such as medical care for the mother.[34]

Millions of women report difficulty obtaining needed preventative medical care. Study after study shows the importance of preventative care, both in terms of health benefits and the critical role preventative medicine can play in containing medical costs.[35] Yet women are more likely than men to go without needed preventative medical screenings due to cost. Even when compared to men with similar insurance coverage (or lack thereof), women are more likely to see cost barriers to receiving preventative care. The gender disparity is particularly sharp amongst the underinsured: nearly a quarter (23 percent) of underinsured women report foregoing preventative medical screenings due to cost, as compared to 16 percent of underinsured men.

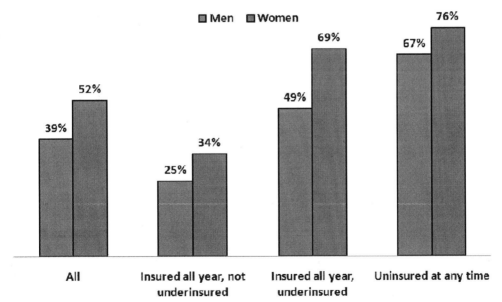

'Going without needed medical care due to cost" is defined as a positive response to one or more of the following: not filling a needed prescription because of cost; skipping recommended test, treatment, or follow up due to cost; having a medical condition and not visiting a doctor due to cost; not getting needed specialist care due to cost. Underinsured is defined as insured all year but experienced one of the following: medical expenses equaled 10% or more of income, medical expenses equaled 5% or more of income if low income (<200% of the federal poverty line), or deductibles equaled 5% or more of income. Non-elderly adults are ages 19-64.

Source: The Common wealth Fund Biennial Health Insurance Survey, 2007.

Figure 9. Non-Elderly Adults Going Without Needed Medical Care Due to Cost, by Insurance Status and Gender.

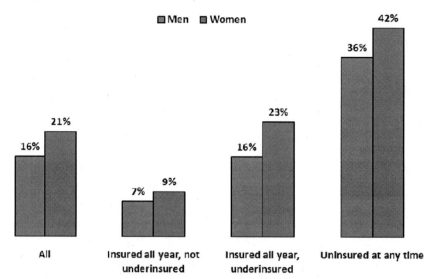

Source: The Common wealth Fund Biennial Health Insurance Survey, 2007.

Figure 10. Non-Elderly Adults Foregoing Needed Medical Screening Due to Cost, by Insurance Status and Gender.

Perhaps unsurprisingly, the same groups of women who are most likely to lack health insurance coverage are likely to report problems receiving necessary medical care. 67 percent of uninsured women report that they delayed receiving needed medical care due to cost.[36] Disparities in access to preventative care are particularly troubling because of the important health benefits of preventative medicine.

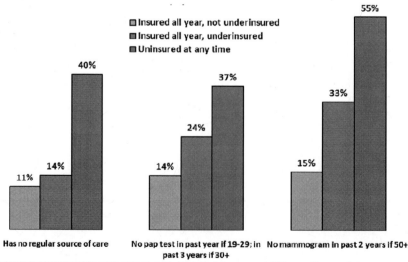

Source: The Commonwealth Fund Biennial Health Insurance Survey, 2007.

Figure 11. Non-Elderly Women's Lack of Access to Preventative Medicine, by Insurance Status.

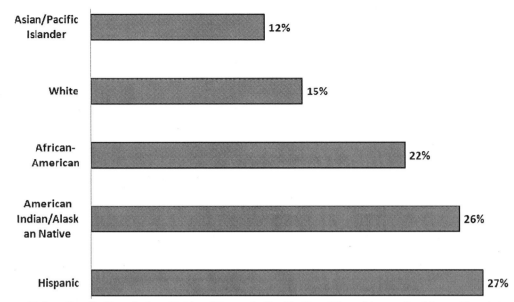

Source: Kaizer Family Foundation, Putting Women's Health Care Disparities on the Map, citing data from the Center for Disease Control and Prevention, 2004-2006.

Figure 12. Share of Non-Elderly Women Reporting NO Doctor's Visit Last Year Due to Cost, by Race/Ethnicity.

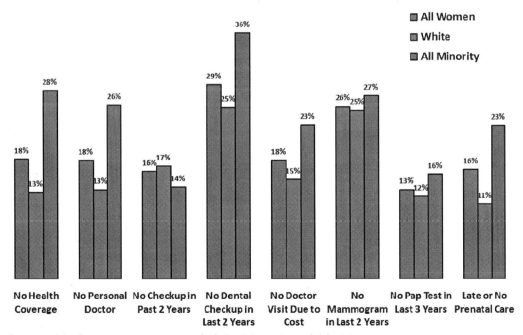

All minorities includes African-Americans, Hispanics, Asian/Pacific Islanders, Native Americans, and Alaskan Natives.

Source: Kaizer Family Foundation, Putting Women's Health Care Disparities on the Map, citing data from the Center for Disease Control and Prevention, 2004-2007.

Figure 13. Share of Non-Elderly Women Reporting Difficulty Obtaining Health Care, by Race.

Uninsured women are far less likely than other women to receive recommended preventative care. Over half (55 percent) of women over age 50 have not received the recommended mammogram, a critical screen for breast cancer that allows providers to catch cancer in its early and treatable stages when conducted on a regular basis. Over a third (37 percent) of uninsured women have not received the recommended pap smear, a critical screen allowing for early detection of cervical cancer. And 40 percent of uninsured women do not have access to a regular doctor.

Significant and troubling racial disparities in women's access to preventative care exist. The high cost of medical care and lack of access to affordable health insurance coverage are likely to explain much of the disparity. Nearly a quarter (23 percent) of minority women report that they were unable to visit a doctor due to cost, as compared to 15 percent of white women. Lack of access to medical care due to cost is particularly problematic for Native American and His-panic women, with 26 percent and 27 percent respectively reporting no doctor's visit in the last year due to prohibitive costs. Access to dental coverage remains highly unequal, with 36 per-cent of all minority women reporting no dental check-up in the last two years as compared to 25 percent of white women. Some preventative medical care remains underutilized by *all* women, regardless of race. Despite recommendations from the American Cancer Society that all women over 40 receive annual mammogram exams, a quarter of all women report no mammogram in the last two years.[37]

Women's reproductive health is severely compromised by un- and under-insurance, with consequences for both women and their children.

The average American woman will spend roughly five years being pregnant, recovering from pregnancy or trying to get pregnant, and three decades trying to avoid an unintended pregnancy.[38] Women's specific health concerns regarding pregnancy and childbirth, access to safe and affordable contraception, and the severe consequences of sexually transmitted diseases require continuous engagement with the health care system.

The consequences of poor access to reproductive health care are severe for women. Women are more likely than men to contract serious sexually-transmitted diseases, including genital herpes, gonorrhea, and Chlamydia, and limited access to regular medical care reduces the likelihood of early detection and effective treatment of these diseases.[39] Women without health insurance are 30 percent less likely to use contraceptive methods requiring a prescription, which are more effective at preventing unintended pregnancies than over-the-counter birth control methods alone.[40] Reproductive health care providers often provide the screenings for female-specific diseases (including breast, cervical, ovarian, uterine, and endometrial cancers) that are less likely to prove fatal with early screening and treatment. Yet limited access to regular care diminishes the likelihood of preventative screenings, as noted above, and further compromises women's reproductive health.

Women's limited access to quality, affordable health care also compromises children's health. Quality pre-natal and post-partum care is strongly linked to healthy outcomes for new infants as well as their mothers.[41] Large disparities in maternal mortality and infant health persist by race and income, suggesting a link between health care access and health outcomes.[42]

While lack of health care coverage remains a critically important barrier to women's receipt of adequate medical care, work-family balance challenges stand in the way of millions of women's access to quality health care.

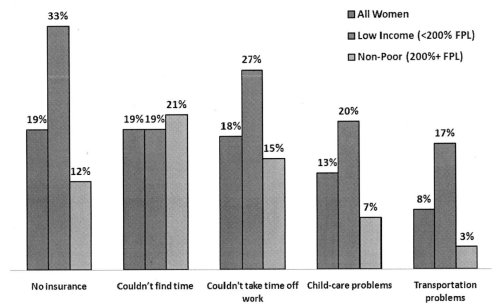

Source: The Kaiser Family Foundation, 2004 Kaiser Women's Health Survey.

Figure 14. Women's Reasons for Delaying or Foregoing Needed Care, by Income.

18 percent of all women report that they delayed or did not receive needed medical care because they were unable to take time off work. Over a quarter (27 percent) of all low-income women report that an inability to take time off work prohibited them from obtaining needed medical care. Similarly, 20 per-cent of all low-income women report that child-care problems kept them from getting needed care. Taken together, these data suggest that health care reform is only the beginning of the solution. Without national policies that assist families in balancing work and life responsibilities, millions of Americans – especially the working poor – will remain unable to access needed medical care.

Inadequate insurance coverage not only puts women's physical health in danger; it also imperils women's financial health. Women bear a heavier financial burden due to un- and under-insurance than do un- and under-insured men.

37 percent of women had medical bill problems in the last year, as compared to 29 percent of men. Amongst the under-insured, 57 percent of women had medical bill problems as compared to 47 percent of men. Amongst those with no insurance at all, the share of both men and women with medical bill problems are even more dramatic – 60 percent of uninsured women and 51 percent of uninsured men.

Many Americans are taking desperate measures to cope with the medical bills that pile up following an illness. Women are more likely than men to deplete their savings accounts in order to pay medical bills. One-third (33 percent) of under-insured women deplete their savings to pay medical bills, as compared to a quarter (25 percent) of under-insured men. The disparity is comparable amongst the uninsured (34 percent of uninsured women as compared to 29 percent of uninsured men).

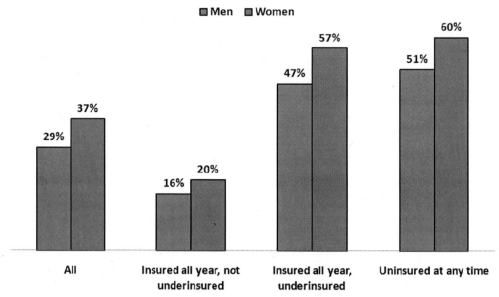

"Medical bill problems" are defined as one or more of the following: problems or inability to pay medical bills; contacted by a collection agency regarding unpaid medical bills; had to change way of life to pay medical bills. Underinsured is defined as insured all year but experienced one of the following: medical expenses equaled 10% or more of income; medical expenses equaled 5% or more of income if low income (<200% of the federal poverty line); or deductibles equaled 5% or more of income. Non-elderly adults are ages 19-64.

Source: The Commonwealth Fund Biennial Health Insurance Survey, 2007.

Figure 15. Non-Elderly Adults with Medical Bill Problems in the Last Year, by Insurance Status and Gender.

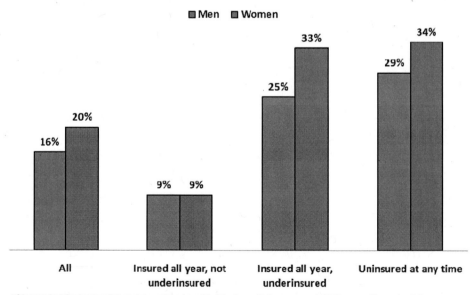

Underinsured is defined as insured all year but experienced one of the following: medical expenses equaled 10% or more of income; medical expenses equaled 5% or more of income it low income (<200% of the federal poverty line); or deductibles equaled 5% or more of income. Non-elderly adults are ages 19-64.

Source: The Commonwealth Fund Biennial Health Insurance Survey, 2007.

Figure 16. Non-Elderly Adults Depleting Savings to Pay Medical Bills, by Insurance Status and Gender.

Comprehensive health-care reform is critical to women's physical and financial health. By simultaneously addressing coverage issues and health care costs, Congress will be tackling two problems that weigh heavily on women and their families – lack of access to affordable coverage and skyrocketing medical costs for those who do have insurance. Specifically:

- *A ban on gender rating* will put an end toward discriminatory practices that charge women substantially more than similarly-situated men for the same health benefits policies. America's health insurers support this reform, recognizing that gender rating is unfair to our nation's mothers and daughters.[43]

- *A ban on denial of coverage based on pre-existing conditions ("guaranteed issue")* will ensure that individuals are not denied insurance coverage because of a medical condition. For millions of breast cancer survivors and others with diseases specific to women, guaranteed issue will make insurance coverage accessible and affordable.

- Inclusive *health insurance "exchanges"* will expand access to health insurance coverage for the millions of women who are not offered employer-based coverage or for those whom employer-based offerings are not adequate or affordable, especially those who work part-time and are thus ineligible for benefits and for women who lose their coverage when an older spouse becomes eligible for Medicare.

- By requiring *well-visits and preventative medicine with no cost-sharing* as part of any policy offered by an insurer participating in the health insurance exchange, health care reform will expand access to necessary and cost-effective preventative screenings and treatments for all women. *Caps on out-of-pocket spending* for any policy offered through the health insurance exchange will insure that a medical crisis no longer comes with the risk of a family financial crisis. *Prohibiting insurers from nullifying previously-offered coverage after costs have been incurred (no "rescissions")* will give families peace of mind in knowing that their health insurance policies must cover what they promise to cover; the rules of the game can no longer be changed mid-way through the process. For the millions of women diagnosed requiring medical attention each year, this security is key.

- The goal of health care reform is to provide affordable health insurance to all Americans, whether or not they have access to employer-provided health insurance benefits. A *public option* may be one of the cheapest ways to ensure that all Americans have access to an affordable, quality insurance plan that meets certain standards.

- *Public subsidies* to help middle-income families pay for health insurance coverage will be a boon for women, whose earnings are typically lower than men's.[44] *Medicaid expansions* will disproportionately benefit women, who are more likely than men to be poor.[45]

The proposals under discussion would allow the millions of American women who are satisfied with their health care coverage and their medical care to maintain the status quo. But it would provide an important and urgent set of solutions for the 64 million women without adequate health insurance. The time has come for comprehensive health care reform.

Expanding Access to Paid Sick Leave:
The Impact of the Healthy Families Act
on America's Workers

A Report by the Joint Economic Committee Representative
Carolyn B. Maloney,
Chair
Senator Charles E. Schumer,
Vice Chair

March 2010

Executive Summary

Paid sick leave is a critical element of job security for American workers, yet forty percent of employees in the private sector today have no such leave.[1] For many workers, a day home sick – or day off of work to care for a sick child – means forgoing a paycheck. At a time when millions of families are living paycheck to paycheck, the lack of paid sick leave forces sick employees to go to work and sick children to attend classes. Going to work sick or "presenteeism" is a public health issue, with sick workers spreading contagious disease to fellow co-workers and customers. The reduced productivity of workers who come to work sick and spillover impacts on other employees is bad for businesses.[2] The provision of paid sick leave through the Healthy Families Act would dramatically expand access to paid sick leave, with salutary effects for society as a whole as well as the families for whom it would impact.

This report represents the first estimates of the impact of the Healthy Families Act (S. 1152 and H.R. 2460) on access to paid sick leave. The bill would guarantee that workers in the United States at firms that employ at least 15 employees accrue at least one hour of paid sick leave for every 30 hours worked.

Using a combination of published and unpublished data from the Bureau of Labor Statistics, the Joint Economic Committee estimates:

- As a result of the Healthy Families Act, at least 30.3 million additional workers would have access to paid sick leave.[3]
- The Healthy Families Act would significantly expand access to paid sick leave for many of America's most vulnerable workers, including lower-wage workers, women, and minorities.[4]
  - o Almost half of the increased access to paid sick leave (14.7 million additional workers) would accrue to workers in the bottom wage quartile.
  - o Nearly half (13.3 million workers) of the increased access to paid sick leave would accrue to women workers.
  - o Almost one-third of the increased access to paid sick leave would accrue to minority workers, including 3.9 million additional African-American workers and 5.6 million additional Latino workers.
- The Healthy Families Act would also significantly expand access to paid sick leave for workers in professions with critical public health implications. For instance, 5.9

million additional food service and preparation workers would have access to paid sick leave due to the Healthy Families Act.[5]

Introduction

Paid sick leave is a critical element of job security and quality for American workers, yet forty percent of private sector workers today have no such leave.[6] Paid sick leave not only gives workers the opportunity to regain their health. Paid leave also allows employees to return to work fully productive, and helps stop the spread of disease to co-workers and customers. As a result, paid sick leave can reduce employers' overall costs while simultaneously contributing to the health of the nation. The United States is amongst only a handful of nations that has no legislation requiring paid sick leave for workers.[7] Voters agree that paid sick days are a critical aspect of job quality. 86 percent of Americans favor a law that guarantees paid sick leave for all workers.[8]

The recession has hammered home the impossible choice a sick worker faces when forced to decide between a paycheck and his or her health. The weak labor market means that many families are living paycheck-to-paycheck, and simply cannot afford to forgo money or to put their job in jeopardy. Yet millions of workers are unable to miss work without forgoing a paycheck – or risking job loss. 17 percent of Americans report that they have lost a job or were told they would lose their job if they took time off due to personal or family illness.[9]

Evidence suggests that employers have been rolling back sick leave coverage in recent years, particularly for low-wage workers who are already struggling to make ends meet. In New York City, for instance, paid sick leave coverage for near-poor workers decreased from 56 percent in 2007 to just 33 percent in 2009.[10] As a result, millions of employees go to work sick every day, exposing their colleagues and customers to illness and dragging down productivity. 68 percent of workers without paid sick leave have gone to work with symptoms of a contagious illness such as the flu, compared to 53 percent of those with paid sick leave.[11] A worker who goes to work sick rather than staying home and resting may end up even sicker, eventually leading to longer absenteeism from work.

The H1N1 outbreak in the spring of 2009 further highlighted the problem with the status quo of no federal policy around paid sick leave. The Centers for Disease Control and Prevention (CDC) recommended "social-distancing" as a strategy for prevention, asking workers with flu-like symptoms to remain home and away from others until 24 hours after all symptoms have resolved.[12] Yet millions of workers face economic hardship if they heed the CDC's advice, because remaining home means forgone wages. When Americans were asked about likely problems they would encounter with staying home for the standard course of the H1N1 virus, the most frequent answer (44 percent) was that they or a household member would "lose pay and have money problems," and 25 percent reported that they would be likely to lose their job or business.[13]

To make matters worse, workers in occupations with critical public health implications have very low rates of access to paid leave. For instance, just 27 percent of food preparation and food service workers have access to paid sick leave. Similarly, just 27 percent of child care workers have access to paid sick leave.[14] These workers are amongst America's lowest-paid, with average annual wages of around $20,000 – half the national average annual wage.[15]

The Healthy Families Act (S. 1152 and H.R. 2460) would have a substantial impact on job quality and job security for American workers. The Healthy Families Act would guarantee that workers in the United States at firms that employ at least 15 employees accrue at least one hour of paid sick leave for every 30 hours worked. As a result of this legislation, at least 30.3 million additional workers would have access to paid sick leave.[16] The Healthy Families Act would significantly expand access to paid sick leave for many of America's most vulnerable workers, including lower-wage workers, women, and minorities. The Healthy Families Act would also significantly expand access to paid sick leave for workers in professions with critical public health implications, including food services.

The Healthy Families Act Expands Paid Sick Leave Access for Private Sector Workers

The Healthy Families Act would dramatically expand access to paid sick leave for private-sector workers. Currently, just 61 percent of the private-sector workforce (62.4 million workers) has access to paid sick leave. This means that nearly 40 million private-sector workers do not have access to paid sick leave today.[17] 30.3 million additional workers would receive coverage under the Healthy Families Act, bringing coverage levels up to over 90 percent in the private-sector workforce.[18]

Specifically, the Healthy Families Act would increase access to paid sick leave for all workers in firms with 15 or more employees. Today, just 64 percent (53.8 million) of those workers have access to paid sick leave. The Healthy Families Act would guarantee that all workers in those firms had access to paid sick leave, adding coverage to 30.3 million new workers with the end result that all 84.1 million Americans in firms with more than 15 employees would have access to paid leave.[19]

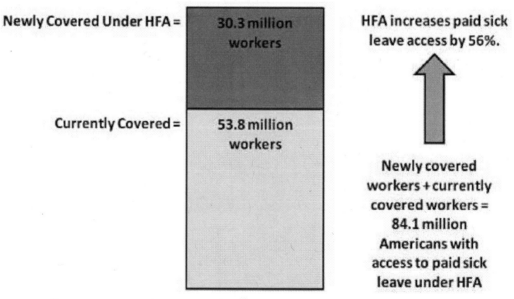

Source: Joint Economic Committee calculations based on unpublished data from the Bureau of Labor Statistics 2009 National Competition Survey.

Note: All figures reflect paid sick leave access at establishments of 15 employees or more, because the healthy Families Act would not impact coverage at smaller firms. As a result, current access to paid sick leave for the total population is larger than the figures here indicate.

Figure 1. Over 30 Million Additional Workers Gain Access to Paid Sick Leave Under the Healthy Families Act.

The Healthy Families Act Expands Access
to Paid Sick Days for Lower-Wage Workers

Low-wage workers are far less likely than higher-wage workers to have access to paid sick leave today. Only 33 percent of workers in the bottom quartile of the wage distribution currently have access to paid sick leave, compared to 81 percent of workers in the top quartile of the wage distribution.[20]

Today, just 35 percent (7.9 million) of workers in the bottom quartile in firms with 15 or more employees have access to paid sick leave. By expanding coverage to workers in these firms, the Healthy Families Act would cover 14.7 million new workers in the bottom wage quartile and resulting in a total of 22.6 million lower-wage workers with access to paid leave. Nearly half (48.6 percent) of all workers with new access to paid sick leave under the Healthy Families Act would be amongst America's lowest-paid.[21]

Millions of these low-wage workers are employed in occupations with high levels of interpersonal contact, including child care, food service, and home health care. As a result of their occupations, these workers are at high risk of spreading disease if they report to work sick.

Yet these workers are also likely to incur a serious financial hardship if they stay home. In absence of paid sick leave, low-wage workers face a choice between a much-needed paycheck and the health of themselves and their children. Moreover, poverty strongly correlates with poor health in the United States.[22] As a result, lower-wage workers may be at a greater risk of illness than higher-wage workers, making access to paid sick leave particularly important for precisely those workers with the lowest levels of current access.

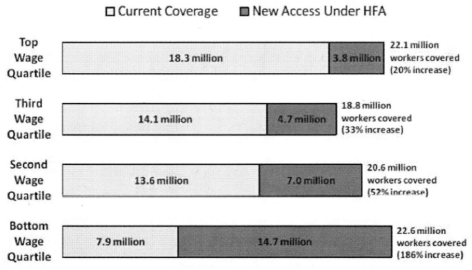

Source: Joint Economic Committee calculations Based on uinpublished data from the Bureau of Labor Statistics 2009 National Compensation Survey.

Note: All figures reflect paid sick leave access at establishments of 15 employees or more, because the healthy Families Act would not impact coverage at smaller firms. As a result, current access to paid sick leave for the total population is larger than the figures here indicate.

Figure 2. 14.7 Million More Low-Wage Workers Will Have Access to Paid Sick Leave under the Healthy Families Act.

The Healthy Families Act Expands
Access to Paid Sick Days for Women

Because the economic hardship associated with a day of unpaid leave is particularly acute for women, access to paid sick leave is of particularly importance for this group of workers. This is especially true for female heads of household, who are solely responsible for their families' wellbeing. Largely because of their sole-earner status, female headed households are amongst the nation's poorest, with nearly 29 percent of female-headed households falling below the poverty level.[23]

Two-thirds (64.3 percent) of mothers work outside the home, and women's earnings make up a substantial share of family income.[24] The typical working wife now brings home 42.2 percent of her family's earnings, which means that families are dependent on women's earnings for their financial well-being.[25] While women's work outside the home is of paramount importance, mothers still bear primary responsibility for a child's health.[26] 80 percent of mothers assume primary responsibility in the family for taking their children to doctor's appointments. Half of all working mothers must miss work if their child is sick, compared to 30 percent of working fathers. And half of all working mothers who do stay home with children when they are sick report that they do not get paid when they must do so.[27] Access to paid sick leave is thus of particular importance for working women because of the double burden they face – both self-care and care for an ill child.

Currently, more than a third (37 percent) of working women in establishments with more than 15 employees lacks access to paid sick leave. The Healthy Families Act would expand access to paid sick days to an additional 13.3 million female workers in these firms, raising the number of women with paid sick leave access to over 40.9 million. This represents a 48 percent increase in the share of working women with access to paid sick leave.[28]

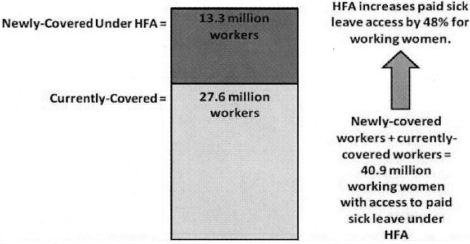

Source: Joint Economic Committee calculations based on unpublished data from the Bureau of the Labor Statistics 2009 National Compensation Survey and the March Current Population Survey.

Note: All figures reflect paid sick leave access at establishments of 15 employers or more, because the healthy families Act would not impact coverage at smaller firms. As a result,current access to paid sick leave for the total population is larger than the figures here indicate.

Figure 3. Over 13 Million Additional WEorking Women Gain Access to Paid Sick Leaveunder the Healthy Families Act.

The Healthy Families Act Expands
Access to Paid Sick Days for Minorities

Minority workers are amongst the nation's most economically vulnerable. 57 percent of working -poor families have at least one non-white parent.[29] Over a quarter of working-poor families (28 percent) have at least one Latino parent, and one-fifth include at least one African-American parent.[30] As a result, these workers are amongst those least able to give up a day's pay in exchange for a day home sick, or home with a sick child.

Yet African-American and Latino workers currently have limited access to paid sick leave. In establishments with 15 or more employees, nearly 40 percent of African-Americans have no paid sick days. Similarly, nearly half (49 percent) of all Latino employees in businesses with more than 15 employees have no access to paid sick leave. The Healthy Families Act would substantially expand access to paid sick leave for minority workers. Under the Act, paid sick leave for African-American workers in covered firms would expand by 60 percent, covering 3.9 million additional African-American workers and resulting in a total of at least 10.5 million African-American workers with paid sick leave coverage. Paid sick leave for Latino workers in covered firms would expand by 78 percent, covering an additional 5.6 million Latino workers and resulting in a total of at least 12.8 million Latino workers with paid sick leave coverage.[31]

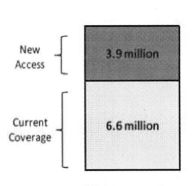

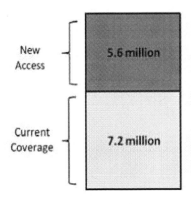

Source: Joint Economic Committee calculations based on unpublished data from the Bureau of the Labor Statistics 2009 National Compensation Survey and the March Current Population Survey.

Note: All figures reflect paid sick leave access at establishments of 15 employees or more, because the Healty Families Act would not impact coverage at smaller firms. As a result, current access to paid sick leave for the total population is larger than the figures here indicate.

Figure 4. 3.9 Million More African-American and 5.6 Million More Latino Workers Will Have Access to Paid Sick Leave under the Healthy Families Act.

The Healthy Families Act Expands
Access to Paid Sick Days
for Occupations with Key
Public Health Implications

Many common infectious diseases are transmitted in workplaces, particularly in workplaces with high degrees of direct contact with the public. For instance, food service workers prepare food consumed directly by the public. Child care workers surrounded by young children and parents incur substantial interpersonal contact. Because of the enhanced danger of contagion for occupations such as these, it is critical that sick employees stay home rather than come to work ill. Moreover, many of those workers in occupations with critical public health implications are amongst America's lowest-paid. Child care workers earn an average of $20,350 annually, while food preparation workers typically earn an average of $20,220 annually.[32] These figures are less than half the national average annual wage for all occupations, $42,270, which suggests that workers in these occupations are also amongst the nation's most economically vulnerable and therefore, amongst the least likely to be able to afford to forgo a day's pay in order to recover at home and avoid spreading infectious illnesses.

Despite the importance of access to paid leave for these critical occupations, food preparation workers and "personal care workers" are amongst the least likely to have such benefits today.[33] Just 28 percent of child care workers in establishments of 15 or more employees have access to paid sick leave today. 48 percent of personal care workers in such establishments have access to paid sick leave today.[34] The Healthy Families Act would substantially expand access to paid sick leave for workers in these occupations with critical public health implications.

Under the Act, paid sick leave for food services workers in covered firms would expand by 259 percent, covering 6.0 million additional food service workers and resulting in a total of at least 8.2 million food service workers with paid sick leave coverage. Paid sick leave for personal care workers in covered firms would expand by 107 percent, covering an additional 1.4 million personal care workers and resulting in a total of at least 2.7 million personal care workers with paid sick leave coverage.[35]

Conclusion

American workers can ill-afford to choose between their health and a paycheck, particularly in today's economic climate. Yet the status quo requires the majority to do just that, as the lack of federal legislation mandating access to paid sick days means that millions of employees must forgo their earnings if they are to stay home to care for their own health or that of a sick child.

The status quo represents not only poor public health policy, as workers sick on the job and children ill at school contribute to the spread of contagious disease. It's also poor economic policy, as sick workers create a drag on their own and co-workers' productivity.

The Healthy Families Act would insure that all workers in firms with 15 or more employees are able to earn paid sick leave, insuring a healthier and more productive America. As the analysis above has detailed, the impact of the Healthy Families Act would be substantial for all Americans, but it would be particularly beneficial for a number of especially vulnerable groups of workers. Lower-wage workers, who are more likely to be unable to weather the blow of a day without pay, would benefit from this legislation. Female workers, who are both more economically vulnerable than their average male counterparts and are more likely to be responsible for their family's health and well-being, would benefit. Minorities, who are more likely to be in lower-wage jobs and therefore less likely to be able to go a day without pay, benefit from this legislation. And occupations with critical public health implications – including the low-paid fields of food service and personal care workers – would benefit immensely.

Paid sick leave is a critical element for workers' economic security. The dramatic expansion of access to paid sick leave under the Healthy Families Act would play a critical role in ensuring that families maintain stable economic footing in unsteady times.

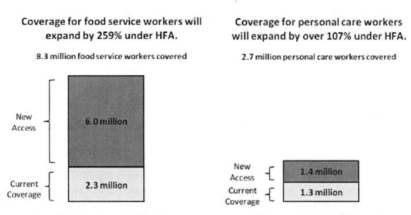

Source: Joint Economic Committee calculations based on unpublished data from the Bureau of the Labor Statistics 2009 National Compensation Survey and the March Current Population Survey.

Note: All figures reflect paid sick leave access at establishments of 15 employees or more, because the Healty Families Act would not impact coverage at smaller firms. As a result, current access to paid sick leave for the total population is larger than the figures here indicate.

Figure 5. 6.0 Million More Food Service Workers and 1.4 Million More Personal Care Workers Will Have Access to Paid Sick Leave under the Healthy Families Act.

Testimony of Ellen Galinsky President and Co-Founder and James T. Bond Vice President for Research Families and Work Institute 267 Fifth Avenue, 2nd Floor New York, NY 10016 (212) 465-2044

Before the *United States Joint Economic Committee*
Hearing on *"New Evidence on the Gender Pay Gap for Women and Mothers in Management"*

July 23, 2009

The Impact of the Recession on Employers

Acknowledgments

We are deeply grateful to members of the Board of Directors of the Families and Work Institute (FWI) who encouraged us to spend our own funds to conduct this timely study on

The Impact of the Recession on Employers and for their astute guidance in suggesting the actual questions we should pursue.

Our biggest thanks go to Board member Ted Childs of Ted Childs LLC and to Lois Backon, FWI's Vice President. It is because of their creative and committed leadership of FWI's Work Life Legacy Awards event—as well as because of FWI's Director of Development Carol BryceBuchanan's passionate leadership of the Institute's Corporate Leadership Circle—that we have the unrestricted funding to be able to do the right study, at the right time!

Our thanks to the work-life scholars and work-life leaders who were so thorough and thoughtful in their reviews of the study's questionnaire, especially Kathleen Christensen of the Alfred P. Sloan Foundation and Katie Corrigan and Chai Feldblum of Workplace Flexibility 2010 at Georgetown Law Center.

We want to acknowledge the outstanding efforts of management and staff of Harris Interactive, Inc., especially David Krane, Vice President, Kaylan Orkis, Research Associate, and Humphrey Taylor, Chairman of The Harris Poll. We also thank the many U.S. employers who took part in the telephone interviews.

We are indeed lucky to have such an exemplary staff at Families and Work Institute— they have supported this study in so many ways. First and foremost is Kerstin Aumann, who provided wise research counsel every step of the way. Kelly Sakai and Shanny Peer provided extremely helpful feedback on the many drafts of this questionnaire. We also thank John Boose for his terrific design for the report and Barbara Norcia-Broms for her careful proof reading. We are grateful to Natalie Elghossain for her skillful assistance in compiling and analyzing the quotes from the open-ended responses of employers and to Courtney Dern for her invaluable assistance in putting the final touches on this study.

Overview of Findings

We all know that the recession has taken a severe toll on employers and on their human resource practices and policies, but no one has been quite sure how severe. Families and Work Institute's new nationally representative study of 400 employers reveals that two thirds (66%) of employers have suffered declining revenues over the past year, with another 28% reporting that the revenues have held more or less steady. Only 6% have experienced growth.

Employers have had to respond, and most (77%) have done so by finding ways to cut or control costs. Among those that have seen their revenues decline, nine in ten have turned to cost-cutting measures—most frequently decreasing or eliminating bonuses, eliminating salary increases, laying off employees and instituting hiring freezes. Layoffs are, in fact, commonplace, as we know from monthly unemployment figures from the U.S. Department of Labor, Bureau of Labor Statistics. In fact, 64% of the employers needing to turn to cost-cutting strategies have reduced the number of employees on their payrolls.

Despite this very bad news, it does appear that that between 34% to 44% of employers are trying to help employees manage the recession—they help employees who have been laid off find jobs, they help employees manage their own finances more effectively, and they connect them to publicly funded benefits and services.

There has been a great deal of debate about what is happening with flexibility during the recession. Since many employers saw flexibility tied to improving retention,[1] would they reduce the workplace flexibility they offer during times of layoffs?

The answer is a resounding no. Most employers are either maintaining the workplace flexibility they offer (81%) or increasing it (13%) during the recession. Perhaps they view flexibility as affecting employee engagement, or perhaps they want to focus on retaining the key employees who remain. While more than a quarter (28%) have turned to involuntary reduction in hours, a comparable percentage (29%) have used voluntary reductions in hours. And perhaps surprisingly, 57% report giving employees some or a lot of say about the schedules they now work.

We know from national unemployment figures that more men than women have lost jobs in the recession, and this study similarly finds that men are more likely than women to work for employers that have laid off employees. But the differences don't stop there—men are also more likely to work for employers that have reduced working hours, changed the scheduling of work hours and reduced salaries.

In addition, employees from for-profit firms are at greater risk of negative financial outcomes during the recession than those at nonprofits. Beyond these findings, there are fewer major differences than expected among employers with varying employee populations in how they are handling the recession, including those with more hourly employees or more unionized employees. Although our most recent study of employers found that small and large employers were equally flexible,[2] this study now finds that large employers are more likely (25%) than small employers (12%) to have increased flexible work options such as flexible schedules and flexible workplace options because of the recession.

Introduction

Economic recessions are associated with significant revenue and earning declines for most employers, and, consequently, with higher rates of unemployment and underemployment for American employees—as well with as other changes in life on the job.

In order to better understand the impact of the current recession on the U.S. labor force and on employers, the Families and Work Institute (FWI) surveyed a random sample of U.S. employers with 50 or more employees in May of 2009. Please see the information in Research Design and Methodology on page 25 for a description of the study design and implementation.

Although the popular media has addressed this issue at some length in recent months, the information presented has been largely anecdotal or based on surveys of specific populations, such as consultants surveying their clients or membership organizations surveying their members. It is important to move beyond speculation to see how a nationally representative sample of employers is dealing with the recession and its impact on its human resource policies and practices. That is the purpose of this study.

Study Questions

This study is designed to address the following questions among a nationally representative sample of U.S. employers with 50 or more employees:

1. What percentage of employers have taken steps to reduce labor and operational costs in the past 12 months?
2. Among these, what specific cost reduction strategies have they used?
3. What are employers doing to help employees deal with the recession?
4. What is happening with workplace flexibility during the recession?

5. Do the strategies employers use for dealing with the recession differ for employers that have larger proportions of women or men; of hourly or salaried employees; of unionized or non-unionized employees? Do they differ for employers that are nonprofit or for-profit? And do they differ for employers of various sizes?

6. What are employers doing that they think would serve as useful examples for other employers? Throughout the report, we include employers' responses to this open-ended question.

Overall Findings

Table 1 addresses the first two study questions—the percentage of employers that have taken steps to reduce labor and operational costs in the past 12 months and the specific cost reduction strategies they have used.

The most obvious indication of the recession's impact on employers is that two thirds (66%) of employers report that their revenues declined in the past 12 months.

- In addition, 28% of employers say revenues remained at approximately the same level, while only 6% report higher revenues.
- *Most employers (77%) have made some effort to reduce or control costs during the recession.*
- Among employers that have experienced lower revenues, 90% have taken steps to reduce labor and operational costs versus 50% of other employers.

In response to our open-ended question about promising practices, some employers reported that they have turned to their employees for suggestions on cost-cutting measures. These include informal requests to more formal procedures:

We generated a cost-savings program where employees submitted cost-saving ideas—the implementing of employees' ideas is going to save a lot of money.

We have organized an active cost committee that is made up of administration and laborers that have meetings once a month and make recommendations.

Decreasing or eliminating bonuses, eliminating salary increases, laying off employees and instituting hiring freezes are the most frequent strategies employers have used to control costs.

As can be seen in Table 1, among those employers that implement cost-saving strategies, 69% have decreased or eliminated bonuses and salary increases; 64% have laid off employees to reduce costs; 61% have implemented a hiring freeze; and 57% have eliminated all travel that is not essential to their businesses.

Other strategies have been used much less frequently, though some of these other strategies to reduce costs may have actually saved jobs—for example, reductions in hours to lower labor costs, increased telecommuting to save on occupancy costs and increased use of compressed workweeks.

In their comments, employers describe some of these practices:

We've had employees go a week a month without working and without pay, and we do this on a revolving basis throughout the location or department. It has worked well to share the pain and maintain morale.

The biggest [strategy] is using compressed workweeks, because it doesn't have an impact on employees' wages, but has an impact on operational costs.

We reduced working hours. That was our biggest cost-saving strategy. Our employees and unions supported that choice.

Table 1. What have employers done to reduce costs during the past 12 months?

Reduction of costs during recession	% of employers
Employer has taken at least one step to reduce labor and operational costs in the past 12 months	77%

Among those employers who have taken steps to reduce labor and operational costs in the past 12 months (maximum N=304), what proportion have used each strategy

1. Decreasing/eliminating bonuses and salary increases	69%
2. Layoffs	64%
3. Hiring freeze	61%
4. Eliminating all travel that is not essential to business	57%
5. Freezing promotions	35%
6. Reducing health care benefits or increasing employee costs	29%
7. Voluntary reductions in hours	29%
8. Involuntary reductions in hours	28%
9. Reducing salaries/wages	27%
10. Increasing use of compressed workweeks	22%
11. Reducing employer contributions to 401(k) or 403(b) plans	21%
12. Increasing telecommuting to save on occupancy costs	19%
13. Hiring workers who earn less	13%
14. Outsourcing work or moving employees into contract work	11%
15. Reducing sick time	8%
16. Offering buyouts or other inducements for early retirement	7%
17. Encouraging phased retirement by working reduced hours	7%
18. Reducing paid vacation time	7%
19. Eliminating the legacy costs of a defined-benefit pension	4%
20. Eliminating health care benefits for retirees	2%

Table 2 addresses the third study question: what are employers doing to help employees deal with the recession? We see such initiatives as having the potential to help employees and employers alike. For example, by reducing stress, health care costs could go down; by treating employees with respect, helping them manage the recession, giving them input and providing them with flexibility to meet personal or family needs, employee engagement could increase.

Between 34% to 44% of employers are helping their employees weather the recession by helping those who have been laid off find other work, providing information on how to manage their own finances and connecting them to publicly funded benefits and services.

Among employers that have laid off employees, 43% have provided them with help to find other work and/or manage this transition. One employer says:

> On a fairly personal level, I would like to say that the Human Resources departments work rather closely with former employees to update résumés, remarket their skills and basically just help them get re-employed. It's not a formal program, but we work very hard at it.

More than one third of employers communicate about the financial situation of their organization very often, and another 41% do so somewhat often. An employer says:

> We have board meetings twice per month, and we have an open door policy.
> Communication is the key—to be available to listen to employees and their concerns.

Additionally, more than one third of employers (34%) report providing special support to help employees manage their own financial situations. This includes helping employees deal with their own finances more effectively in the downturn:

> We have a financial advisor who we make available to our employees. He actually comes into our office which makes it more convenient to our employees.
> We use our EAP provider to provide financial counseling and assistance that we use to assist employees with their finances. We do this both because of the economic crisis and as a benefit to our employees. [In addition], a group of other businesses in the area has identified resources that are available in the community. When a local business is in need, this is a way we have used to become proactive—to assist those who may become victims of the current financial situation.

Employers also provide help in managing stress:

> We have a motivated association program concerned with stress. It is directed to employees that have financial stress, family stress.

And companies report helping others in their community who need assistance:

> We have made donations for clothes, toys and food for people in the community, for people in need. We're having a big garage sale and will donate in the community.

Employer efforts to refer low-income employees to public programs are not new or necessarily related to the current recession. Indeed, there have been various public, NGO and private employer initiatives addressing this issue in recent years in response to the fact that even in the best of times, various public programs (e.g. EITC, child care subsidies, free tax preparation, SCHIP) are underutilized by those who are eligible and could benefit from them. We find that more than two in five employers nationally (44%) are currently making some effort to encourage employee enrollment in public programs or to connect employees to community services.

Table 2. Specific steps taken by employers to support employees

Specific steps by employers to support employees	Overall % of employers
Among those employers that have laid off employees: Do you provide any assistance to employees who have been laid off to help them find other work or to manage this transition? (N=192)	
Yes	43%
No	37
All employers: How often do you communicate with your employees about the financial situation of your organization? (N=398)	
Very often	34%
Somewhat often	41
Not often	25
All employers: Are you providing any special support to employees to help them manage their own financial situations during this recession? (N=396)	
Yes	34%
No	66
All employers: Do you make a special effort to inform employees or laid-off employees who are potentially eligible for publicly funded benefits or services about the availability of these benefits and services? (N=383)	
Yes	44%
No	36

A very large majority of employers is either maintaining the workplace flexibility they offer (81%) or increasing it (13%) during the recession.

Table 3 addresses the fourth study question: what is happening with workplace flexibility during the recession?

- Among employers that have encouraged employees to choose flexible work arrangements (telecommuting, compressed workweeks, voluntary reduced hours and phased retirement), the majority (57%) of employers give employees a great deal or some input into decisions about using those arrangements.
- Among employers that have implemented reduced work hours—both mandatory and voluntary—to reduce costs, a large majority (83%) has maintained the same level of benefits for employees.
- In addition, fully 81% of employers have maintained existing flexible work options during the recession and 13% have actually increased those options, while 6% have reduced them.
- Finally, 26% of employers have specifically used flexible workplace options to minimize the need for layoffs.

Table 3. Workplace flexibility during the recession

Flexible workplace options during the recession	Overall % of employers
Among those employers that have encouraged flexible work arrangements (telecommuting, compressed workweeks, voluntary reduced hours, phased retirement): How much input or choice have employees had about working under the flexible arrangements now in place? (N=156)	
A lot/Some	57%
Not much/None	44
Among those employers that relied upon reduced work hours (phased retirement, voluntary part time, and mandatory part time): Do you still provide the same level of benefits to employees who work reduced hours? (N=134)	
Yes	83%
No	18
All employers: Have you reduced, maintained or increased flexible work options such as flexible schedules or flexible workplace options because of the current economic downturn? (N=375)	
Reduced	6%
Maintained	81
Increased	13
All employers: Have you used flexible workplace options to minimize the need to lay off employees? (N=394)	
Yes	26%
No	74

Although we didn't ask about this in our survey, some employers report that they have tried to find ways to improve morale and to bring fun into the workplace during these trying times:

> We've just incorporated incentives—games to increase morale when the employees go above and beyond. [These are] low-cost or non-monetary incentives.
>
> We're looking at creative ways to have fun in the workplace at low cost. These include secret pal, potlucks, raffles, fund drives, etc.

Employers who report helping their employees manage the recession make statements such as this one:

> Don't impair your most important asset—your human asset.

How Have Employers with Different Characteristics Responded to the Recession?

In the remainder of the report, we address the fifth study question: do the strategies employers use for dealing with the recession differ for employers that have larger proportions of women or men; of hourly or salaried employees; of unionized or non-unionized employees? Do they differ for employers that are nonprofit or for-profit? And do they differ for employers of various sizes?

Employers that Differ in the Proportion
of Women and Men

Men have been disproportionately affected by the recession. They are more likely than women to work for employers that have laid off employees, reduced working hours, changed the scheduling of work hours and reduced salaries.

As shown in Table 4, employers with larger proportions of men than women on the payroll are more likely to have taken steps to reduce costs (80% versus 69%). Specifically:

- Employers with more men on the payroll are more likely to have laid off employees (71% versus 50%). Regarding layoffs, unemployment rates for men have exceeded those for women since the beginning of the recession. In May of 2009, when this survey was conducted, the unemployment rate for men was 9.8% versus 7.5% for women.[3] Men, of course, are more likely to be employed in goods-producing industries where job losses have been the greatest.

- Employers with more men on the payroll are more likely to have frozen promotions (39% versus 26%) as well as to have required employees to work reduced hours (35% versus 17%), which typically means lower wages. National statistics from the U.S. Department of Labor also show that men are more likely to be working reduced hours today (under 35 hours a week) than in the past—up from 9.5% in 2007 to 10.2% in 2008. In contrast, women's level has remained stable—23.5% in 2007 and 23.6% in 2008.[4]

- In addition, employers with more men on the payroll rely more heavily on compressed workweeks (27% versus 15%) to control costs.

- In contrast—although the numbers are quite small, employers with more women on the payroll are more likely (6% versus 1%) to have eliminated health care benefits for retirees. This action has significant implications not only for retirees, but for those nearing retirement as well, especially women since they live longer than men on average and tend to have fewer financial resources.

Employers with a larger proportion of women than men are more likely to communicate about the organizations' financial situation and to connect employees to publicly funded benefits and services.

Table 5 details how employers that vary in the proportion of women to men help employees manage the recession.

- Employers with more women on the payroll than men are more likely to inform employees or laid-off employees who are potentially eligible for publicly funded benefits or services about the availability of these benefits and services (51% versus 40%). This may be because women are more likely to earn lower wages and to live in low-income families than men and to be single parents.[5]

- Employers where half or more of the employees are women are also more likely to keep the employees informed about the financial situation of the organization.

Table 4. How have employers' strategies to reduce costs in response to the current recession varied in relation to the proportion of women employees?

Strategy to reduce cost	Overall %	Women < 50%	Women 50% +	Sig.
Have taken any steps to reduce costs	77%	80%	69%	*
1. Decreasing/eliminating bonuses and salary increases	69%			ns
2. Layoffs	64%	71%	50%	***
3. Hiring freeze	61%			ns
4. Eliminating all travel that is not essential to business	57%			ns
5. Freezing promotions	35%	39%	26%	*
6. Reducing health care benefits or increasing employee costs	29%			ns
7. Voluntary reductions in hours	29%			ns
8. Involuntary reductions in hours	28%	35%	17%	**
9. Reducing salaries/wages	27%			ns
10. Increasing use of compressed workweeks	22%	26%	15%	*
11. Reducing employer contributions to 401(k) or 403(b) plans	21%			ns
12. Increasing telecommuting to save on occupancy costs	19%			ns
13. Hiring workers who earn less	13%			ns
14. Outsourcing work or moving employees into contract work	11%			ns
15. Reducing sick time	8%			ns
16. Offering buyouts or other inducements for early retirement	7%			ns
17. Encouraging phased retirement by working reduced hours	7%			ns
18. Reducing paid vacation time	7%			ns
19. Eliminating the legacy costs of a defined-benefit pension	4%			ns
20. Eliminating health care benefits for retirees	2%	1%	6%	*

Table 5. Specific steps taken by employers to support employees that vary in proportion of women to men employees

Specific steps by employers to support employees	Overall %	Women < 50%	Women 50%+	Sig.
Among those employers that have laid off employees: Do you provide any assistance to employees who have been laid off to help them find other work or to manage this transition? (N=192)				ns
Yes	43%			
No	56			
All employers: How often do you communicate with your employees about the financial situation of your organization? (N=398)				**
Very often	34%	28%	43%	
Somewhat often	41	43	36	
Not often	25	28	21	
All employers: Are you providing any special support to employees to help them manage their own financial situations during this recession? (N=396)				ns
Yes	34%			
No	66			
All employers: Do you make a special effort to inform employees or laid-off employees who are potentially eligible for publicly funded benefits or services about the availability of these benefits and services? (N=383)				*
Yes	44%	40%	51%	
No	36	60	49	

As shown in Table 6, there are no statistically significant differences in how employers with higher proportions of women versus men are using workplace flexibility during the recession.

Employers that Differ in the Proportion of Hourly Employees

There are few differences between employers with larger or smaller proportions of hourly employees in how they control costs during the recession—only two differences were found. Employers where more than half of the workforce is hourly are more likely to have reduced health care coverage or to require larger co-pays, and they are more likely to call for voluntary reductions in hours.

Table 7 compares the strategies for cost controls used by employers with larger and smaller proportions of hourly employees during the recession:

- Employers with more hourly employees on the payroll are more likely to have reduced health care benefits or increased cost sharing by employees, by way of higher premiums (33% versus 22%).
- Employers with more hourly employees are also more likely to rely upon "voluntary reductions in hours" to control costs. Voluntary part-time work is the most common

arrangement. Whether employees have truly free choice—uninfluenced by their
employers—cannot be determined with certainty from our data.

**Table 6. Workplace flexibility during the recession among employers that vary in
proportion of women to men employees**

Flexible workplace options during the recession	Overall %	Women < 50%	Women 50%+	Sig.
Among those employers that have encouraged flexible work arrangements (telecommuting, compressed workweeks, voluntary reduced hours, phased retirement): How much input or choice have employees had about working under the flexible arrangements now in place? (N=156) A lot/Some Not much/None	 57% 44			ns
Among those employers that relied upon reduced work hours (phased retirement, voluntary part time and mandatory part time): Do you still provide the same level of benefits to employees who work reduced hours? (N=134) Yes No	 83% 18			ns
All employers: Have you reduced, maintained or increased flexible work options such as flexible schedules or flexible workplace options because of the current economic downturn? (N=375) Reduced Maintained Increased	 6% 81 13			ns
All employers: Have you used flexible workplace options to minimize the need to lay off employees? (N=394) Yes No	 26% 74			ns

As shown in Table 8, there is only one difference between employers with a higher versus a
lower proportion of hourly employees.

*By a large margin, salaried employees are more likely than hourly employees (55%
versus 36%) to receive help finding other work and to manage the transition when laid off.*

*Employers with a larger percentage of hourly employees on the payroll are more likely to
have used flexible workplace options to minimize the need to lay off employees (30% versus
20%).*

Thus, although employers with more hourly employees are less likely to provide help to
employees who have been laid off, they are more likely to have taken steps to reduce the need
for layoffs.

Employers that Differ in the Proportion
of Unionized Employees

The proportion of unionized employees in the U.S. workforce has decreased significantly
in recent years. Consequently, there are relatively few employers with large proportions of
unionized employees on the payroll. Indeed, 88% of employers have fewer than 25% of

employees who belong to a union. Since that was the lowest percentage group in our measured distribution, we compare employers with fewer than 25% unionized employees with those that have more.

Table 7. How have employers' strategies to reduce costs in response to the current recession varied in relation to the proportion of hourly employees?

Strategy to reduce cost	Overall %	Hourly <= 50%	Hourly > 50%	Sig.
Have taken any steps to reduce costs	77%			ns
1. Decreasing/eliminating bonuses and salary increases	69%			ns
2. Layoffs	64%			ns
3. Hiring freeze	61%			ns
4. Eliminating all travel that is not essential to business	57%			ns
5. Freezing promotions	35%			ns
6. Reducing health care benefits or increasing employee costs	29%	22%	33%	*
7. Voluntary reductions in hours	29%	21%	34%	*
8. Involuntary reductions in hours	28%			ns
9. Reducing salaries/wages	27%			ns
10. Increasing use of compressed workweeks	22%			ns
11. Reducing employer contributions to 401(k) or 403(b) plans	21%			ns
12. Increasing telecommuting to save on occupancy costs	19%			ns
13. Hiring workers who earn less	13%			ns
14. Outsourcing work or moving employees into contract work	11%			ns
15. Reducing sick time	8%			ns
16. Offering buyouts or other inducements for early retirement	7%			ns
17. Encouraging phased retirement by working reduced hours	7%			ns
18. Reducing paid vacation time	7%			ns
19. Eliminating the legacy costs of a defined-benefit pension	4%			ns
20. Eliminating health care benefits for retirees	2%			ns

Table 8. Specific steps by employers to support employees that vary in proportion of hourly employees

Specific steps by employers to support employees	Overall %	Hourly <= 50%	Hourly > 50%	Sig.
Among those employers that have laid off employees: Do you provide any assistance to employees who have been laid off to help them find other work or to manage this transition? (N=192)				*
Yes	43%	55%	36%	
No	56	45	64	
All employers: How often do you communicate with your employees about the financial situation of your organization? (N=398)				ns
Very often	34%			
Somewhat often	41			
Not often	25			
All employers: Are you providing any special support to employees to help them manage their own financial situations during this recession? (N=396)				ns
Yes	34%			
No	66			
All employers: Do you make a special effort to inform employees or laid-off employees who are potentially eligible for publicly funded benefits or services about the availability of these benefits and services? (N=383)				ns
Yes	44%			
No	36			

There is only one difference in the cost control strategies used by employers with more and fewer union employees on the payroll: offering buyouts for early retirement.

- As shown in Table 10, 18% of employers with 25% or more union employees have offered buyouts or other inducements for early retirement versus 6% of other employers.

Table 9. Workplace flexibility during the recession among employers that vary in the proportion of hourly employees

Flexible workplace options during the recession	Overall %	Hourly <= 50%	Hourly > 50%	Sig.
Among those employers that have 'encouraged' flexible work arrangements (telecommuting, compressed workweeks, voluntary reduced hours, phased retirement): How much input or choice have employees had about working under the flexible arrangements now in place? (N=156)				ns
A lot/Some	57%			
Not much/None	44			

Flexible workplace options during the recession	Overall %	Hourly <= 50%	Hourly > 50%	Sig.
Among those employers that relied upon reduced work hours (phased retirement, voluntary part time and mandatory part time): Do you still provide the same level of benefits to employees who work reduced hours? (N=134) Yes No	 83% 18			ns
All employers: Have you reduced, maintained or increased flexible work options such as flexible schedules or flexible workplace options because of the current economic downturn? (N=375) Reduced Maintained Increased	 6% 81 13			ns
All employers: Have you used flexible workplace options to minimize the need to lay off employees? (N=394) Yes No	 26% 74	 20% 80	 30% 70	*

Table 10. How have employers' strategies to reduce costs in response to the current recession varied in relation to the proportion of unionized employees?

Strategy to reduce cost	Overall %	Union <25%	Union 25%+	Sig.
Have taken any steps to reduce costs	77%			ns
1. Decreasing/eliminating bonuses and salary increases	69%			ns
2. Layoffs	64%			ns
3. Hiring freeze	61%			ns
4. Eliminating all travel that is not essential to business	57%			ns
5. Freezing promotions	35%			ns
6. Reducing health care benefits or increasing employee costs	29%			ns
7. Voluntary reductions in hours	29%			ns
8. Involuntary reductions in hours	28%			ns
9. Reducing salaries/wages	27%			ns
10. Increasing use of compressed workweeks	22%			ns
11. Reducing employer contributions to 401(k) or 403(b) plans	21%			ns
12. Increasing telecommuting to save on occupancy costs	19%			ns
13. Hiring employees who earn less	13%			ns
14. Outsourcing work or moving employees into contract work	11%			ns
15. Reducing sick time	8%			ns
16. Offering buyouts or other inducements for early retirement	7%	6%	18%	**
17. Encouraging phased retirement by working reduced hours	7%			ns
18. Reducing paid vacation time	7%			ns
19. Eliminating the legacy costs of a defined-benefit pension	4%			ns
20. Eliminating health care benefits for retirees	2%			ns

There are no differences between employers with higher proportions and a lower proportion of unionized employees in their specific efforts to support employees during the recession, as shown in Table 11.

Table 11. Specific steps taken by employers to support employees that vary in proportion of unionized employees

Specific steps by employers to support employees	Overall %	Union <25%	Union 25%+	Sig.
Among those employers that have laid off employees: Do you provide any assistance to employees who have been laid off to help them find other work or to manage this transition? (N=192) Yes No	 43% 56			ns
All employers: How often do you communicate with your employees about the financial situation of your organization? (N=398) Very often Somewhat often Not often	 34% 41 25			ns
All employers: Are you providing any special support to employees to help them manage their own financial situations during this recession? (N=396) Yes No	 34% 66			ns
All employers: Do you make a special effort to inform employees or laid-off employees who are potentially eligible for publicly funded benefits or services about the availability of these benefits and services? (N=383) Yes No	 44% 36			ns

Only one significant difference is shown in Table 12:

- Employers with more unionized employees on the payroll are more likely to have reduced flexible work options and less likely to have increased them because of the recession.

Nonprofit Versus for-Profit Organizations

Employees at for-profit firms are at greater risk of negative financial outcomes during the recession than are employees at nonprofits.

As shown in Table 13, for-profit employers are much more likely (71% versus 54%) to report lower revenues during the previous 12 months. So not surprisingly, they are much more likely (82%) to have taken some steps to reduce costs during the recession than nonprofit employers (63%). The extent of this difference is, however, unexpected since donations to nonprofits are reported to be decreasing, costs have risen and endowments have declined.[6]

- For-profit employers are more likely (74%) than nonprofit employers (54%) to have decreased or eliminated bonuses and salary increases.
- For-profit employers are much more likely to lay off employees (70% versus 43%).
- For-profit employers are more likely to reduce contributions to retirement plans (25% versus 10%).

Table 12. Workplace flexibility during the recession among employers that vary in proportion of unionized employees

Flexible workplace options during the recession	Overall %	Union <25%	Union 25%+	Sig.
Among those employers that have 'encouraged' flexible work arrangements (telecommuting, compressed workweeks, voluntary reduced hours, phased retirement): How much input or choice have employees had about working under the flexible arrangements now in place? (N=156)				ns
A lot/Some	57%			
Not much/None	44			
Among those employers that relied upon reduced work hours (phased retirement, voluntary part time and mandatory part time): Do you still provide the same level of benefits to employees who work reduced hours? (N=134)				ns
Yes	83%			
No	18			
All employers: Have you reduced, maintained or increased flexible work options such as flexible schedules or flexible workplace options because of the current economic downturn? (N=375)				*
Reduced	6%	6%	11%	
Maintained	81	80	85	
Increased	13	13	4	
All employers: Have you used flexible workplace options to minimize the need to lay off employees? (N=394)				ns
Yes	26%			
No	74			

In addition, nonprofit employers are more likely (44%) than for-profit employers (30%) to help employees manage their own financial situations during the recession, as shown in Table 14. Helping their own employees may be an extension of their missions for a number of nonprofits—to help those in need.

We found no significant differences between nonprofit and for-profit employers in the use of flexible workplace options, as shown in Table 15.

Employers that Differ in Size

When analyzing employer size as an independent variable, it is unnecessary to weight sample data for size of employer as is done elsewhere in this report. Thus, we use unweighted sample data giving us roughly equal numbers of employers in each size category: 50 – 99, 100 – 999 and 1000 or more.

To simplify the presentation and interpretation of employer-size comparisons, we exclude medium-size employers (100 – 999) from the comparisons reported below, comparing only employers with fewer than 100 employees (small) and those with 1000 or more employees (large). Generally, the responses of medium-size employers fall between those of small and large.

Table 13. How have employers' strategies to reduce costs in response to the current recession varied in relation to their nonprofit or for-profit status?

Strategy to reduce cost	Overall %	Nonprofit	For-Profit	Sig.
Have taken any steps to reduce costs	77%	63%	82%	***
1. Decreasing/eliminating bonuses and salary increases	69%	54%	74%	**
2. Layoffs	64%	43%	70%	***
3. Hiring freeze	61%			ns
4. Eliminating all travel that is not essential to business	57%			ns
5. Freezing promotions	35%			ns
6. Reducing health care benefits or increasing employee costs	29%			ns
7. Voluntary reductions in hours	29%			ns
8. Involuntary reductions in hours	28%			ns
9. Reducing salaries/wages	27%			ns
10. Increasing use of compressed workweeks	22%			ns
11. Reducing employer contributions to 401(k) or 403(b) plans	21%	10%	25%	**
12. Increasing telecommuting to save on occupancy costs	19%			ns
13. Hiring employees who earn less	13%			ns
14. Outsourcing work or moving employees into contract work	11%			ns
15. Reducing sick time	8%			ns
16. Offering buyouts or other inducements for early retirement	7%			ns
17. Encouraging phased retirement by working reduced hours	7%			ns
18. Reducing paid vacation time	7%			ns
19. Eliminating the legacy costs of a defined-benefit pension	4%			ns
20. Eliminating health care benefits for retirees	2%			ns

Table 14. Specific steps taken by employers to support employees that vary in relation to their nonprofit or for-profit status

Specific steps by employers to support employees	Overall %	Nonprofit	For-Profit	Sig.
Among those employers that have laid off employees: Do you provide any assistance to employees who have been laid off to help them find other work or to manage this transition? (N=192)				ns
Yes	43%			
No	56			
All employers: How often do you communicate with your employees about the financial situation of your organization? (N=398)				ns
Very often	34%			
Somewhat often	41			
Not often	25			
All employers: Are you providing any special support to employees to help them manage their own financial situations during this recession? (N=396)				**
Yes	34%	44%	30%	
No	66	56	71	
All employers: Do you make a special effort to inform employees or laid-off employees who are potentially eligible for publicly funded benefits or services about the availability of these benefits and services? (N=383)				ns
Yes	44%			
No	36			

Table 15. Workplace flexibility during the recession among nonprofit and for-profit employers

Flexible workplace options during the recession	Overall %	Nonprofit	For-Profit	Sig.
Among those employers that have 'encouraged' flexible work arrangements (telecommuting, compressed workweeks, voluntary reduced hours, phased retirement): How much input or choice have employees had about working under the flexible arrangements now in place? (N=156)				ns
A lot/Some	57%			
Not much/None	44			
Among those employers that relied upon reduced work hours (phased retirement, voluntary part time and mandatory part time): Do you still provide the same level of benefits to employees who work reduced hours? (N=134)				ns
Yes	83%			
No	18			
All employers: Have you reduced, maintained or increased flexible work options such as flexible schedules or flexible workplace options because of the current economic downturn? (N=375)				ns
Reduced	6%			
Maintained	81			
Increased	13			
All employers: Have you used flexible workplace options to minimize the need to lay off employees? (N=394)				ns
Yes	26%			
No	74			

Table 16. How have employers' strategies to reduce costs in response to the current recession varied in relation to their employee size?

Strategy to reduce cost	Overall %	<100 employees	1000+ employees	Sig.
Have taken any steps to reduce costs	77%			ns
1. Decreasing/eliminating bonuses and salary increases	69%			ns
2. Layoffs	64%			ns
3. Hiring freeze	61%			ns
4. Eliminating all travel that is not essential to business	57%	51%	68%	*
5. Freezing promotions	35%			ns
6. Reducing health care benefits or increasing employee costs	29%			ns
7. Voluntary reductions in hours	29%			ns
8. Involuntary reductions in hours	28%			ns
9. Reducing salaries/wages	27%			ns
10. Increasing use of compressed workweeks	22%			ns
11. Reducing employer contributions to 401(k) or 403(b) plans	21%			ns
12. Increasing telecommuting to save on occupancy costs	19%	13%	33%	**
13. Hiring employees who earn less	13%			ns
14. Outsourcing work or moving employees into contract work	11%			ns
15. Reducing sick time	8%			ns
16. Offering buyouts or other inducements for early retirement	7%	3%	17%	**
17. Encouraging phased retirement by working reduced hours	7%			ns
18. Reducing paid vacation time	7%			ns
19. Eliminating the legacy costs of a defined-benefit pension	4%			ns
20. Eliminating health care benefits for retirees	2%			ns

Three significant differences are reported in Table 16:

- Large employers are more likely (68%) than small employers (51%) to eliminate all travel that is not directly related to doing business. Employers with 1000 or more employees are more likely to have employees as well as clients in a variety of locations and are, thus, affected to a greater extent than small employers by travel expenses.

- Large employers are more likely (33% versus 13%) to have increased telecommuting to reduce occupancy costs.
- Large employers are more likely (17% versus 3%) to offer buyouts or other inducements for early retirement.
- As shown in Table 17, large employers are much more likely (66%) than small employers (33%) to help laid-off employees find other work and to manage the transition. This difference may be explained by a number of factors. Large employers are more likely to have human resource professionals on staff who can address these issues and to have contracts with EAP vendors and other business and professional service firms that provide outplacement and counseling services. In addition, providing such services may be important to the organization's reputation in the communities where they operate and among their peers.
- Large employers are more likely (44% versus 25%) to help employees manage their own financial situations during the recession. As above, large employers typically have more resources to provide this sort of support.

Large employers are more likely (25%) than small employers (12%) to have increased flexible work options such as flexible schedules and flexible workplace options because of the recession.

- Finally, as shown in Table 18, large employers are more likely (37%) than small employers (23%) to have used flexible workplace options to minimize the need to lay off employees.

Table 17. Specific steps taken by employers to support employees that vary in relation to employee size

Specific steps by employers to support employees	Overall %	<100 employees	1000+ employees	Sig.
Among those employers that have laid off employees: Do you provide any support to these employees to Do you provide any assistance to employees who have been laid off to help them find other work or to manage this transition? (N=192)				***
Yes	43%	33%	66%	
No	56	67	34	
All employers: How often do you communicate with your employees about the financial situation of your organization? (N=398)				ns
Very often	34%			
Somewhat often	41			
Not often	25			
All employers: Are you providing any special support to employees to help them manage their own financial situations during this recession? (N=396)				**
Yes	34%	25%	44%	
No	66	75	56	
All employers: Do you make a special effort to inform employees or laid-off employees who are potentially eligible for publicly funded benefits or services about the availability of these benefits and services? (N=383)				ns
Yes	44%			
No	36			

Table 18. Workplace flexibility during the recession among employers that vary in relation to employee size

Flexible workplace options during the recession	Overall %	<100 employees	1000+ employees	Sig.
Among those employers that have 'encouraged' flexible work arrangements (telecommuting, compressed workweeks, voluntary reduced hours, phased retirement): How much input or choice have employees had about working under the flexible arrangements now in place? (N=156)				ns
A lot/Some	57%			
Not much/None	44			
Among those employers that relied upon reduced work hours (phased retirement, voluntary part time and mandatory part time): Do you still provide the same level of benefits to employees who work reduced hours? (N=134)				ns
Yes	83%			
No	18			
All employers: Have you reduced, maintained or increased flexible work options such as flexible schedules or flexible workplace options because of the current economic downturn? (N=375)				**
Reduced	6%	7%	3%	
Maintained	81	81	73	
Increased	13	12	25	
All employers: Have you used flexible workplace options to minimize the need to lay off employees? (N=394)				*
Yes	26%	23%	37%	
No	74	77	63	

Conclusion

Obviously, the impact of the recession on employers is a moving target, subject to continual change. It is our intention that this "snapshot in time"—May 2009—of a representative group of employers will provide a picture of the trends, both the negatives and the positives. This study makes it clear that employers are reducing labor and operational costs. This study also indicates that employers recognize that retaining and engaging employees are critical strategies to organizational strength during the recession and beyond.

Research Design and Methodology

Dun & Bradstreet drew a random sample of employers with 50 or more employees from its database. It's coverage of employers of this size is quite good, and we know of no other privately available database that rivals it. Harris Interactive conducted 400 20-minute telephone interviews with Directors of Human Resources or persons with primary responsibility for human resources in (mainly smaller) organizations without HR directors. Interviews were conducted in

May of 2009. The response rate was 21%. The maximum sampling error (i.e., margin of error) is approximately +/- 5%.

Employer size is defined as small = 50 – 99; medium = 100 – 999; and large = 1000 or more. Because smaller employers far outnumber larger employers in the U.S., employers were sampled to provide similar numbers in each size category to obtain reliable population estimates for employers of all sizes. Then, the proportions of employers of different sizes in the sample were weighted to their proportions in the population of employers in the U.S. (as appropriate). Only our analyses of employer size as an independent variable use unweighted sample data. The sample excludes federal, state and local government entities, including public universities. It includes, however, private nonprofit organizations.

We report absolute "differences" as statistically significant only when there is at least less than one chance in 20 ($p < .05$ or "*") that they occurred by chance. The symbols "**" and "***" indicate that absolute differences are less likely than "one in 100" or "1 in 1000" times, respectively, to have occurred by chance. When no significant difference ("ns") is found among groups, the reader should assume that overall sample %s apply to the groups being compared. Only the findings from tests of *linear* relationships are reported in order to simplify interpretation and presentation.

Testimony of Karen Nussbaum
Executive Director, Working America 815 16th St.,
N.W. Washington, D.C. 20006 202-637-5137

Before the United States Joint Economic Committee
Hearing on "Balancing Work and Family in the Recession:
How Employees and Employers are Coping"

July 23, 2009

"Thank you, Chair Maloney, Vice-Chair Schumer, and Ranking Member Brownback.

My name is Karen Nussbaum. I am here today representing a lifetime of experience representing the concerns of working women: as the founder and director of 9to5, the National Association of Working Women; the Director of the Women's Bureau of the U.S. Department of Labor, the highest seat in the federal government devoted to women's issues; assistant to the president of the AFL-CIO; and currently as the executive director of Working America, the community affiliate of the AFL-CIO, an organization of 2.5 million working women and men who do not have a union on the job. My professional experience as a working women's advocate – and an advocate for working men and families – spans all occupations, union and non-union.

The Deteriorating Work-Family Balance

I am glad to be here today in the company of Ellen Galinsky and Cynthia Calvert to discuss this important issue. For generations, the problem of work and family was solved simply -- pay a family wage to a single breadwinner. Accepted norms governed employer-employee relationships, strengthened by unions and collective bargaining. This solution did not work for everyone – around 40% of African American women worked throughout the first half of the 20th century, while single women of all races did not earn a family wage. But the post-World War II economic boom saw a common increase in standard of living across all income groups, families were tended to and communities benefitted from the volunteer activities of their members. The American middle class blossomed in these years.

A 1974 Business Week editorial signaled a shift in employer strategy. In the face of rising international competition, Business Week advised cutting wages and benefits and warned, "It will be a bitter pill for most Americans to swallow – the idea of doing with less so that banks and big businesses can have more." This signaled the inception of a low road strategy, in which employers reduced wages and benefits for most workers, creating a privileged group of professional workers at the top at the expense of a broad middle class; drafted low-wage workers, particularly women, into the workforce; and made a concerted effort to reduce worker bargaining power.

This strategy has proven effective for employers and disastrous for workers and their families. Working and middle-class people shared in the postwar boom, but after 1973, workplace standards were steadily eroded and most Americans ended up doing with less.

- Median family income stagnated, and actually dropped from 2000-2006.[1]
- Defined benefit pensions became a thing of the past – 25 years ago more than 80% of large and medium-sized firms offered defined benefit pensions; today, less than a third do.[2]
- Nearly half of private sector workers have no paid sick leave.[3]
- Nearly a quarter of workers have no paid vacation or holidays,[4] and Americans work, on average, a month longer each year than in 1983.[5]
- More and more women are working multiple jobs and non-standard hours – more than one out of four regularly work nights or weekends; and nearly half of all women work different schedules than spouses or partners.[6]

And banks and big businesses – until they crashed – did get more.

- Between 1948 and 2001, in each cyclical recovery, corporate profits grew an average of 14% while worker salaries grew at half that rate. Between 2001 and 2004, while workers' incomes shrank by 0.6%, corporate profits grew 62.2%.[7]
- From 1987 to 2005, the percentage of Americans without health insurance grew from 12.9% to 15.9%,[8] while from 2002 to 2005 alone, insurance company profits soared by nearly 1000%.[9]

A Return to Standards

Once known as "cafeteria benefits," work and family policies such as child care or flextime were seen as options that could be chosen to fit personal needs above and beyond the basic benefits. While some employees – primarily urban professionals – were making choices at the cafeteria, the great majority of working people no longer even had meat and potatoes.

Some leaders, such as former General Electric CEO Jack Welch, say that there is "no such thing as work-life balance,"[10] that working women have no choice but to sacrifice either work or family. But Ellen Galinsky's impressive work demonstrates that work/life policies are viable and widespread, increase productivity and personal satisfaction. Her research demonstrates that pursuing work/life policies in a recession is *good* for the bottom line.

However, after a 30-year experiment with voluntary adoption of work/family measures in the workplace, we know that reasonable standards will not penetrate the workplace without enforcement. A small minority of professional workers will have the benefits and arrangements they require, but the majority of workers will be subject to work schedules beyond their control, minimal or no benefits and no paid leave to care for their families.

As we decide how to cope with recession, we have the perfect opportunity to take the next step and create workplace standards that are good for the bottom line and for working families.

Freedom to Join a Union
and Bargain Collectively

The most effective and flexible way to create customized improvements at the work place is by enabling working people to talk directly with employers about what is needed – otherwise known as collective bargaining.

A recent study by the Labor Project for Working Families found that, among hourly workers, 46 percent of unionized workers receive full pay while on leave compared to 29 percent of nonunionized workers, while companies with 30 percent or more unionized workers are five times as likely as companies with no unionized workers to pay the entire family health insurance premium.[11] The Employee Free Choice Act would restore the right to collective bargaining, which would help create a contemporary version of work/life balance.

Health Care

Health care costs are crippling families and employers and crowding out the possibility of other workplace improvements. With health insurance expenses the fastest-growing cost component for employers,[12] employers do that offer health coverage are finding it difficult to compete, both with companies in countries that have universal coverage and with employers in the U.S. that do not offer benefits. Meanwhile, workers' out-of-pocket costs have soared from $1,320 in 2001 to $3,597 in 2008[13] and medical debt is a factor in 62 percent of personal bankruptcies.[14]

Solving the health care crisis would create a new floor for the work/family balance, boosting disadvantaged families while reassuring middle-class ones that one piece of bad luck would not plunge them into bankruptcy.

Work/Family Standards

In addition, there are key work/family standards which provide the framework for moving forward.

- Paid sick days
  - Paid sick days help reduce the spread of illness in workplaces, schools and child care facilities, yet 79 percent of low-income workers – the majority of whom are women –do not have a single paid sick day.[15]
  - Congress should support The Healthy Families Act (H.R. 2460), which would provide full-time employees with seven paid sick days per year – and a prorated amount for part-time employees – to be used for short-term illness, to care for a sick family member or for routine medical care.
- Paid family leave
  - The Family and Medical Leave Act has been a great success. Since 1993, workers have used the FMLA more than 100 million times.[16] Yet, half of the private-sector workforce is excluded from it and 4 out of 5 eligible employees who need

leave could not take it because it was unpaid.[17] FMLA coverage should be expanded and wage replacement be added.

- Control over work hours/flexible work hours
  - o Flexibility in regards to workers' work/life balance is particularly important given that Americans work nearly nine weeks (350 hours) longer each year than Western Europeans.[18] In 1970, fewer than half (38 percent) of U.S. women with school-age children were in the labor market. By 2000, more than two-thirds (67 percent) were on the job.[19] In the U.S., two-thirds of working couples with kids put in overtime.[20] Flextime helps solve the common conflict between lengthening work hours and our personal obligations. Flextime gives a worker more control over her or his schedule on an hourly, daily, weekly, seasonal or annual basis. If Workers are expected to flex to the job, the job should flex back. I'd like to recognize Chair Maloney for her leadership on this issue and ongoing commitment to working families across the country. Securing a flexible workplace for women and families is essential to balancing the daily demands of work and personal life, and the Working Families' Flexibility Act seeks to advance that cause.
- Paycheck fairness
  - o The Paycheck Fairness Act is not strictly a work/family policy but it does seek to restore balance – in the wages paid to women and men. (H.R. 12) would close loopholes in the Equal Pay Act of 1963 and is long overdue.
- Misclassification of employees
  - o Misclassification of employees allows employers to save on taxes and benefits, and harms workers and their families by excluding them from health insurance, workers compensation, minimum wage and overtime pay, and family and medical leave or unemployment benefits.
- Child care and pre-school
  - o Affordable child care is a must for single mothers, families that require two incomes to get by, and women who choose to continue working while their children are you.
  - o Early childhood education would not only benefit children but would enable their parents to save on childcare costs and potentially return to the workforce sooner if they chose.

Conclusion

It has taken decades to achieve basic workplace standards – in some cases it has been more than a century of struggle: overtime after 40 hours, no child labor, non-discrimination, and more recently, unpaid family leave. Many benefits workers took for granted in the 1950s are now seriously eroded. We are now far behind all other industrial countries both in standards and practice and we have seen that without the standards, we will not have the practice.

Now is the time to put the next generation of basic workplace safeguards in place.

Testimony of Cynthia Thomas Calvert
Deputy Director, The Center for WorkLife
Law UC Hastings College of the Law 200
McAllister St. San Francisco, CA 94102

Before the United States Joint Economic Committee Hearing on "Balancing Work and Family in the Recession: How Employees and Employers are Coping"

July 23, 2009

Balancing Work and Family
in the Recession

Introduction

"Chairman Maloney, Vice Chairman Schumer, Ranking Members Brady and Brownback, and Members of the Joint Economic Committee, thank you for inviting me to speak about work/family balance in the current economy. My name is Cynthia Thomas Calvert, and I am the Deputy Director of the Center for WorkLife Law at the University of California Hastings College of the Law. I have been researching work/life and flexible work issues for more than twenty years, the last ten of which have been with WorkLife Law's Director, Distinguished Professor of Law Joan Williams. I am the co-author, with Professor Williams, of the only legal treatise on family responsibilities discrimination, *WorkLife Law's Guide to Family Responsibilities Discrimination*, and of *Solving the Part-Time Puzzle: The Law Firm's Guide to Balanced Hours*. As part of my work at WorkLife Law, I manage a hotline for employees who believe they are facing FRD. My testimony today will be based largely on information learned from the hotline.

Although I will be speaking today primarily about the employee's perspective, it is important to note that WorkLife Law also includes the perspective of the employer. WorkLife Law is a nonprofit research and advocacy group with a unique "six stakeholder" model that brings together employees, employers, plaintiffs' employment lawyers, management-side employment lawyers, unions, and public policymakers. WorkLife Law works with these groups to educate them about FRD and flexible work bias, and to craft business-based solutions.

In addition to maintaining the hotline, WorkLife Law has pioneered the research of family responsibilities discrimination ("FRD").[1] We maintain a database of nearly 2000 FRD cases and track trends in FRD litigation. We publish an email alert for employers about recent developments in FRD and provide resources and training materials for employers and their lawyers to use to prevent FRD in the workplace. We educate plaintiffs' and employers' lawyers about FRD case law, and provide technical assistance to policymakers who seek to address FRD and flexible work bias through public policy. We are currently developing a database of union arbitration decisions that involve FRD, and we provide training and information to unions as well. By working with all stakeholders, we obtain and present nuanced and balanced viewpoints that enable us to create usable and effective strategies for preventing and addressing discrimination against caregivers and flexible workers.

Bias against Employees
with Family Responsibilities

FRD, also known as caregiver discrimination,[2] is employment discrimination based on family caregiving responsibilities. It manifests itself in many ways, including:

- refusing to hire pregnant women;
- not promoting mothers of young children;
- punishing male employees for taking time off to care for their children; and
- giving unwarranted negative evaluations to employees who take leave to care for aging parents.

FRD is typically caused by unexamined bias about how employees with family caregiving responsibilities will or should act. For example, a supervisor may assume that a man who is taking care of his dying father will be distracted, and therefore not promote him, even though the man continues to perform at the same high level he always has. Although FRD is certainly not confined to women, a large segment of the unexamined biases that cause FRD is maternal wall bias: bias against women because they are or one day may be mothers.[3] A common bias is that a pregnant woman will not be a good employee because she will have poor attendance or will not be as committed to her job once she is a mother, which can lead a supervisor to terminate her. An illustration of a bias based on beliefs about how caregivers should act comes from an employee who contacted WorkLife Law's hotline: her supervisor apparently believed that mothers should be at home with their children, so the supervisor cut her hours to less than half of full-time, telling her that this would allow her to see more of her kids.

Flexible Work Bias

We are very encouraged by the findings of the Families and Work Institute showing that many work/family programs provided by employers are relatively unchanged by the recession.[4] These findings are consistent with what WorkLife Law has learned from the employers with whom it works: the business reasons for offering flexibility, such as retention of good workers and increased productivity and morale, have not changed.

Unfortunately, what also has remained unchanged is the prevalence of flexible work bias. Flexible work bias mirrors and often overlaps with family responsibilities bias. Employees who work flexibly often encounter unspoken and often unrecognized assumptions on the part of supervisors and co-workers about their commitment, dependability, worth, ambition, competence, availability, and suitability for promotion. These assumptions affect how supervisors perceive flexible workers and their performance, which in turn affects the assignments they receive, and how their work is evaluated and rewarded. While employers may not be changing their work/family programs, employees may engage in "bias avoidance" by not taking advantage of such programs for fear of being marginalized or penalized at work— behavior that may be exacerbated by today's economic climate in which most employees have at least some fear of losing their jobs.

Here is an example of how flexible work bias commonly plays out in the workplace, which is drawn from calls to our hotline: Tonya is a hard worker who regularly receives raises and is given training opportunities to enable her to be prepared for a promotion. Once Tonya begins to work reduced hours and to work some of the hours from home, attitudes toward her change. She doesn't get the challenging assignments anymore, because supervisors reserve those for the "go-getters" in the department who are more committed to their work and can be counted on to complete assignments on time. Tonya no longer receives training opportunities, because her employer assumes that she does not want a promotion and, even if she does, those opportunities should be reserved for employees who are the "future" of the company. Tonya, who used to be able to arrive at and leave the office as desired, now finds that her hours are scrutinized. When she is out of the office, everyone assumes it is for schedule-related reasons, even if the real reason is a visit to a customer. Tonya's work product is reviewed more closely now, as if it may contain more errors due to inattention or incompetence. She receives a more critical performance review, and, consequently, a proportionately lesser raise than when working standard hours. She begins to understand that her future with the company has become cloudy, or perhaps has vanished completely. Interestingly, supervisors in other departments, who work with Tonya but are unaware of her change in schedule, think she is doing the same great job as ever, as do her customers.

This example shows how subtle, often unrecognized assumptions can add up to create a significant flexible work bias that sets up a lesser "flex track," much like maternal wall or caregiver bias sets up a "mommy track" in the workplace. Other common examples of flexible work bias include hostile situations in which supervisors actively try to get rid of workers on flexible schedules, either by creating situations that justify termination or by making work so unpleasant that the employees will quit.

WorkLife Law Hotline

The flexible work bias and caregiver bias largely explain why FRD and related claims come to our WorkLife Law hotline. Many of the employees who contact us are facing personnel actions based on biased assumptions, not on their actual performance.

WorkLife Law has been running the hotline since 2003. In the first five years of our hotline's operation, we received a total of approximately 315 inquiries. The volume of calls to our hotline then increased dramatically. In 2008, we received approximately 125 inquiries, double our previous annual average, with the bulk of the calls coming in the last quarter. This year, in the six-month period between January and July 15 alone, we have had approximately 92 inquiries, which suggests that we will receive more than 175 inquiries for this calendar year.

The inquiries come mostly from women, but also from some men. Men can face caregiver bias and flexible work bias, and it is important to note that they also often face hostile gender bias: if they are somewhat involved with their families, such as coaching soccer, they are "great guys"; if they engage in regular caregiving, they are "wimps," no longer viewed as team players, and seen as lacking the drive necessary to get ahead.

Calls and emails to the hotline come from all types of workers. We have heard, for example, from workers in retail, manufacturing, public safety, education, corporate management, and law firms. We hear from hourly workers, department managers, and vice presidents. We hear primarily from pregnant women and parents of young children, and we also hear from adult children of aging parents, employees with sick or disabled spouses, and grandparents who are guardians of their grandchildren.

Hotline Inquiries in the Recessionary Period

Many of the hotline calls suggest that employers are targeting family caregivers and flexible workers for termination. Some of this appears to be attributable to hostile forms of bias, such as in the case of one caller who reported that when she was pregnant, her supervisor told her that he had doubts she could get her work done once she had children and she was really inconveniencing him and her department. When she asked after returning from maternity leave if she could work a flexible schedule, he told her no, that she could quit if she couldn't hack it. In the ensuing weeks, he acted abusively toward her and she did in fact quit.

Another example that suggests hostility involves a scientist who worked for Shell Oil. Shell Oil has a reputation for having very effective flexible work policies,[5] but as this example suggests, a terrific policy can quickly be undone by a single supervisor.

This call came into our hotline in January of this year, from Tobi Kosanke. Tobi now has a lawyer, and has filed a complaint with the EEOC. The following allegations are from that complaint. Tobi worked from home, examining thin sections of rock through a microscope. This arrangement was created because her daughter was born with a medication-resistant disease that requires her to be breastfed frequently and Tobi has health issues that prevent her from pumping milk at work. The arrangement worked well, Tobi was very productive, had happy clients, and won special recognition awards. After a couple of years, she got a new supervisor who referred to her telecommuting arrangement as "a mess" she would have to fix. The new supervisor moved Tobi to a new team and told her to return her microscope to the company. The supervisor then told Tobi to be in the office 30 hours per week or work part-time and take a pay cut, even though the supervisor was aware that these schedules would not allow Tobi to feed her child. Tobi took FMLA leave and tried to wean her child, but was not successful. Faced with a choice between a paycheck and her daughter's health, she says she asked to work part-time or take a sabbatical, but the company terminated her instead.

It should be noted, however, that many terminations that are not based on *hostile* bias may involve bias nonetheless. An equally likely, although untested, reason for termination of family caregivers and flexible workers in the current economy may be the pressure supervisors feel to show good results with fewer resources as their budgets shrink. They may feel that they have to weed out underperformers and trim personnel costs to maintain their bottom line. The problem arises when supervisors assume that those employees with caregiving responsibilities or who telecommute or work flexible schedules are the "underperformers." Thus, the supervisors' response to this pressure is no less based on bias: when they take personnel actions based not on actual employee performance but on assumptions of how caregivers and flexible workers should or will perform, they are engaging in discrimination.

We have received other inquiries from employees in the past eighteen months who have had their flexible work arrangements eliminated, some of whom were told the elimination was for economic reasons. Some reported that their employers eliminated the company's flex time policy and telecommuting policy. These callers unanimously expressed their needs for flexibility and feelings of near desperation at facing unemployment because of their inability to work a standard schedule. Several were working part-time for caregiving reasons, but were told that they must return to full-time work or be terminated. The economic rationale for this is hard to understand. Requiring employees to return to full-time work, at greater pay and with benefits, costs employers money unless the employers are banking on reducing number of employees on the payroll by forcing the employees to quit.

In another indication that employers may be using the recession as an excuse to terminate family caregivers, since January 2008, we have received 45 inquiries from women who were terminated shortly before, during, or shortly after their pregnancies. Several of these terminations were carried out by supervisors who expressly questioned the new mothers' ability to combine work and family, but most were more circumspect. Several women were told there was not enough work, but these women told us that it was because their work had been given to others. Several were told their positions were eliminated for budgetary reasons, but the circumstances raise questions: one was not given the option of applying for other open positions, one said there was enough funding to move another employee to full-time hours and provide him benefits, and two reported that their employer hired other employees in their department after terminating them.

One example from this group is particularly instructive.[6] An employee had performed well at a large company for more than six years. She had a child, and everything was fine. Her manager worked with her on her schedule, and was happy as long as she was getting her work done. That is lesson one: a little flexibility on the manager's part allowed the company to retain a good worker. She became pregnant again, and soon before she left on leave, she had a new manager. The new manager changed her schedule, putting her on late night and very early morning shifts that she could not work because of the lack of public transportation at those hours. That is lesson two: WorkLife Law has noticed a pattern in court cases and calls to the hotline in which flexibility works fine for everyone until a new manager arrives. The manager may feel a mandate to reorganize the department or may lack a personal relationship with the employees and an understanding of their value to the organization. But whatever the reason, the pattern typically includes the termination of flexibility and action to terminate the employee.

This employee was the sole breadwinner for her family, however, so she did her best to make it work with her new manager. When she went out on leave, others were hired to do her work. She returned to work as planned, and asked if she could take one day a week off or work from home one day a week. She didn't receive an answer. Instead, she was laid off at the end of last year as part of a recession-based, company-wide RIF. She was the only person in her department who was let go, despite her seniority and record of satisfactory performance. This is lesson three: having a child and asking for flexibility are two key trigger points for bias and discrimination.

Almost a third of the inquiries in the past eighteen months have come from employees who feel squeezed between job and family demands. Some of the most heart-wrenching stories come from this group, involving employees who literally weigh the need to put food on the table against the need to provide for the safety and care of dependents. Three recent callers told of being fired because they missed work because their children were hospitalized, even though they had alerted their employer to the reason for their absences. Another caller missed one day of work because her childcare failed and she could not leave her toddler unattended; she was fired even though others in her company missed days of work for other reasons and were not fired. In some of these instances, it appears that the employer has created the situation to force the employees to quit so the employer can avoid paying unemployment and perhaps reduce the likelihood of a lawsuit. In one such situation, a single mother who had been working successfully for nearly a year was placed on a schedule of rotating shifts by a new supervisor, making it impossible for her find childcare. Another with special needs children was told she would have to work large amounts of overtime, although others in her department were not required to. Another caller, a brand new mother, worked overtime for weeks on end, and when she finally asked for a break – which just meant a return to standard hours for a period of time – she was fired.

While flexible work options would resolve most of these situations, the hotline callers state that their supervisors have refused their requests for flexibility, or that they have received a message that their use of such options would impact their careers negatively. Another way to state this is that in workplaces where flexible work bias is weak or nonexistent, employees will resolve work/family conflict through flexible work schedules. Where the bias is too great, they feel they cannot. In one of the strongest examples of bias, some part-time employees reported the belief that they were being targeted for layoffs before employees working standard schedules.[7] In today's economy, employees simply cannot afford to do anything that would threaten their jobs.

In conclusion, bias against family caregivers and flexible workers is a pressing problem in the workforce. Its effect on employees is clear, but we also need to remember that these biases damage employers' bottom lines. They cost employers not just in terms of legal liability, but also in terms of unscheduled absenteeism, worker attrition, smaller available talent pool, lowered productivity and morale, higher health costs, and poorer customer service.[8] Employers and employees will both benefit from bias prevention programs and from effective systems to address bias as it occurs.

We appreciate the Committee holding this hearing and we stand ready to assist in any way in your efforts going forward.

D. Retirement Security

Social Security Provides Economic
Security to Women

A Factsheet by the Joint Economic Committee Representative
Carolyn B. Maloney,
Chair

October 28, 2010

Across the United States, Social Security plays an important role in retirement security—especially for women. Women 65 and over make up nearly 10 percent of the adult U.S. population. In Florida, older women make up 12.4 percent of the adult population, compared to 5.3 percent of the adult population in Alaska. The vast majority of these women receive Social Security. In 2009, over 20 million women aged 65 and older received Social Security benefits, either from retirement benefits, survivors' insurance or disability insurance (see table).

Women are less likely than men to have income outside of Social Security to rely on in retirement,[1] with Social Security accounting for two-thirds of all income for women aged 65 and over.[2] A woman who reaches age 65 can expect to live an additional 20 years.[3] For these women, Social Security is an essential source of income post-retirement, providing a life-long stream of income that is protected against inflation.

Social Security benefits, while modest, are a substantial source of income for older Americans, providing annual benefits of roughly $12,000 for women 65 and over. These benefits are especially critical in reducing poverty among older women. Without Social Security benefits, over half of women 65 and over would be living in poverty. With Social Security, the poverty rate for older women falls to 12 percent. Among widows, the impact of Social Security is particularly striking – 58 percent of widows would be living in poverty if not for Social Security (see figure below).

As policymakers debate future changes to Social Security, they must be mindful of the important role Social Security plays providing economic security and peace of mind to millions of American women.

Social Security Benefits Reduce the Poverty Rate for Older Women, Especially Widows
Percent of Women 65 and Older Living Below the Poverty Threshold, by Marital Status, 2009

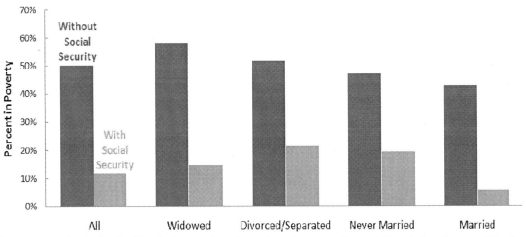

Source: JEC Majority Staff calculations based on data from the Current Population Survey, March 2010.

Across the Country, Over 20 Million Older Women Rely on Social Security Benefits			
	Women Aged 65 and Older As Percent of Adult Population	Number of Women Aged 65 and Older Receiving Social Security Benefits	Average Monthly Benefit of Women Aged 65 and Older Receiving Benefits
United States	9.8%	20,274,175	$1,009
Alabama	10.6%	350,580	$958
Alaska	5.3%	24,098	$947
Arizona	9.8%	400,721	$1,019
Arkansas	10.8%	219,997	$938
California	8.6%	1,936,591	$1,004
Colorado	7.9%	263,989	$973
Connecticut	10.5%	265,555	$1,112
Delaware	10.6%	66,016	$1,067

	Women Aged 65 and Older As Percent of Adult Population	Number of Women Aged 65 and Older Receiving Social Security Benefits	Average Monthly Benefit of Women Aged 65 and Older Receiving Benefits
Across the Country, Over 20 Million Older Women Rely on Social Security Benefits			
District of Columbia	8.7%	30,326	$945
Florida	12.4%	1,500,784	$1,002
Georgia	8.2%	529,712	$982
Hawaii	10.6%	93,812	$1,030
Idaho	8.9%	97,543	$957
Illinois	9.6%	824,600	$1,043
Indiana	10.0%	457,588	$1,050
Iowa	11.2%	246,714	$990
Kansas	10.0%	197,775	$1,028
Kentucky	10.0%	301,065	$930
Louisiana	9.6%	279,676	$891
Maine	11.1%	109,827	$926
Maryland	9.3%	346,725	$1,043
Massachusetts	10.2%	461,518	$1,022
Michigan	10.1%	731,503	$1,066
Minnesota	9.5%	355,993	$1,002
Mississippi	10.2%	204,285	$931
Missouri	10.4%	439,305	$987
Montana	10.2%	72,086	$946
Nebraska	10.3%	129,945	$983
Nevada	8.4%	145,052	$1,017
New Hampshire	9.7%	94,663	$1,038
New Jersey	10.3%	623,706	$1,126
New Mexico	9.9%	128,844	$924
New York	10.2%	1,322,678	$1,075
North Carolina	9.7%	650,506	$1,000
North Dakota	10.8%	51,301	$910
Ohio	10.6%	841,981	$987
Oklahoma	10.3%	263,810	$969
Oregon	9.7%	273,355	$1,011
Pennsylvania	11.6%	1,059,007	$1,031
Rhode Island	10.9%	83,099	$1,027
South Carolina	10.3%	330,669	$990
South Dakota	10.8%	63,335	$912
Tennessee	10.0%	452,099	$980
Texas	8.1%	1,263,999	$952
Utah	7.2%	121,702	$977
Vermont	10.1%	48,016	$1,000
Virginia	9.1%	496,283	$1,000
Washington	8.8%	412,776	$1,036
West Virginia	11.5%	154,221	$954
Wisconsin	10.0%	420,371	$1,024
Wyoming	8.8%	34,373	$980

Source: JEC Majority Staff calculations based on data from U.S. Census Bureau, American Community Survey, 2009, and Social Security Administration, Office of Research, Statistics, and Policy Analysis, OASDI Beneficiaries by State and Country, 2009, Tables 2 and 3.

End Notes for Part I

[1] Joint Economic Committee Majority Staff analysis of the Current Establishment Survey from the Bureau of Labor Statistics.

[2] Ibid.

[3] Boushey, Heather. 2009. "The New Breadwinners." In Boushey, Heather and Ann O'Leary, eds. *The Shriver Report: A Women's Nation Changes Everything.* Washington, DC: Center for American Progress. (http://www.shriverreport.com/awn/economy.php).

[4] Becker, Gary. 2010. "The Revolution in the Economic Empowerment of Women." (http://www.beckerposner-blog.com/2010/01/the-revolution-in-the-economic-empowerment-of-women-becker.html). See also Becker, Gary, et. al. 2010. "The Market for College Graduates and the Worldwide Boom in the Higher Education of Women." *American Economic Review* 100(2): 229-233.

[5] Lacey, T. Alan and Benjamin Wright. 2009. "Occupational Employment Projections for 2018." *Monthly Labor Review*, November: 82-123 (http://www.bls.gov/opub/mlr/2009/11/).

[6] Boushey, Heather. 2009. "The New Breadwinners." In Boushey, Heather and Ann O'Leary, eds. *The Shriver Report: A Women's Nation Changes Everything.* Washington, DC: Center for American Progress.

[7] Joint Economic Committee Majority Staff analysis of the Current Population Survey from the Bureau of Labor Statistics, originally published in Joint Economic Committee Majority Staff. 2010. "Women in the Economy 2010: 25 Years of Progress But Challenges Remain." (http://jec.senate.gov/public/index.cfm?p=Reports1&ContentRecord_id=f5b62c08-227f-42b2-89d5-886a60f22131&ContentType_id=efc78dac-24b1-4196-a730-d48568b9a5d7&Group_id=c120e658-3d60-470b-a8a1- 6d2d8fc30132).

[8] Bureau of Labor Statistics. 2009. *Women in the Labor Force: A Databook.* Table 24. (http://www.bls.gov/cps/wlf-databook2009.htm).

[9] Boushey, Heather. 2009. "The New Breadwinners." In Boushey, Heather and Ann O'Leary, eds. *The Shriver Report: A Women's Nation Changes Everything.* Washington, DC: Center for American Progress.

[10] Joint Economic Committee Majority Staff analysis of the Current Population Survey from the Bureau of Labor Statistics, originally published in Joint Economic Committee Majority Staff. 2010. "Women in the Economy 2010: 25 Years of Progress But Challenges Remain." (http://jec.senate.gov/public/index.cfm?p=Reports1&ContentRecord_id=f5b62c08-227f-42b2-89d5-886a60f22131&ContentType_id=efc78dac-24b1-4196-a730-d48568b9a5d7&Group_id=c120e658-3d60-470b-a8a1- 6d2d8fc30132).

[11] Bradbury, Katherine and Jane Katz. 2005. "Wives' Work and Family Income Mobility." Public Policy Discussion Papers Number 04-3. Boston, MA: Federal Reserve Bank of Boston. (http://www.bos.frb.org/economic/ppdp/2004/ppdp0403.pdf).

[12] Joint Economic Committee Majority Staff analysis of unpublished Current Population Survey data from the Bureau of Labor Statistics, originally published in Joint Economic Committee Majority Staff. 2010. "Working Mothers in the Great Recession." (http://jec.senate.gov/public/?a=Files.Serve&File_ id=c8242af9- a97b-4a97-9a9d-f7f7999911ab).

[13] Ibid.

[14] Boushey, Heather. 2009. "Women Breadwinners, Men Unemployed." Washington, DC: Center for American Progress. (http://www.americanprogress.org/issues/2009/07/breadwin_women.html).

[15] Silverstein, Micheal. 2008. *The Female Economy: What Women Want.* PowerPoint presentation on the United States shared with the Joint Economic Committee.

[16] Hira, Tahira and Cazilia Lobel. 2006. "Gender Differences in Investment Behavior." NASD Investor Education Foundation.(http://www.finrafoundation.org/web/groups/foundation/@foundation/documents/foundation/p118 417.pdf).

[17] Joy, Lois et al. 2007. "The Bottom Line: Corporate Performance and Women's Representation on Boards." New York, NY: Catalyst. (http://www.catalyst.org/publication/200/the-bottom-line-corporateperformance-and-womens-representation-on-boards).

[18] "Women and Profits: Companies That Smash the Glass Ceiling Also Enjoy Higher Profits, a New Study Indicates." *Harvard Business Review* (November 2001): 20. The article cites research by Roy. D. Adler, Executive Director of the Glass Ceiling Research Center at Pepperdine University.

[19] Brown, David A. H. et. al. 2002. *Women on Boards: Not Just the Right Thing ... But the "Bright" Thing.* Conference Board of Canada. (http://www.europeanpwn.net/files/women_on_boards_canada.pdf).

[20] McKinsey & Company. 2009. *Women Matter 3: Women Leaders, a Competitive Edge In and After the Crisis.* (http://www.mckinsey.com/locations/swiss/news_publications/pdf/Women_Matter_3_English.pdf).

[21] U.S. Department of Commerce Economics and Statistics Administration for the White House Council on Women and Girls. 2010. *Women-Owned Businesses in the 21ˢᵗ Century.* (http://www.esa.doc.gov/WOB/).

[22] Gaumer, Zachary and David Glass. 2008. "Health Care Sector Growth." For MedPAC. (http://www.medpac.gov/transcripts/health%20care%20sector%20growth%20final.pdf).

[23] Bureau of Labor Statistics. 2009. *Women in the Labor Force: A Databook.* U.S. Department of Labor. (http://www.bls.gov/cps/wlf-databook2009.htm).

[24] Lacey, T. Alan and Benjamin Wright. 2009. "Occupational Employment Projections for 2018." *Monthly Labor Review*, November: 82-123 (http://www.bls.gov/opub/mlr/2009/11/).

[25] Joint Economic Committee Majority Staff analysis of the Current Population Survey from the Bureau of Labor Statistics, originally published in Joint Economic Committee Majority Staff. 2010. "Women in the Economy 2010: 25 Years of Progress But Challenges Remain." http://jec.senate.gov/public/index.cfm?p= Reports1&ContentRecord_id=f5b62c08-227f-42b2-89d5- 886a60f22131&ContentType_id=efc78dac-24b1-4196-a730-d48568b9a5d7&Group_id=c120e658-3d60-470b-a8a1- 6d2d8fc30132).

[26] U.S. Census Bureau, Current Population Survey, Annual Social and Economic Surveys. (http://www.census.gov/hhes/www/income/data/historical/people/index.html).

[27] Joint Economic Committee Majority Staff analysis of the Current Population Survey from the Bureau of Labor Statistics, originally published in Joint Economic Committee Majority Staff. 2010. "Large Gender Pay Gap for Older Workers Threatens Economic Security of Older Women." (http://jec.senate.gov/ public//index.cfm?a=Files.Serve&File_id=6dc3f726-69e4-46e6-bd8e684f9a2772d5&SK= 86C7 D841 AE4DA8D0A87EBD4CF8BADB4B).

[28] Bureau of Labor Statistics. 2009. *Women in the Labor Force: A Databook.* U.S. Department of Labor. (http://www.bls.gov/cps/wlf-databook2009.htm).

[29] Government Accountability Office (GAO). September, 2010. *Women in Management: Analysis of Female Managers' Representation, Characteristics, and Pay.* Washington, D.C.: Government Accountability Office. (http://www.gao.gov/new.items/d10892r.pdf).

[30] Government Accountability Office (GAO). April, 2009. *Women's Pay: Gender Pay Gap in the Federal Workforce Narrows as Differences in Occupation, Education, and Experience Diminish.* Washington, D.C.: Government Accountability Office. (http://www.gao.gov/products/GAO-09-279).

[31] U.S. Census Bureau, Current Population Survey, Annual Social and Economic Surveys. (http://www.census.gov/hhes/www/cpstables/032010/perinc/new03_000.htm). Note, however, that all of these figures compare all male and female workers over the age of 25, rather than comparing full-time, full-year workers. As a result, the magnitude of these pay gap figures may be influenced by differences in men's and women's work schedules, amongst other things.

[32] Dey, Judy Goldberg and Catherine Hill. 2007. *Behind the Pay Gap.* Washington, D.C.: AAUW Educational Foundation.

[33] Bertrand, Marianne, Claudia Goldin, and Lawrence Katz. 2008. "Dynamics of the Gender Gap for Young Professionals in the Corporate and Financial Sectors." NBER Working Paper 14681. Cambridge, MA: National Bureau of Economic Research.

[34] Carter, Nancy M. and Christine Silva. 2010. "Pipeline's Broken Promise." New York: Catalyst, Inc.

[35] See for instance Waldfogel, Jane. 1997. "The Effect of Children on Women's Wages." *American Sociological Review* 62(2): 209-217; Budig, Michelle and Paula England. 2001. "The Wage Penalty for Motherhood." *American Sociological Review* 66(2): 204-225; Anderson, Deborah J. et. al. 2003. "The Motherhood Wage Penalty Revisited: Experience, Heterogeneity, Work Effort, and Work-Schedule Flexibility." *Industrial and Labor Relations Review* 56(2).

[36] Budig, Michelle and Paula England. 2001. "The Wage Penalty for Motherhood." *American Sociological Review* 66(2).

[37] General Accounting Office (GAO). October, 2003. *Women's Earnings: Work Patterns Partially Explain Difference Between Men's and Women's Earnings.* Washington, D.C.: General Accounting Office. (http://www.gao.gov/new.items/d0435.pdf).

[38] General Accounting Office (GAO). October, 2003. *Women's Earnings: Work Patterns Partially Explain Difference Between Men's and Women's Earnings.* Washington, D.C.: General Accounting Office. (http://www.gao.gov/new.items/d0435.pdf).

[39] Correll, Shelly et al. "Getting a Job: Is There a Motherhood Penalty?" *American Journal of Sociology* 112(15): 1297-1338.

[40] Joint Economic Committee Majority Staff analysis of the Current Population Survey and U.S. Census Bureau data, originally published in Joint Economic Committee Majority Staff. 2010. "The Earnings Penalty for Part-

Time Work: An Obstacle to Equal Pay." (http://jec.senate.gov/public/index.cfm?a= Files.Serve&File_id=00e50917-a323-49d6-8214- d961bf2f732d).

[41] Institute for Women's Policy Research. 2005. "Memo to John Roberts: The Gender Wage Gap is Real." Washington, DC: IWPR. (http://www.americanprogressaction.org/issues/2008/pdf/equal_pay.pdf).

[42] Arons, Jessica. December, 2008. "Lifetime Losses: The Career Wage Gap." Washington, DC: Center for American Progress. (http://www.americanprogressaction.org/issues/2008/pdf/equal_pay.pdf).

[43] Lang, Ilene. President, Catalyst, Inc. Testimony to the Joint Economic Committee. (http://www. catalyst. org/etc/Catalyst_Written_Testimony.pdf); Catalyst, Inc. November 2010. "Women CEOs of the Fortune 500." (http://www.catalyst.org/publication/322/women-ceos-of-the-fortune-1000); Soares, Rachel, et. al. December 2010. "Catalyst 2010 Census: Fortune 500 Women Executive Officers and Top Earners." New York, NY: Catalyst, Inc. (http://www.catalyst.org/publication/459/23/2010- catalyst-census-fortune-500-women-executive-officers-and-top-earners); Soares, Rachel, et. al. December 2010. "Catalyst 2010 Census: Fortune 500 Women Board Directors. New York, NY: Catalyst, Inc. (http://www.catalyst.org/ publication/ 460/23/2010-catalyst-census-fortune-500-women-board-directors).

[44] Ibid.

[45] Joy, Lois et. al. 2007. "The Bottom Line: Corporate Performance and Women's Representation on Boards." New York, NY: Catalyst. (http://www.catalyst.org/publication/200/the-bottom-line-corporateperformance-and-womens-representation-on-boards).

[46] "Women and Profits: Companies That Smash the Glass Ceiling Also Enjoy Higher Profits, a New Study Indicates." *Harvard Business Review* (November 2001): 20. The article cites research by Roy. D. Adler, Executive Director of the Glass Ceiling Research Center at Pepperdine University.

[47] OECD. 2007. "Babies and Bosses -- Reconciling Work and Family Life: A Synthesis of Findings for OECD Countries."See Chart 5.1.(http://www.oecd.org/document/45/0,3343,en_2649_34819_ 39651501 _1_1_1_1,00.html#Selection). Following the publication of the OECD study, in June 2010, the Australian government passed legislation enacting a paid parental leave program scheduled to go into effect on January 1, 2011. (http://www.fahcsia.gov.au/sa/families/progserv/ paid_parental /Pages /default.aspx).

[48] Sasha Corporation. "Compilation of the Cost of Turnover Studies." (http://www.sashacorp.com/turnframe.html).

[49] Joint Economic Committee Majority Staff analysis of unpublished Current Population Survey data, originally published in Joint Economic Committee Majority Staff. 2010. "Expanding Access to Paid Sick Leave: The Impact of the Healthy Families Act on America's Workers." (http://jec.senate.gov/ public/index.cfm?a=Files.Serve&File_id=abf8aca7-6b94-4152-b720-2d8d04b81ed6).

[50] Nichol, Kristin L. 2001. "Cost-Benefit Analysis of a Strategy to Vaccinate Healthy Working Adults Against Influenza." *Archives of Internal Medicine* 161 (March 12): 749 – 759.

[51] Goetzel, Ron Z., Stacey R. Long, Ronald J. Ozminkowski, Kevin Hawkins, Shaohung Wang, and Wendy Lynch. 2004. "Health, Absence, Disability, and Presenteeism Cost Estimates of Certain Physical and Mental Health Conditions Affecting U.S. Employers." *Journal of Occupational and Environmental Medicine* 46 (April): 398-412. See also Lovell, Vicky. 2005. "Valuing Good Health: An Estimate of Costs and Savings for the Healthy Families Act." Washington, DC: Institute for Women's Policy Research. (http://www.iwpr.org/pdf/B248.pdf).

[52] Families and Work Institute. 2009. "When Work Works: 2009 Guide to Bold Ideas for Making Work Work." New York: Families and Work Institute.(http://familiesandwork.org/site/research/reports /2009boldideas.pdf).

[53] See Corporate Voices for Working Families. 2005. *Business Impacts of Flexibility: An Imperative for Expansion*. Washington, D.C.

[54] Data from the National Association of Child Care Resource and Referral Agencies, published in Joint Economic Committee Majority Staff. 2010. "Women in the Economy 2010: 25 Years of Progress But Challenges Remain." (http://jec.senate.gov/public/index.cfm?p=Reports1&ContentRecord_id=f5b62c08-227f42b2-89d5-886a60f22131&ContentType_id=efc78dac-24b1-4196-a730-d48568b9a5d7&Group_id=c120e658- 3d60-470b-a8a1-6d2d8fc30132).

[55] Heymann, Jody. "Can Working Families Ever Win?" *Boston Review*. Orginally published in February/March 2002. (http://www.bostonreview.net/BR27.1/heymann.html#12).

[56] Heckman, James. January 10, 2006. "Catch 'Em Young." *Wall Street Journal*, page A14.

[57] The American Recovery and Reinvestment Act injected extra funding into children's programs for 2010, but the trajectory of decreased spending on children as a share of the federal budget is expected to resume course when that funding expires at the close of the year. See First Focus. 2010. *Children's Budget 2010*. Washington, DC: First Focus. (http://www.firstfocus.net/library/reports/childrens-budget-2010).

[58] Isaacs, Julia. 2009. "Supporting Young Families and Children: A Strategy That Pays." Washington, DC: Brookings Institution and First Focus. (http://www.brookings.edu/~/media/Files/rc/articles /2008/winter_children_families_isaacs/winter_children_families _isaacs.pdf).

[59] U. S. Census Bureau, Current Population Survey. 2009. Table POV01: Age and Sex of All People, Family Members and Unrelated Individuals Iterated by Income-to-Poverty Ratio and Race. (http://www.census.gov/hhes/www/cpstables/032010/pov/new01_100_01.htm).

[60] Johnson, Richard W. and Joshua M. Wiener. 2006. "A Profile of Frail Older Americans and Their Caregivers." Washington, DC: Urban Institute. (http://www.urban.org/UploadedPDF/311284_older_americans.pdf).

[61] Johnson, Richard W. and Anthony T. Lo Sasso. 2006. The Impact of Elder Care on Women's Labor Supply. *Inquiry* 43(3): 195-210.

[62] Papke, Leslie E. et al. 2008. "Retirement Security for Women: Progress to Date and Policies for Tomorrow." Washington, DC: Retirement Security Project. (http://www.pewtrusts.org/uploadedFiles/ wwwpewtrustsorg/Reports/Retirement_security/RSPPB_Women_FINAL_4.2.2008.pdf).

[63] Joint Economic Committee Majority Staff analysis of the Current Population Survey, originally published in Joint Economic Committee Majority Staff. 2010. "Social Security Provides Economic Security to Women." (http://jec.senate.gov/public/?a=Files.Serve&File_id=d0036901-2da3-4387-b77fd33afffe6f7f).

[64] Wolff, Jennifer I. and Judith D. Kasper. 2006. Caregivers of Frail Elders: Updating a National Profile. *The Gerontologist* 46(3): 344-356. See also White-Means, Shelly and Rose M. Rubin. 2008. "Retirement Security for Family Elder Caregivers with Labor Force Employment." Washington, DC: National Academy for Social Insurance.   (http://www.nasi.org/sites/default/files/research/White-Means_and_Rubin_January_2009_Rockefeller.pdf).

[65] Joint Economic Committee Majority Staff. 2009. "Comprehensive Health Reform: An Essential Prescription for Women."   (http://jec.senate.gov/public/index.cfm?a=Files.Serve&File_id=1b11097b-90cb-4806-   8da8-16be5fdafe7a).

[66] Galinsky, Ellen. President, Families and Work Institute. July 23, 2009. Testimony to the Joint Economic Committee. "Balancing Work and Family in the Recession: How Employees and Employers Are Coping."

[67] Kornbluh, Karen. 2005. "The Joy of Flex." *Washington Monthly*. (http://www.newamerica.net/node/7355).

[68] Lovell, Vicky. 2005. "Valuing Good Health: An Estimate of Costs and Savings for the Healthy Families Act," Washington DC: Institute for Women's Policy Research. (http://www.iwpr.org/pdf/B248.pdf).

[69] Senator Christopher Dodd. 2003. "Dodd Introduces Bill to Expand Historic Family and Medical Leave Act." (http://dodd.senate.gov/?q=node/3270/print&pr=press/Releases/03/0205.htm).

[70] See Boushey, Heather. 2009. "Helping Breadwinners When It Can't Wait: A Progressive Program for Family Leave Insurance." Washington, DC: Center for American Progress. (http://www.americanprogress. org/issues/2009/06/fmla.html); See also the Family Leave Insurance Act of 2009, introduced by Representatives Pete Stark (D-CA), Lynn Woolsey (D-CA), George Miller (D-CA), and Carolyn Maloney (D-NY), modeled on California's paid family leave program. For a comprehensive Family Security Insurance policy proposal encompassing paid family leave, see Workplace Flexibility 2010 and the Berkeley Center on Health, Economic, and Family Security. 2010. *Family Security Insurance: A New Foundation for Economic Security*. (http://www.law.berkeley.edu/files/chefs/family_security_ insurance_ 2010_Final_web.pdf).

[71] Joint Economic Committee Majority Staff. 2009. "Vicious Cycle: How Unfair Credit Card Practices are Squeezing Consumers and Undermining the Recovery." (http://jec.senate.gov/public/index. cfm?p=Reports1&ContentRecord_id=355f9ac1-5056-8059-76d9-   8b95b3c0a95b&ContentType_id= efc78dac-24b1-4196-a730-d48568b9a5d7&Group_id=c120e658-3d60-470b-a8a1-6d2d8fc30132& MonthDisplay=5&YearDisplay=2009)

[72] Warren, Elizabeth. 2009. "Feminomics: Women and Bankruptcy." (http://www.huffingtonpost.com/elizabeth-warren/feminomics-women-and-bank_b_395667.html).

[73] Surveys suggest that women are currently less financially-savvy than men, a fact that may be remedied with the clear presentation of the details of financial transactions as mandated by the Dodd-Frank Act. See, for instance, FINRA. 2009. "Financial Capability in the United States." (http://www.finrafoundation.org/ web/groups/foundation/@foundation/documents/foundation/p120535.pd_f).

[74] Dill, Janette S., and John Cagle. 2010. Caregiving in a Patient's Place of Residence: Turnover of Direct Care Workers in Home Care and Hospice Agencies. *Journal of Health and Aging* 22:713-733; Whitebook, Marcy et al. 2004. *Then and Now: Changes in Child Care Staffing*. Berkeley, CA: Center for the Child Care Workforce. (http://www.eric.ed.gov/ERICWebPortal/search/detailmini.jsp?_   nfpb=true&_   &ERICE xtSearch_SearchValue_0=E D452984&ERICExtSearch_SearchType_0=no&accno=ED452984).

[75] Long Island Care at Home & Osborne vs. Evelyn Coke; Bureau of Labor Statistics. 2010. "Home Health Aides and Personal and Home Care Aides." *Occupational Outlook Handbook, 2010-2011 Edition.* (http://www.bls.gov/oco/ocos326.htm).

End Notes for "Women in the Recession: Mothers and Families Hit Hard"

[1] Joint Economic Committee, "Equality in Job Loss: Women Are Increasingly Vulnerable to Layoffs During Recessions" July 22, 2008.

[2] Bureau of Labor Statistics (BLS), Current Population Survey (CPS), Table 4. Number of families by presence and age of own children under 18 years old, type of family, employment status of parents, race and Hispanic or Latino ethnicity, 2008 annual averages. The Current Population Survey is a monthly survey of about 50,000 households conducted by the Bureau of the Census for the Bureau of Labor Statistics. The sample is scientifically selected to represent the civilian non-institutional population. See www.census.gov/cps/ for more information on this survey.

[3] BLS, Current Employment Statistics. The last seven months available data are for August 2008 through February 2009.

[4] BLS, Current Population Survey, unpublished tables. These data are not seasonally adjusted. According to the CPS, a "family" is a group of two persons or more (one of whom is the head of the household) residing together and related by birth, marriage, or adoption. Thus, female heads of households may include households where the dependents are the aging parents rather than children of the head of household. We note that the CPS discontinued the use of the word "head of household" in March 1980 and replaced it with "householder."

[5] This is the sum of the unemployed and the marginally attached. *Ibid.*

[6] *Ibid.*

[7] *Ibid.*

[8] BLS, Current Population Survey, Table A-1. Employment status of the civilian population by sex and age, various months. These data are seasonally adjusted.

[9] BLS, Current Population Survey, unpublished tables.

[10] *Ibid.* We note that the April 2009 data show a reduction in the unemployment rate. However, this is a highly volatile series and it is not possible to extrapolate a change in trend from a single observation. This hold for figures 4-7.

[11] *Ibid.*

[12] *Ibid.*

[13] Although none of the data used for Figures 4 -7 are seasonally adjusted, a seasonal trend is only visible for Hispanic female heads of households, shown in Figure 7. The peak in the unemployment rate during the last recession and the spike in unemployment during month 12 of the current recession are for December. This strong seasonality may indicate that Hispanic women who maintain families are more likely to be employed in occupations that have strong seasonal trends. *Ibid.*

End Notes for "Understanding the Economy: Working Mothers in the Great Recession"

[1] Bureau of Labor Statistics, Current Employment Survey.

[2] Ibid.

[3] April's strong employment growth showed women gained 86,000 jobs last month, far fewer than the 204,000 jobs gained by men in April. Bureau of Labor Statistics, Current Employment Survey, April 2010.

[4] The Joint Economic Committee released a report on working mothers last year. See Women in the Recession: Working Mothers Face High Rates of Unemployment, May 28, 2009.

[5] Data is from Tables 4, 4a, and 6 using data from the Current Population Survey.

[6] Unless otherwise specified, mother refers to a woman with her own children under the age of 18. Married mothers are those with a spouse who is present. Single mothers include married mothers with an absent spouse; divorced, separated, and widowed mothers; and mothers who have never been married.

[7] See Joint Economic Committee report: The Earnings Penalty for Part-Time Work, April 20, 2010.

[8] Many child care centers do not offer prorated part-time child care meaning that the per-hour cost for part-time care is higher than for full-time care.

End Notes for "Testimony of Lisa M. Maatz

[1] Jared Bernstein and Christina Romer. *The Job Impact of the American Recovery and Reinvestment Act*. Retrieved March 5, 2009, from http://otrans.3cdn.net/ee40602f9a7d8172b8_ozm6bt5oi.pdf.

[2] U.S. Census Bureau and the Bureau of Labor Statistics. (August 2008). *Annual Demographic Survey*. Retrieved December 11, 2008, from http://pubdb3.census.gov/macro/032008/perinc/new05_000.htm.

[3] National Committee on Pay Equity. (September 2007). *The Wage Gap Over Time: In Real Dollars, Women See a Continuing Gap*. Retrieved December 11, 2008, from http://www.pay-equity.org/infotime.html.

[4] U.S. Census Bureau and the Bureau of Labor Statistics. (August 2008). *Annual Demographic Survey*. Retrieved December 11, 2008, from http://pubdb3.census.gov/macro/032008/perinc/new05_000.htm.

[5] Institute for Women's Policy Research. (July 2008). *Improving Pay Equity Would Mean Great Gains for Women*. Retrieved December 11, 2008 from http://www.iwpr.org/pdf/payequityrelease.pdf.

[6] AAUW Educational Foundation. (March 2003). *Women at Work*. Washington, DC.

[7] National Women's Law Center. (2005). *Tools of the Trade: Using the Law to Address Sex Segregation in High School Career and Technical Education*. Retrieved December 11, 2008, from http://www.nwlc.org/pdf/NWLCToolsoftheTrade05.pdf.

[8] See, for example, Blau, Francine and Lawrence Khan. *The Gender Pay Gap: Going, Going ... But not Gone*. Paper presented at the Cornell University Inequality Symposium, October 2002.

[9] AAUW Educational Foundation. (2007). *Behind the Pay Gap,* by Catherine Hill and Judy Goldberg Dey. Washington, DC.

[10] American Community Survey; http://factfinder.census.gov/servlet/STTable?_bm=y&- geo_id=01000US&- qr_name=ACS_2005_EST_G00_S1101&-ds_name=ACS_2005_EST_G00_

[11] AAUW Educational Foundation. (2007). *Behind the Pay Gap,* by Catherine Hill and Judy Goldberg Dey. Washington, DC.

[12] This is in keeping with research that shows that a "motherhood penalty" applies to most women but less to women who maintain continuous work force attachment (Lundberg & Rose, 2000).

[13] DiPrete, Thomas A., & Claudia Buchmann. (2006, February). Gender-specific trends in the value of education and the emerging gender gap in college completion. *Demography*, 43(1), 1-24.

[14] Authors calculation from tables produced by the U.S. Department of Labor, Bureau of Labor Statistics. (2006). Median Usual Weekly Earnings, Employed Full Time, Wage and Salary Workers, 25 Years and Older. Retrieved April 16, 2007 from http://www.bls.gov/cps/.

End Notes for "Testimony of Randy Albelda"

[1] In 2007, year-round, full-time women earners made $35,102 while men earned $45,113. Carmen DeNavas-Walt, Bernadette D. Proctor, and Jessica C. Smith, U.S. Census Bureau, Current Population Reports, P60-235, *Income, Poverty, and Health Insurance Coverage in the United States: 2007*, U.S. Government Printing Office, Washington, DC, 2008; Table 1.

[2] Ibid, Table A-2.

[3] U.S. Department of Labor, U.S. Bureau of Labor Statistics, Highlights of Women's Earnings in 2007, Report 1008, October 2008, Chart 1 (accessed 4-23-09 at http://www.bls.gov/cps/cpswom2007.pdf).

[4] Lalith Munasinghe, Tania Reif and Alice Henriques, "Gender gap in wage returns to job tenure and experience. Labour Economics, 2008: 1296-1916. This study looked at US men's and women job experience in the early part of their careers with longitudinal data (National Longitudinal Survey of Youth) for the years 1979-1994 (ages 14-22 in 1979 (making the sample between 29-37 years old in 1994). They found men with high school degrees or less worked an average of 6.7 years compared to women's 5.9 years. For those with more than a high school degree, the average amount of work experience was 7.8 years for men and 7.3 years for women. Men worked, on average, about 6 more hours per week than did women. Men accrued 15 percent higher wage

growth from an additional year of experience than women. Similar results can be found in Audrey Light and Manuelita Ureta, "Early-Career Work Experience and Gender Wage Differentials" *Journal of Labor Economics* 1995,13 (1) and Pamela Loprest, "Gender Differences in Wage Growth and Job Mobility" *American Economic Review* 1992, 82 (5).

[5] In 2007, 35 percent of all women ages 25-64 in the labor force had a college degree compared to 33 percent of men. Conversely, 42 percent of men ages 25-64 in the labor force had a high school diploma or less education compared to 35 percent of women. Calculated by author from data provided in U.S. Department of Labor, U.S. Bureau of Labor Statistics, *Women in the Labor Force: A Databook (2008 Edition)* Table 8, (accessed 4-23-09 at http://www.bls.gov/cps/wlf-table8-2008.pdf).

[6] Francine Blau and Lawrence Kahn, "The US Gender Pay Gap in the 1990s: Slowing Convergence," Industrial *and Labor Relations Review*, 2006, 60(1):45–66.

[7] Judy Goldberg Dey and Catherine Hill, *Behind the Pay Gap*, Washington DC: American Association of University Women Educational Foundation, 2007.

[8] Judith McDonald and Robert Thornton, "Do New Male and Female College Graduates Receive Unequal Pay?" *Journal of Human Resources*, 2007, 52(1): 32-48.

[9] U.S. Department of Labor, U.S. Bureau of Labor Statistics, *Women in the Labor Force: A Databook (2008 Edition)* Table 18, (accessed 4-23-09 at http://www.bls.gov/cps/wlf-table8-2008.pdf).

[10] The authors use Current Population Survey data and look at average hourly wages for full-time workers. Francine Blau and Lawrence Kahn, "The Gender Pay Gap" The Economists' Voice, Berkeley Electronic Press, 2007: 1-6.

[11] Stephen Stanley and T.D. Jarrell, "Declining Bias and Gender Wage Discrimination? A Meta-Regression Analysis. *Journal of Human Resources*, 2004, 36(3): 828-838.

[12] Melissa Binder et al. "Gender Pay Differences for the Same Work: Evidence from a United States Public University" forthcoming, *Feminist Economics*.

[13] Francine Blau and Lawrence Kahn, "The US Gender Pay Gap in the 1990s: Slowing Convergence," Industrial *and Labor Relations Review*, 2006, 60(1):45–66.

[14] David Neumark, using equally experienced male and female "pseudo" applicants, found high-priced restaurants were much more likely to both interview or offer jobs to men ("Sex Discrimination in Restaurant Hiring: An Audit Study," *Quarterly Journal of Economics*, 1996, 111(3): 915–41). Claudia Golden and Cecilia Rouse found that the probability that women would advance and be hired by symphony orchestras was higher when auditions were "blind" (i.e. the gender of the applicant auditioning was unknown) than when they were not ("Orchestrating Impartiality: The Impact of 'Blind' Auditions on Female Musicians," *American Economic Review*, 2000, 90(4): 715–41).

[15] In 2007, the median weekly salary of someone in construction occupations was $619 but as a secretary was $583; for a production occupations the week median salary was $559 compared to $494 for a retail salesperson. U.S. Department of Labor, U.S. Bureau of Labor Statistics, *Women in the Labor Force: A Databook (2008 Edition)* Table 18 (accessed 4-23-09 at http://www.bls.gov/cps/wlf-table8-2008.pdf).

[16] Paula England, Michelle Budig and Nancy Folbre, "Wages of Virtue: The Relative Pay of Care Work" *Social Problems* 2002;49(4):455-474; and Nancy Folbre, *The Invisible Heart: Economics and Family Values*, New York: New Press, 2001.

[17] Randy Albelda, Mignon Duffy and Nancy Folbre, "Taking Care: The Costs and Contributions of Care Work in Massachusetts" University of Massachusetts, forthcoming.

[18] See Randy Albelda, Robert Drago and Steven Shulman, *Unlevel Playing Fields: Understanding Wage Inequality and Discrimination*, Boston, MA: Economics Affairs Bureau 2004, Chapter 7; Joan Williams, *Unbending Gender: Why Family and Work Conflict and What to Do About It*. New York: Oxford University Press, 2001; Robert Drago, *Striking a Balance: Work, Family*, Life, Boston, MA: Dollars and Sense, 2007.

[19] Wendy Single-Rushton and Jane Waldfogel, "Motherhood and Women's Earnings in Anglo-American, Continental European, and Nordic Countries" *Feminist Economics* 2007,13(2): 55-91; Joni Hersh and Leslie Stratton., "Housework and Wages" *Journal of Human Resources* 2002, 37(1):217-229; and Deboarah Anderson, Melissa Binder and Kate Krause, "Experience, Heterogeneity, Work Effort and Work-Schedule Flexibility" Industrial and Labor Relations Review, 2003, 56(2): 273-294; and Michelle Budig and Paula England, "The Wage Penalty for Motherhood" *American Sociological Review*, 2001, 66(2), 204-225

[20] U.S. Census Bureau, *America's Families and Living Arrangements: 2007*, Tables F1 and FM-1, (accessed 2-13-09 from http://www.census.gov/population/socdemo/hh-fam/cps2007/tabF1-all.xls and http://www.census.gov/population/socdemo/hh-fam/fm1.xls.

[21] Ibid.

[22] U.S. Department of Labor, U.S. Bureau of Labor Statistics, *Women in the Labor Force: A Databook (2008 Edition),* Tables 23 and 24 (accessed 4-23-09 at http://www.bls.gov/cps/wlf-table8-2008.pdf).

[23] Heather Boushey, *Equal Pay for Breadwinners*, Washington, DC: Center for American Progress, 2009.

[24] John Schmitt *Unions and Upward Mobility for Women Workers,* Washington DC: Center for Economic and Policy Research, 2008.

End Notes for Testimony of Andrew Sherrill before the United States Joint Economic CommitteeHearing on "Equal Pay for Equal Work? New Evidence on the Persistence of the Gender Pay Gap"

[1] GAO, Women's Earnings: Work Patterns Partially Explain Difference between Men's and Women's Earnings, GAO-04-35 (Washington, D.C.: Oct. 31, 2003).

[2] GAO, Women's Earnings: Federal Agencies Should Better Monitor Their Performance in Enforcing Anti-Discrimination Laws, GAO-08-799 (Washington, D.C.: Aug. 11, 2008).

[3] GAO, Women's Earnings: Gender Pay Gap in the Federal Workforce Narrows as Differences in Occupation, Education, and Experience Diminish, GAO-09-279 (Washington, D.C.: Mar. 17, 2009).

[4] The CPDF does not include information for certain executive branch agencies, such as the intelligence services, agencies in the judicial branch, and most agencies in the legislative branch. The CPDF also does not include the U.S. Postal Service or members of the armed forces.

[5] In this report, measurable factors are those factors for which we have CPDF data.

End Notes for Testimony of Andrew Sherrill before the United States Joint Economic Committee Hearing on "New Evidence on the Gender Pay Gap for Women and Mothers in Management

[1] GAO, *Women in Management: Analysis of Selected Data from the Current Population Survey*, GAO-02- 156 (Washington, D.C.: Oct. 23, 2001).

[2] GAO, *Women in Management: Analysis of Female Managers' Representation, Characteristics, and Pay*, GAO-10-892R (Washington, D.C.: Sept. 20, 2010).

[3] We reported on the years 2000 through 2007 to avoid concerns about the role of the recession that began in December, 2007 and to avoid any complications to the analysis due to the change of survey questions in the data set we used that were made in 2008. The ACS became nationally representative in 2000, and thus was not available for the analysis we did in the 2001 report on women in management.

[4] We excluded agriculture because, according to the Bureau of Labor Statistics, farmers may have other sources of income, such as from federal subsidies, which may not be reported in ACS as income and would complicate our analysis on pay differentials. We excluded mining because we found a relatively limited number of observations in the mining industry. According to ACS, group quarters is a place where people live or stay, in a group living arrangement that is owned or managed by an entity or organization providing housing and/or services for the residents. Examples include college residence halls, nursing homes, group homes, military barracks, correctional facilities, and mental hospitals.

[5] Our definition of individuals working full time were those who, over the past 12 months, reported usually working greater than or equal to 35 hours per week and 50 weeks per year, and reported positive wages earned.

[6] When we looked at all industries together, we also adjusted for industry sector.

[7] Our definition of individuals working part-time included those who were not working full time, but reported usually working some hours per week, weeks worked, and wages earned, all over the past 12 months.

End Notes for Testimony of Ilene H. Lang
President and Chief Executive Officer, Catalyst, Inc. before the United States Joint Economic Committee Hearing on "New Evidence on the Gender Pay Gap for Women and Mothers in Management"

[1] Bureau of Labor Statistics, Annual averages tables from the 2009 Current Population Survey (2010).

[2] *Digest of Education* Statistics (National Center for Education Statistics, 2009).

[3] Michael J. Silverstein and Kate Sayre, with John Butman, *Women Want More: How to Capture Your Share of the World's Largest, Fastest-Growing Market* (New York: HarperCollins, 2009).

[4] Catalyst, *Women CEOs of the Fortune 1000* (2010).

[5] Rachel Soares, Nancy M. Carter, and Jan Combopiano, *2009 Catalyst Census: Fortune 500 Women Board Directors* (Catalyst, 2009).

[6] Rachel Soares, Nancy M. Carter, and Jan Combopiano, *2009 Catalyst Census: Fortune 500 Women Executive Officers and Top Earners* (Catalyst, 2009).

[7] Bureau of Labor Statistics, Annual averages tables from the 2009 Current Population Survey (2010).

[8] *Digest of Education* Statistics (National Center for Education Statistics, 2009) and Nathan E. Bell, *Graduate Enrollment and Degrees: 1999 to 2009* (Council of Graduate Schools, 2010).

[9] Pyramid statistics do not sum to 100.0% because categories are not mutually exclusive. *Fortune* 500 Total Employees, Low-Mid Officers & Managers and Professionals, and Senior Officers & Managers: Unpublished aggregate EEOC data for 2009 *Fortune* 500 companies based on 2009 EEO-1 survey; *Fortune* 500 Executive Officer and Top Earner positions: Rachel Soares, Nancy M. Carter, and Jan Combopiano, *2009 Catalyst Census:* Fortune *500 Women Executive Officers and Top* Earners (Catalyst, 2009); *Fortune* 500 board seats: Rachel Soares, Nancy M. Carter, and Jan Combopiano, *2009 Catalyst Census:* Fortune *500 Women Board Directors* (Catalyst, 2009); *Fortune* 500 CEOs: Catalyst, *Women CEOs of the* Fortune *1000* (2010).

[10] The chart displays the percent of women CEOs at the time *Fortune* magazine publishes their annual *Fortune* 500 list. Catalyst, *Women CEOs in the* Fortune *Lists: 1972-2010* (2010); the most recent data displays the percent of women CEOs. Catalyst, *Women CEOs of the* Fortune *1000* (2010).

[11] Catalyst, *2005 Catalyst Census of Women Corporate Officers and Top Earners of the* Fortune *500* (2006); Catalyst, *2006 Catalyst Census of Women Corporate Officers and Top Earners of the* Fortune *500* (2007); Catalyst, *2007 Census of Women Corporate Officers and Top Earners of the* Fortune *500* (2007); Catalyst, *2008 Catalyst Census of Women Corporate Officers and Top Earners of the* Fortune *500* (2008); Rachel Soares, Nancy M. Carter, and Jan Combopiano, *2009 Catalyst Census:* Fortune *500 Women Executive Officers and Top Earners* (Catalyst, 2009).

[12] Catalyst, *2005 Catalyst Census of Women Board Directors of the* Fortune *500* (2006); Catalyst, *2006 Catalyst Census of Women Board Directors of the* Fortune *500* (2007); Catalyst, *2007 Catalyst Census of Women Board Directors of the* Fortune *500* (2007); Catalyst, *2008 Catalyst Census of Women Board Directors of the* Fortune *500* (2009); Rachel Soares, Nancy M. Carter, and Jan Combopiano, *2009 Catalyst Census:* Fortune *500 Women Board Directors*.

[13] Rachel Soares, Nancy M. Carter, and Jan Combopiano, *2009 Catalyst Census* (Catalyst, 2009).

[14] Unpublished aggregate EEOC data for 2009 *Fortune* 500 companies based on 2009 EEO-1 survey.

[15] Catalyst, *Women CEOs of the* Fortune *1000* (2010).

[16] Rachel Soares, Nancy M. Carter, and Jan Combopiano, *2009 Catalyst Census:* Fortune *500 Women Board Directors* (Catalyst, 2009).

[17] Rachel Soares, Nancy M. Carter, and Jan Combopiano, *2009 Catalyst Census:* Fortune *500 Women Executive Officers and Top* Earners (Catalyst, 2009).

[18] Unpublished aggregate EEOC data for 2009 *Fortune* 500 companies based on 2009 EEO-1 survey.

[19] Unpublished aggregate EEOC data for 2009 *Fortune* 500 companies based on 2009 EEO-1 survey.

[20] Unpublished aggregate EEOC data for 2009 *Fortune* 500 companies based on 2009 EEO-1 survey.

[21] Unpublished aggregate EEOC data for 2009 *Fortune* 500 companies based on 2009 EEO-1 survey.

[22] Catalyst, *2006 Catalyst Census of Women Board Directors of the* Fortune *500* (2007); Catalyst, *2007 Catalyst Census of Women Board Directors of the* Fortune *500* (2007); Catalyst, *2008 Catalyst Census of Women Board Directors of the* Fortune *500* (2009); Rachel Soares, Nancy M. Carter, and Jan Combopiano, *2009 Catalyst Census:* Fortune *500 Women Board Directors*; Catalyst, *2006 Catalyst Census of Women Corporate Officers and Top Earners of the* Fortune *500* (2007); Catalyst, *2007 Census of Women Corporate Officers and*

Top Earners of the Fortune *500* (2007); Catalyst, *2008 Catalyst Census of Women Corporate Officers and Top Earners of the* Fortune *500* (2008).

[23] Catalyst, *2006 Catalyst Census of Women Board Directors of the* Fortune *500* (2007); Catalyst, *2007 Catalyst Census of Women Board Directors of the* Fortune *500* (2007); Catalyst, *2008 Catalyst Census of Women Board Directors of the* Fortune *500* (2009); Rachel Soares, Nancy M. Carter, and Jan Combopiano, *2009 Catalyst Census:* Fortune *500 Women Board Directors*; Catalyst, *2006 Catalyst Census of Women Corporate Officers and Top Earners of the* Fortune *500* (2007); Catalyst, *2007 Census of Women Corporate Officers and Top Earners of the* Fortune *500* (2007); Catalyst, *2008 Catalyst Census of Women Corporate Officers and Top Earners of the* Fortune *500* (2008).

[24] Catalyst, *2006 Catalyst Census of Women Board Directors of the* Fortune *500* (2007); Catalyst, *2007 Catalyst Census of Women Board Directors of the* Fortune *500* (2007); Catalyst, *2008 Catalyst Census of Women Board Directors of the* Fortune *500* (2009); Rachel Soares, Nancy M. Carter, and Jan Combopiano, *2009 Catalyst Census:* Fortune *500 Women Board Directors*; Catalyst, *2006 Catalyst Census of Women Corporate Officers and Top Earners of the* Fortune *500* (2007); Catalyst, *2007 Census of Women Corporate Officers and Top Earners of the* Fortune *500* (2007); Catalyst, *2008 Catalyst Census of Women Corporate Officers and Top Earners of the* Fortune *500* (2008).

[25] Current Population Survey, Bureau of Labor Statistics, "Table 2: Employment status of the civilian noninstitutional population 16 years and over by sex, 1973 to date," *Annual Averages 2009* (2010). http://www.bls.gov/cps/cpsaat2.pdf

[26] *Digest of Education* Statistics (National Center for Education Statistics, 2009) and Nathan E. Bell, *Graduate Enrollment and Degrees: 1999 to 2009* (Council of Graduate Schools, 2010).

[27] *Digest of Education* Statistics (National Center for Education Statistics, 2009) and Nathan E. Bell, *Graduate Enrollment and Degrees: 1999 to 2009* (Council of Graduate Schools, 2010).

[28] ** Category includes the following degrees: Chiropractic, Dentistry, Law, Medicine, Optometry, Osteopathic Medicine (D.O.), Pharmacy (Pharm.D.), Podiatry (D.P.M., D.P., or Pod.D.), Theology (M.Div., M.H.L., B.D., or Ordination), Veterinary Medicine (D.V.M.). National Center for Education Statistics, Digest of Education Statistics, "Table 268: Degrees conferred by degree-granting institutions, by level of degree and sex of student: Selected years, 1869-70 through 2017-18" (2008).

[29] Catalyst, *2005 Catalyst Census of Women Corporate Officers and Top Earners of the* Fortune *500* (2006); Catalyst, *2006 Catalyst Census of Women Corporate Officers and Top Earners of the* Fortune *500* (2007); Catalyst, *2007 Census of Women Corporate Officers and Top Earners of the* Fortune *500* (2007); Catalyst, *2008 Catalyst Census of Women Corporate Officers and Top Earners of the* Fortune *500* (2008); Rachel Soares, Nancy M. Carter, and Jan Combopiano, *2009 Catalyst Census:* Fortune *500 Women Executive Officers and Top Earners* (Catalyst, 2009).

[30] Nancy M. Carter and Christine Silva, *Pipeline's Broken Promise* (Catalyst, 2010).

[31] Nancy M. Carter and Christine Silva, *Pipeline's Broken Promise* (Catalyst, 2010).

[32] Catalyst, *The Bottom Line: Connecting Corporate Performance and Gender Diversity* (2004).

[33] Catalyst, *The Bottom Line: Connecting Corporate Performance and Gender Diversity* (2004).

[34] Lois Joy, Nancy M. Carter, Harvey M. Wagner, and Sriram Narayanan, *The Bottom Line: Corporate Performance and Women's Representation on Boards* (Catalyst, 2007).

[35] Lois Joy, Nancy M. Carter, Harvey M. Wagner, and Sriram Narayanan, *The Bottom Line: Corporate Performance and Women's Representation on Boards* (Catalyst, 2007).

[36] Lois Joy, Nancy M. Carter, Harvey M. Wagner, and Sriram Narayanan, *The Bottom Line: Corporate Performance and Women's Representation on Boards* (Catalyst, 2007).

[37] Lois Joy, *Advancing Women Leaders: The Connection Between Women Board Directors and Women Corporate Officers* (Catalyst, 2008).

[38] Lois Joy, *Advancing Women Leaders: The Connection Between Women Board Directors and Women Corporate Officers* (Catalyst, 2008).

[39] Lois Joy, *Advancing Women Leaders: The Connection Between Women Board Directors and Women Corporate Officers* (Catalyst, 2008).

[40] Rachel Soares, Nancy M. Carter, and Jan Combopiano, *2009 Catalyst Census:* Fortune *500 Women Executive Officers and Top Earners* (Catalyst, 2009); Rachel Soares, Nancy M. Carter, and Jan Combopiano, *2009 Catalyst Census:* Fortune *500 Women Board Directors*; Unpublished aggregate EEOC data for 2009 *Fortune 500* companies based on 2009 EEO-1 survey.

[41] Catalyst, *2006 Catalyst Census of Women Board Directors of the* Fortune *500* (2007); Catalyst, *2007 Catalyst Census of Women Board Directors of the* Fortune *500* (2007); Catalyst, *2008 Catalyst Census of Women*

Board Directors of the Fortune *500* (2009); Rachel Soares, Nancy M. Carter, and Jan Combopiano, *2009 Catalyst Census:* Fortune *500 Women Board Directors*; Catalyst, *2006 Catalyst Census of Women Corporate Officers and Top Earners of the* Fortune *500* (2007); Catalyst, *2007 Census of Women Corporate Officers and Top Earners of the* Fortune *500* (2007); Catalyst, *2008 Catalyst Census of Women Corporate Officers and Top Earners of the* Fortune *500* (2008).

[42] Rachel Soares, Nancy M. Carter, and Jan Combopiano, *2009 Catalyst Census:* Fortune *500 Women Executive Officers and Top Earners* (Catalyst, 2009).

[43] Nancy M. Carter and Christine Silva, *Pipeline's Broken Promise* (Catalyst, 2010).

[44] *Digest of Education* Statistics (National Center for Education Statistics, 2009) and Nathan E. Bell, *Graduate Enrollment and Degrees: 1999 to 2009* (Council of Graduate Schools, 2010).

[45] Bureau of Labor Statistics, Annual averages tables from the 2009 Current Population Survey (2010).

[46] Anika K. Warren, *Cascading Gender Biases, Compounding Effects: An Assessment of Talent Management Systems* (Catalyst, 2009).

[47] Scott Page*, The Difference: How the Power of Diversity Creates Better Groups, Firms, Schools, and societies* (Princeton University Press, 2007); Fidan Ana Kurtus, "The Effect of Heterogeneity on the Performance of Employees and Organizational Divisions of the Firm," (paper presented at the annual conference of the Society for Labor Economics, New York, NY, May 9-10, 2008); Corinne Post and Emilio De Lia, et al "Capitalizing On Thought Diversity For Innovation," *Research Technology Management* ,vol. 2, no. 6 (Nov/Dec 2009): p. 14-25.

End Notes for Testimony Data

[1] 2009 analysis is based on 496 companies. Catalyst excluded four companies due to specific events: two declared bankruptcy, one was acquired, and one delisted with the SEC.

[2] Employees are defined as "any individual on the payroll of an employer who is an employee for purposes of the employers withholding of Social Security taxes except insurance sales agents who are considered to be employees for such purposes solely because of the provisions of 26 USC 3121 (d) (3) (B) (the Internal Revenue Code)."

[3] Equal Employment Opportunity, Standard Form 100, Employer Information Report EEO-1 Instruction Booklet (2006) http://www.eeoc.gov/employers/eeo1survey/2007instructions.cfm.

[4] Current Population Survey, Bureau of Labor Statistics, "Table 18: Employed persons by detailed industry, sex, race, and Hispanic or Latino ethnicity," 2009 Annual Averages (2010).

[5] By definition, female-dominated industries would be those in which men account for 25% or less of all those employed in the field. In 2009, only one 2-digit NAICS code industry qualified as female-dominated: Health Care and Social Assistance. However, this industry has fewer than 10 companies in the 2009 *Fortune* 500 list, making comparisons inappropriate.

[6] Please refer to each publication's methodology section or appendix for more detailed information about the methodology (e.g., verification rates for each year).

[7] Please refer to the definitions section of the appendix for the definition of Executive Officer.

[8] Please refer to each publication for more detailed information about the number of companies included in the race/ethnicity data analysis.

[9] § 240.3b-7 Definition of "executive officer." [47 FR 11464, Mar. 16, 1982, as amended at 56 FR 7265, Feb. 21, 1991] (http://ecfr.gpoaccess.gov/cgi/t/text/text-idx?c=ecfr&sid=47b43cbb88844faad586861 c05c81595&rgn=div5&view=text&node=17:3.0.1.1.1&idno=17#17:3.0.1.1.1.1.54.45).

[10] *Fortune* Magazine, *Fortune* 500 http://money.cnn.com/magazines/fortune/fortune500/2009/faq/.

[11] Equal Employment Opportunity Commission, Employer Information Report EEO-1 Instruction Booklet (2006). http://www.eeoc.gov/employers/eeo1survey/upload/instructions_form.pdf.

[12] U.S. Census Bureau, Office of Management and Budget, Revisions to the Standards for the Classification of Federal Data on Race and Ethnicity. http://www.census.gov/population/www/socdemo/race/Ombdir15.html.

[13] Equal Employment Opportunity Commission, Employer Information Report EEO-1 Instruction Booklet (2006). http://www.eeoc.gov/employers/eeo1survey/upload/instructions_form.pdf.

[14] Code of Federal Regulations, Amendment from September 08, 2006, § 229.402 (Item 402) Executive compensation.

End Notes for Testimony of Michelle J. Budig before the United States Joint Economic Committee Hearing on "New Evidence on the Gender Pay Gap for Women and Mothers in Management"

[1] U.S. Bureau of Labor Statistics, *Employment and Earnings: January 2010*, Table 7, (accessed 9-22- 2010 at http://www.bls.gov/cps/cpsa2009.pdf).

[2] Misra, Joya, Michelle J. Budig and Irene S. Boeckmann. 2010. "Cross-National Patterns in Individual and Household Employment and Work Hours by Gender and Parenthood." Forthcoming at *Research in the Sociology of Work*. Presented at the 2010 annual meetings of the American Sociological Association (Atlanta, GA).

[3] Lundquist, Jennifer Hickes, Michelle J. Budig, and Anna Curtis. 2009. "Race and Childlessness in America, 1988-2002." *Journal of Marriage and the Family* 71:741-755.

[4] Abma, Joyce C. and Gladys M. Martinez. 2006. "Childlessness Among Older Women in the United States: Trends and Profiles." *Journal of Marriage and the Family* 68:1045-1056.

[5] Jacobs, Jerry and Kathleen Gerson. 2004. *The Time Divide: Work, Family, and Gender Inequality*. Cambridge, MA: Harvard University Press.

[6] http://www.time.com/time/business/article/0,8599,2015274,00.html

[7] Misra, Joya, Michelle J. Budig and Irene S. Boeckmann. 2010. "Cross-National Patterns in Individual and Household Employment and Work Hours by Gender and Parenthood." Forthcoming at *Research in the Sociology of Work*. Presented at the 2010 annual meetings of the American Sociological Association (Atlanta, GA).

[8] Polachek, S.W. 2006. "How the Life-Cycle Human Capital Model Explains Why the Gender Wage Gap Narrowed." Pp. 102-124 in *The Declining Significance of Gender?* F.D. Blau, M.C. Brinton, and D.B. Grusky, eds. New York: Russell Sage Foundation.

[9] Waldfogel, Jane. 1998a. "Understanding the 'Family Gap' in Pay for Women with Children." *Journal of Economic Perspectives* 12(1):137-56.

[10] Waldfogel, Jane. 1998b. "The Family Gap for Young Women in the United States and Britain: Can Maternity Leave Make a Difference?" *Journal of Labor Economics* 16 (3): 505-545.

[11] Anderson, D., M. Binder, and K. Krause. 2003. "The Motherhood Wage Penalty Revisited: Experience, Heterogeneity, Work Effort, and Work-Schedule Flexibility." *Industrial and Labor Relations Review* 56:273-94.

[12] Avellar, S. and P. Smock. 2003. "Has the Price of Motherhood Declined over Time? A Cross-Cohort Comparison of the Motherhood Wage Penalty." *Journal of Marriage and the Family* 65:597-607.

[13] Budig, Michelle J. and Paula England. 2001. "The Wage Penalty for Motherhood." *American Sociological Review* 66:204-25.

[14] Budig, Michelle J. and Melissa J. Hodges. 2010. "Differences in Disadvantage: Variation in the Motherhood Penalty Across White Women's Earnings Distribution." *American Sociological Review* 75 (5): Oct. (In press).

[15] Glauber, R. 2007a. "Marriage and the Motherhood Wage Penalty among African Americans, Hispanics, and Whites." *Journal of Marriage and the Family* 69:951-61.

[16] Taniguchi, H. 1999. "The Timing of Childbearing and Women's Wages." *Journal of Marriage and the Family* 61:1008-19.

[17] Waldfogel, J. 1997. "The Effect of Children on Women's Wages." *American Sociological Review* 62:209-17.

[18] Median earnings taken from IWPR report, "Gender Wage Gap 2009", accessed 9/22/2010, (http://www.iwpr.org/pdf/C350.pdf)

[19] Table taken from Budig, Michelle J. and Melissa J. Hodges. 2010. "Differences in Disadvantage: Variation in the Motherhood Penalty Across White Women's Earnings Distribution." *American Sociological Review* 75(5): Oct.

[20] Correll, Shelley J., Stephen Benard, and In Paik. 2007. "Getting a Job: Is There a Motherhood Penalty?" *American Journal of Sociology* 112:1297–1338.

[21] Glauber, Rebecca. 2007. "Race and Gender in Families and at Work: The Fatherhood Wage Premium." *Gender & Society* 22: 8-30.

[22] Hodges, Melissa J. and Michelle J. Budig. 2010. "Who Gets the Daddy Bonus? Organizational Hegemonic Masculinity and the Impact of Fatherhood on Men's Earnings." *Gender & Society* 24(6):December Issue.

[23] Armenia, Amy, Naomi Gerstel, and Coady Wing. 2009. "Estimating and Predicting Compliance with FMLA: Pressures from Above and Below." Paper presented at the Annual Meetings of the Southern Sociological Society.

[24] Gerstel, Naomi and Amy Armenia. 2009. "Giving and Taking Family Leaves: Right or Privilege." Yale Journal of Law and Feminism. 21(1): 161-184.

[25] Gangl, Markus and Andrea Ziefle. 2009. "Motherhood, Labor Force Behavior, and Women's Careers: An Empirical Assessment of the Wage Penalty for Motherhood in Britain, Germany, and the United States." Demography 46:341–69.

[26] Hochschild, Arlie. 2001. The Time Bind: When Work Becomes Home and Home Becomes Work. Owl Books.

[27] Glass, Jennifer. 2004. "Blessing or Curse? Work-Family Policies and Mothers' Wage Growth Over Time." Work and Occupations 31:367–94.

End Notes for The Earnings Penalty for Part-Time Work: An Obstacle to Equal Pay

[1] One widely cited estimate of the gap in pay shows that women's earnings were 77 percent of men's earnings in 2008, or about $5 per hour less than men. National Committee on Pay Equity, available at http://www.pay-equity.org/info-time.html, 2008 data based on full-time workers. To calculate average hourly wage differences, it is assumed that workers work 40 hours per week.

[2] Bertrand, Marianne, Claudia Goldin, and Lawrence Katz. "The Dynamics of the Gender Gap for Young Professionals in the Financial and Corporate Sectors." December 2009 working paper. See http://www.economics.harvard.edu/.

End Notes for Large Gender Pay Gap for Older Workers Threatens Economic Security of Older Women

[1] Bureau of Labor Statistics. Highlights of Women's Earnings in 2009. June 2010.

[2] See Joint Economic Committee. Women and the Economy 2010: 25 Years of Progress But Challenges Remain. August 2010.

[3] Bureau of Labor Statistics. Highlights of Women's Earnings in 2009. June 2010. Table 2.

[4] CONSAD Research Corporation. An Analysis of the Reasons for the Disparity in Wages Between Men and Women: Final Report. Prepared for U.S. Department of Labor, Employment Standards Administration. January 12, 2009. http://www.consad.com/content/reports/Gender%20Wage%20Gap%20Final%20Report.pdf

[5] For example, and a summary of other relevant work, see Blau, Francine D. and Lawrence M. Kahn, 2006. "The U.S. Gender Pay Gap in the 1990s: Slowing Convergence." Industrial and Labor Relations Review. 60(1): 45-66. http://www.nber.org/papers/w10853.pdf.

[6] See Joint Economic Committee. Women and the Economy 2010: 25 Years of Progress But Challenges Remain. August 2010.

[7] Bureau of Labor Statistics. Current Population Survey. 2009 Annual Averages.

End Notes for C. Access to Benefits

[1] Rustgi, Sheila et al. 2009. Women at Risk: Why Many Women Are Foregoing Needed Health Care. Washington, D.C.: The Commonwealth Fund. (http://www.commonwealthfund.org/~/media/Files/Publications/Issue per-cent20Brief/2009/May/Women percent20at percent20Risk/PDF_1262_Rustgi_women_at_risk_issue_ brief_ Final.pdf).

[2] Himmelstein, David et al. 2009. "Medical Bankruptcy in the United States, 2007: Results of a National Study." The American Journal of Medicine. 122(8)(August 2009). (http://pnhp.org/new_bankruptcy_ study/Bankruptcy-2009.pdf).

[3] Wood, Susan et al. 2009. *Women's Health and Health Care Reform: The Economic Burden of Disease in Women.* Washington, D.C.: The Jacobs Institute of Women's Health at the George Washington University School of Public Health and Health Services.

[4] The most recent data available are for August 2009.

[5] Had the 111th Congress not expanded the State Children's Health Insurance Program (S-CHIP) eligibility this winter, the number of children losing health coverage likely would be even greater.

[6] The most recent data available are for September 2009. See also the Joint Economic Committee's May 2009 report on working mothers in the recession, *Women in the Recession: Working Mothers Face High Rates of Un-employment.* (http://jec.senate.gov).

[7] Schumacher, Jessica R., et al. 2009. "Insurance Disruption Due to Spousal Medicare Transitions: Implications for Access to Care and Health Utilization for Women Approaching Age 65." *Health Services Research* 44(3)(June). (http://www.hsr.org/ hsr/abstract.jsp?aid=44347877138).

[8] Bureau of Labor Statistics Household Survey. Data are for women ages 16-24, with the most recent data available are for September 2009.

[9] Rustgi, Sheila et al. 2009.

[10] Himmelstein, David et al. 2009.

[11] Chavkin, Wendy and Sara Rosenbaum. 2008. "Women's Health and Health Care Reform: The Key Role of Comprehensive Reproductive Health Care." New York, New York: Columbia University Mailman School of Pub-lic Health. (http://www.jiwh.org /attachments/Women percent20and percent20Health percent20Care percent20Re-form.pdf).

[12] Patchias, E. and Waxman J. 2007. *Women and Health Coverage: The Affordability Gap.* Washington, D.C.: The Commonwealth Fund and the National Women's Law Center. (http://www.nwlc.org /pdf/ NWLCCommonwealthHealthInsuranceIssueBrief2007.pdf).

[13] Institute for Women's Policy Research. 2009. *The Gender Wage Gap: 2008.* Washington, D.C.: Institute for Women's Policy Research. (http://www.iwpr.org/pdf/C350.pdf). Cawthorne, Alexandra. 2008. "The Straight Facts on Women in Poverty." Washington, D.C.: Center for American Progress. (http://www. americanprogress.org/issues/2008/10/women_poverty.html).

[14] U.S. Census Current Population Survey. 2009. America's Families and Living Arrangements: 2008. See Table FG5. (http://www.census.gov/population/www/ socdemo/hh-fam/cps2008.html). See also the Kaiser Family Foundation's *2004 Women's Health Survey.* (http://www.kff.org/womenshealth/upload/2004-Kaiser-Women-s-Health-Survey-Presentation.pdf).

[15] Wood, Susan et al. 2009.

[16] Joint Economic Committee calculations from Bureau of Labor Statistics Household Survey. The most recent data available are for September 2009.

[17] The most recent data available are for August 2009.

[18] Joint Economic Committee calculations from Bureau of Labor Statistics Household Survey. The most recent data available are for September 2009.

[19] The Joint Economic Committee's calculations incorporate the number of jobs lost by men and women, the probability that a given individual had an employer-sponsored plan (either as a policy-holder or as a dependent), as well as industry-specific weights to account for the distribution of job losses and health insurance across indus-tries. We compute job-loss related health insurance losses separately for each gender. Data for industry-specific health insurance coverage status by gender comes from the March 2008 Supplement to the Current Population Survey (CPS), which is the most recently available detailed data on health insurance coverage. Data on job loss comes from the Bureau of Labor Statistics' Establishment Survey, from December 2007 through August 2009 representing the most current available detailed data. Data for industry-specific marriage rates by gender are from the June 2009 CPS, the most recent data available. A complete methodological appendix is available from the Joint Economic Committee upon request.

[20] In one recent nationally-representative survey, amongst employers who reported taking steps to reduce costs in the last 12 months, 29 percent reported reducing health care benefits or increasing employee costs as a in the last 12 months. See Galinsky, Ellen and James. T. Bond. 2009. The Impact of the Recession on Employers." Washing-ton, D.C.: Families and Work Institute.

[21] Schumacher, Jessica R., et al. 2009.

[22] National Women's Law Center. 2008. *Nowhere to Turn: How the Individual Health Insurance Market Fails Women.* Washington, D.C.: National Women's Law Center. (http://action.nwlc.org/site/ PageNavigator/nowheretoturn_Report). See the final section on recommended policy prescriptions for a widely-agreed upon fix to the problem of discriminatory gender rating practices.

[23] Joint Economic Committee calculations using data from the U.S. Census Bureau 2009 ASEC Supplement, Table HI08. Health Insurance Coverage Status and Type of Coverage by Selected Characteristics for Children Under 18: 2008. (http://www.census.gov/hhes/www/cpstables/032009/health/h08_000.htm).

[24] Joint Economic Committee calculations from Bureau of Labor Statistics Household Survey, current as of September 2009.See the Joint Economic Committee's May 2009 report on working mothers in the recession, *Women in the Recession: Working Mothers Face High Rates of Unemployment.* (http://jec.senate.gov).

[25] The Joint Economic Committee's calculations incorporate the change in the number of employed female heads-of-household, the number of children impacted by that change, and the probability that those children received health insurance through a mother's employer. Because data on the number of employed female heads-of-household from Bureau of Labor Statistics Household Survey are not seasonally-adjusted, the Joint Economic Committee uses the annual change in the number of employed female heads-of-household from September 2008 to September 2009, rather than the change over the course of the recession. Had the 111th Congress not expanded the State Children's Health Insurance Program (S-CHIP) eligibility this winter, the number of children losing health coverage likely would be even greater.

[26] FamiliesUSA. 2009. *Understanding COBRA and Mini-COBRA Premium Assistance.* Washington, D.C. FamiliesUSA. (http://www.familiesusa.org/issues/private-insurance/understanding-cobrapremium.html).

[27] Bureau of Labor Statistics Household Survey. Data are for women ages 16-24, with the most recent data available are for September 2009.

[28] Collins, Sara R. April 23, 2009. *Young and Vulnerable: The Growing Problem of Uninsured Young Adults and How Policies Can Help.* Washington, D.C.: Commonwealth Fund. (http://www.commonwealthfund.org /~/media/Files/Publications/Testimony/2009/Apr/Testimony percent20Young percent20and percent20Vulnerable/1264_Collins_New_York_Ciy _council_hearing_young_ adults_04232009_testimony.pdf); National Conference on State Legislatures, 2008. *Covering Young Adults Through Their Parents' or Guardians' Health Policy.* (http://www.ncsl.org/issuesresearch/health /healthinsurancedependentstatus/tabid/14497/default.aspx).

[29] Under federal rules, state Medicaid programs must cover pregnant women and children under age 6 whose family incomes are below 133 percent of the federal poverty line and children age 6 to 18 whose family incomes are be-low 100 percent of the federal poverty line. Beyond that, the federal government allows states to set their own eligibility guidelines. In some states, such as Louisiana, out-of-work families qualify for Medicaid only if their in-comes are at least 11 percent *below* the federal poverty line ($2,426 for a family of four). Unemployment benefits are counted as income, which means that many unemployed families find themselves without health insurance, but with too much income to qualify for Medicaid. See Galewitz, Phil. "Medicaid: True or False?" *Kaiser Health News*, July 1, 2009.

[30] Numerous states have already enacted limits to Medicaid eligibility, and several more are considering proposed cuts. See, for example: Kelley, Debbie. "Advocates say Medicaid cuts will hurt developmentally disabled." *Denver Post*, July 1, 2009. (http://www.denverpost.com/breakingnews/ci_12733118); California Budget Project. June 1, 2009. *More Than 1.9 Million Californians Could Lose Access to Health Coverage Under the Governor's May Revision.* Sacramento, CA: California Budget Project. (http://www.cbp.org/documents/090521_Health_Cuts_Statewide_Fact_Sheet.pdf).

[31] Note that the definition of "low-income" varies somewhat here because the data is from a separate survey. Income groups are defined according to absolute dollar values rather than in terms of the federal poverty line. For instance, low-income is defined as under $20,000 rather than 100 percent of the federal poverty line.

[32] Difficulty obtaining needed care is defined as reporting any one of the following four problems: 1) did not fill a needed prescription 2) did not see a needed specialist 3) skipped a recommended medical test, treatment, or follow-up 4) had a medical problem but did not visit a doctor or clinic.

[33] U.S. Census Bureau . *Income, Poverty, and Health Insurance Coverage in the United States: 2008.* (http://www.census.gov/prod/2009pubs/p60-236.pdf)

[34] U.S. Census Current Population Survey. 2009. *America's Families and Living Arrangements: 2008.* See Table FG5. (http://www.census.gov/population /www/socdemo/hh-fam/cps2008.html).

[35] For a literature review on the health benefits of prevention, see Partnership for Prevention. 2007. *Preventative Care: A National Profile on Use, Disparities, and Health Benefits.* Washington, D.C.: Partnership for Prevention. (http://www.prevent.org/images/stories/ 2007/ncpp/ncpp percent20preventive percent20care percent20report.pdf). For a review of the economic arguments for prevention, see Woolf, Steven H. 2009. "A Closer Look at the Economic Arguments for Prevention." *Journal of the American Medical Association* 301(2009):536-538. (http://jama.ama-assn.org/cgi/content/full/301/5/536) (subscription required). See (http://www.rwjf.org/pr/product.jsp?id=38410) for a free abstract.

[36] The Kaiser Family Foundation. *2004 Kaiser Women's Health Survey.*

[37] Note that some studies have found significant racial differences in the timing of mammograms. For instance, a recent study found that 18 percent of white women with breast cancer were inadequately screened with mammography prior to breast cancer, as compared to 34 percent of African-American women with breast cancer. See Smith-Bindman, Rebecca. 2006. "Does utilization of screening mammography explain the racial and ethnic differences in breast cancer?" *Annals of Internal Medicine* 144(8): 614-6. (http://www.ncbi.nlm.nih.gov/pubmed/16618951?ordinal-pos=1&itool=EntrezSystem2.PEntrez.Pubmed.Pubmed_ResultsPanel.Pubmed_DiscoveryPanel.Pubmed_RVAbstractPlus); Chan, Nancy. April 17, 2006. "Mammography screenings for breast cancer show racial and ethnic dis-parities." UCSF News Office. (http://news.ucsf.edu/releases/mammography-screeningsfor-breast-cancer-show-racial-and-ethnic-disparities/).

[38] Chavkin and Rosenbaum. 2008.

[39] Alan Guttmacher Institute. 2002. *Sexual and Reproductive Health: Women and Men.* (http://www.guttmacher.org/ pubs/fb_10-02.pdf).

[40] Culwell, Kelly R. and Joe Feinglass. 2007. "The Association of Health Insurance with Use of Prescription Contraceptives." *Perspectives on Sexual and Reproductive Health* 39(4): 224-230. For data on the efficacy of prescription versus over-the-counter birth control methodologies, see the Mayo Clinic's Birth Control Guide (http://www.nlm.nih.gov/medlineplus/birthcontrol.html).

[41] McCormick, Marie C. and Joanna E. Seigel. 1999. *Prenatal Care: Effectiveness and Implementation.* New York, NY: Cambridge University Press; Butz, Arlene M. et al. 1993. "Infant Health Care Utilization Predicted by Pattern of Prenatal Care." *Pediatrics.* 92(1): 50-54; Conway, Karen Smith and Andrea Kutinova. 2006. "Maternal Health: Does Prenatal Care Make a Difference?" *Health Economics* 15(5): 461-488; Centers for Disease Control and Prevention Health Resources and Services Administration. *Healthy People 2010*, esp. Chapter 16, "Maternal, Infant, and Child Health." (http://www.healthypeople.gov/document/ HTML /Volume2/16MICH.htm#_Toc494699663).

[42] Chavkin and Rosenbaum. 2008.

[43] The health insurance industry's trade group, AHIP, has repeatedly stated its support for a ban on discriminatory rating practices, including gender rating. See, for example, Edney, Anna. 2009. "AHIP Pleads Its Case: Regulate Us." *National Journal.* May 6, 2009. http://undertheinfluence.nationaljournal.com/2009/05/ahip-pleads-its-case-regulate. php). The insurance industry recognizes that discriminatory rating practices drive down coverage rates, as shown in multiple empirical studies. See, for example, Wachenstein, Leigh and Hans Leida. 2007. "The Impact of Guaranteed Issue ad Community Rat-ing Reforms on Individual Insurance Markets." Seattle, WA: Milliman, Inc. (http://www.ahip.org/content/default.aspx?docid=20736). Note that the ban on gender rating practices is often referred to as part of the "guaranteed issue" policy, which would prohibit insurers from denying coverage based on pre-existing conditions, race, gender, or other basic characteristics.

[44] Institute for Women's Policy Research. 2009.

[45] Cawthorne, Alexandra. 2008.

End Notes for Expanding Access to Paid Sick Leave:
The Impact of the Healthy Families Act
on America's Workers

[1] 66 percent of all civilian workers in the United States have access to paid sick leave, according to the Bureau of Labor Statistics. Bureau of Labor Statistics. 2009. "Employee Benefits in the United States, March 2009." Table 6. http://www.bls.gov/news.release/pdf/ebs2.pdf.

[2] For example, see Goetzel, Ron Z., Long, Stacey R., Ozminkowski, Ronald J., Hawkins, Kevin, Wang, Shaohung, and Lynch, Wendy. 2004. "Health, Absence, Disability, and Presenteeism Cost Estimates of Certain Physical and Mental Health Conditions Affecting U.S. Employers." *Journal of Occupational and Environmental Medicine.* Lovell, Vicki. 2004. *No Time to Be Sick: Why Everyone Suffers When Workers Don't Have Paid Sick Leave.* Washington, DC: Institute for Women's Policy Research. Available at http://www.iwpr.org/pdf/B242.pdf. Stewart, W., Matousek, D., and Verdon, C. 2003. *The American Productivity Audit and the Campaign for Work and Health.* The Center for Work and Health, Advance PCS.

[3] This analysis focuses on the impact of the Healthy Families Act on the private-sector workforce only. Private-sector workers have lower levels of access to paid sick leave than do public sector workers. For example,

according to the Bureau of Labor Statistics, 89 percent of state and local government workers have access to paid sick leave as compared to just 61 percent of the private-sector workforce. The Healthy Families Act would apply to both the public and private sector, therefore the Joint Economic Committee's estimates presented in the following analysis likely understate the full impact of the Healthy Families Act on access to paid sick leave. See Bureau of Labor Statistics. 2009. "Employee Benefits in the United States, March 2009." Table 6. http://www.bls.gov/news.release/pdf/ebs2.pdf.

[4] Joint Economic Committee calculations based on unpublished data from the Bureau of Labor Statistics' 2009 National Compensation Survey and the March 2009 Current Population Survey. Methods available from the Joint Economic Committee upon request.

[5] Joint Economic Committee calculations based on unpublished data from the Bureau of Labor Statistics' 2009 National Compensation Survey.

[6] 66 percent of all civilian workers in the United States have access to paid sick leave, according to the Bureau of Labor Statistics. Bureau of Labor Statistics. 2009. "Employee Benefits in the United States, March 2009." Table 6. http://w ww.bls.gov/news.release/pdf/ebs2.pdf.

[7] Heymann, Jody and Alison Earle. 2009. *Raising the Global Floor: Dismantling the Myth That We Can't Afford Good Working Conditions for Everyone.* Stanford, CA: Stanford Politics and Policy. See http://researchtoaction.mcgill.ca/public_html/wfei/index.php.

[8] Smith, Tom W. 2008. "Paid Sick Days: A Basic Labor Standard for the 21st Century." Chicago, IL: National Opinion Research Center. http://www.norc.org/NR/rdonlyres/D1391669-A1EA-4CF4- 9B36-5FB1C1B595 AA/0/PaidSickDaysReport.pdf.

[9] Smith, Tom W. 2008. "Paid Sick Days: A Basic Labor Standard for the 21st Century." Chicago, IL: National Opinion Research Center. http://www.norc.org/NR/rdonlyres/D1391669-A1EA-4CF4- 9B36-5FB1C1 B595AA/0/PaidSickDaysReport.pdf.

[10] Reiss, Jeremy and Nancy Rankin. 2009. "Sick in the City: What the Lack of Paid Leave Means for New Yorkers. An Analysis of Eight Years of Findings From *The Unheard Third.*" New York: Community Service Society/A Better Balance.http://www.abetterbalance.org/cms/index2.php? option=com_docman&task=doc_view&gid= 72&Item id=99999999.

[11] Smith, Tom W. 2008. "Paid Sick Days: A Basic Labor Standard for the 21st Century." Chicago, IL: National Opinion Research Center. http://www.norc.org/NR/rdonlyres/D1391669-A1EA-4CF4- 9B36-5FB1C1 B595AA/0/PaidSickDaysReport.pdf.

[12] Centers for Disease Control and Prevention. October 23, 2009. "CDC Recommendations for the Amount of Time Persons with Influenza-Like Illness Should Be Away from Others." http://www.cdc.gov/ h1n1flu/guidance/exclusion.htm.

[13] Blendon, Robert, G. Steel Fisher, J. Benson, K. Weldon, and M. Herrmann. 2009. "Influenza A (H1N1)/Swine Flu Survey III. http://www.hsph.harvard.edu/news/press-releases/2009- releases/national-survey-americans-influenza-a-h1n1-outbreakfall-winter.html.

[14] Unpublished data from the Bureau of Labor Statistics' National Compensation Survey, March 2009.

[15] Bureau of Labor Statistics. 2008. "May 2008 National Occupational Employment and Wage Estimates." http://www.bls.gov/oes/2008/may/oes_nat.htm#b25-0000.

[16] This analysis focuses on the impact of the Healthy Families Act on the private-sector workforce only. Private-sector workers have lower levels of access to paid sick leave than do public sector workers. For example, according to the Bureau of Labor Statistics, 89 percent of state and local government workers have access to paid sick leave as compared to just 61 percent of the private-sector workforce. The Healthy Families Act would apply to both the public and private sector, therefore the Joint Economic Committee's estimates presented in the following analysis likely understate the full impact of the Healthy Families Act on access to paid sick leave. See Bureau of Labor Statistics. 2009. "Employee Benefits in the United States, March 2009." Table 6. http://www.bls.gov/news.release/pdf/ebs2.pdf.

[17] Current access figures are from unpublished data provided by the Bureau of Labor Statistics National Compensation Survey. These figures are likely to overstate current access to leave because many employers impose a job tenure requirement on workers prior to offering access to paid sick leave. As a result, the Joint Economic Committee's estimate of the impact of the Healthy Families Act is conservative, because the analysis may over-estimate access in the absence of the legislation. Specifically, the Bureau of Labor Statistics' survey is unable to ascertain whether a given worker has met an employers' job tenure requirements, therefore many employers may actually overstate their workforce's access to paid sick leave. Prior research has demonstrated that correcting for workers' job tenure substantially lowers the share of Americans with access to paid sick days relative to the raw data presented by the Bureau of Labor Statistics.

See Lovell, Vicky. 2004. "No Time To Be Sick: Why Everyone Suffers When Workers Don't Have Paid Sick Leave." Washington, DC: Institute for Women's Policy Research. http://www.iwpr.org/pdf/B242.pdf. Unfortunately, due to data restrictions, a similar correction to the Bureau of Labor Statistics most recent data is not possible. Thus the Joint Economic Committee estimates may overstate status-quo access to paid sick leave by relying on the uncorrected Bureau of Labor Statistics data.

[18] Joint Economic Committee calculations based on unpublished data from the Bureau of Labor Statistics' National Compensation Survey.

[19] Joint Economic Committee calculations based on unpublished data from the Bureau of Labor Statistics' National Compensation Survey.

[20] Current access figures for the full population are from unpublished data from the Bureau of Labor Statistics' National Compensation Survey.

[21] Joint Economic Committee calculations based on unpublished data from the Bureau of Labor Statistics' National Compensation Survey.

[22] For a literature review on the relationship between poverty, inequality, and health outcomes, see, for example, Deaton, Angus and Christina Paxson. 2001. "Mortality, Education, Income and Inequality Amongst American Cohorts." In Wise, David, ed. *Themes in the Economics of Aging.* Chicago: University of Chicago Press. http://www.nber.org/papers/w7140.

[23] United States Census Bureau, Current Population Survey, 2009 Annual Social and Economic Supplement. "Table POV04: Families by Age of Householder, Number of Children, and Family Structure, 2008." http://www.census.gov/hhes/www/cpstables/032009/pov/new04_100_01.htm.

[24] Boushey, Heather. 2009. "The New Breadwinners." In Boushey, Heather and Ann O'Leary, eds. *The Shriver Report: A Woman's Nation Changes Everything.* Washington, D.C.: Center for American Progress.

[25] Boushey, Heather. 2009. "The New Breadwinners." In Boushey, Heather and Ann O'Leary, eds. *The Shriver Report: A Woman's Nation Changes Everything.* Washington, D.C.: Center for American Progress.

[26] Salganicoff, Alina and Usha R. Ranji. 2005. *Women and Health Care: A National Profile.* Washington, D.C.: Kaiser Family Foundation. http://www.kff.org/womenshealth/upload/Womenand-Health-Care-A-National-Profile-Key-Findings-from-the-Kaiser-Women-s-Health-Survey.pdf.

[27] Institute for Women's Policy Research. 2007. "Women and Paid Sick Days: Crucial for Family Well-Being." Washington, D.C.: Institute for Women's Policy Research. http://www.iwpr.org/pdf/B254 paidsickdaysFS.pdf.

[28] Joint Economic Committee calculations based on unpublished data from the Bureau of Labor Statistics' 2009 National Compensation Survey and the March 2009 Current Population Survey. Methods available from the Joint Economic Committee upon request.

[29] Working Poor Families Project. 2008. "Still Working Hard, Still Falling Short: New Findings on the Challenges Confronting America's Workers. Baltimore, MD: Annie E. Casey Foundation. http://www.aecf.org/~/media/PublicationFiles/NationalDataBriefFINAL.pdf.

[30] Waldron, Tom, Brandon Roberts, and Andrew Reamer. 2004. "Working Hard, Falling Short: America's Working Families and the Pursuit of Economic Security." Baltimore, MD; and New York, NY: Annie E. Casey Foundation, Ford Foundation, and the Rockefeller Foundation. http://www.caseyfoundation.org/upload/publicationfiles/working%20hard.pdf.

[31] Joint Economic Committee calculations based on unpublished data from the Bureau of Labor Statistics' 2009 National Compensation Survey and the March 2009 Current Population Survey. Methods available from the Joint Economic Committee upon request.

[32] Bureau of Labor Statistics. 2008. "May 2008 National Occupational Employment and Wage Estimates." http://www.bls.gov/oes/2008/may/oes nat.htm#b25-0000.

[33] "Personal care workers" is category provided by the Bureau of Labor Statistics that includes child care and home health workers, and perhaps many others with direct contact with the public – including children, the elderly, the infirm, and others with heightened vulnerability to contagious disease.

[34] Current access figures for the full population are from unpublished data from the Bureau of Labor Statistics' National Compensation Survey.

[35] Joint Economic Committee calculations based on unpublished data from the Bureau of Labor Statistics' 2009 National Compensation Survey.

End Notes for Testimony of Ellen Galinsky President and Co-Founder and James T. Bond Vice President for Research Families and Work Institute 267 Fifth Avenue, 2nd Floor New York, NY 10016 (212) 465-2044

[1] Galinsky, E., Bond, J.T. and Sakai, K. (2008) *National Study of Employers*. New York: Families and Work Institute. http://familiesandwork.org/site/research/reports/2008nse.pdf.

[2] Ibid.

[3] U.S. Department of Labor, Bureau of Labor Statistics (June 2009). "Economic News Release: Employment Situation Summary." http://www.bls.gov/news.release/empsit.nr0.htm.

[4] Galinsky, E., Aumann, K. and Bond, J.T. (2009). *Times Are Changing: Gender and Generationat Work and at Home*. New York: Families and Work Institute. http://familiesandwork.org/site/research/ reports/ Times_Are_Changing.pdf.

[5] Bond, J.T. and Galinsky, E. (November 2006). *What Do We Know About Entry-Level, Hourly Employees?* Research Brief No.1. New York: Families and Work Institute. http://familiesandwork. org/site/research/reports/brief1.pdf.

[6] Salamon, L.M., Geller, S.L. and Spence, K.L. (2009) "Impact of the 2007-09 Economic Recession on Nonprofit Organizations," *Communiqué*, No.14. Baltimore, MD: Center for Civil Society Studies, Johns Hopkins University. http://www.ccss.jhu.edu/pdfs/LP_Communiques/LP_Communique_14.pdf.

End Notes for Testimony of Karen Nussbaum Executive Director, Working America 815 16th St., N.W. Washington, D.C. 20006 202-637-5137

[1] Economic Policy Institute, 2006. "State of Working America." http://www.stateofworkingamerica. org/tabfig/2008/01/03.jpg Accessed 7/19/09.

[2] Jacob Hacker, 2008. Testimony Before Committee on Education and Labor, U.S. House of Representatives Field Hearing on "The Impact of the Financial Crisis on Workers' Retirement Security." http://www.law.berkeley.edu/files/Hacker_Testimony_-_Oct_2008-1(1).pdf Accessed 7/17/09.

[3] Vicky Lovell, Institute for Women's Policy Research, "Women and Paid Sick Days: Crucial for Family Well-Being, 2007."

[4] Center for Economic and Policy Research, 2007. "U.S. Only Advanced Economy That Does Not Guarantee Workers Paid Vacation." http://www.cepr.net/index.php/press-releases/press-releases/us-only-advancedeconomy-that-does-not-guarantee-workers-paid-vacation/ Accessed 7/21/09

[5] Darrell Hutchens and Jeff Milchen, 2003. "Americans Working More, Earning Less." http://www.reclaimdemocracy.org/labor/unpaid_overtime_rules.html Accessed 7/19/09.

[6] AFL-CIO, "Ask A Working Woman Survey 2000," poll conducted by Lake Snell Perry & Assoc., 2000.

[7] Economic Policy Institute, 2004. "When Do Workers Get Their Share?" http://www.epi.org/ economic_snapshots/ entry/webfeatures_snapshots_05272004/ Accessed 7/19/09.

[8] U.S. Census Bureau, "Historical Health Insurance Tables." http://www.census.gov/hhes/www/hlthins/historic/ hlthin05/hihistt1.html Accessed 7/20/09.

[9] AFL-CIO, "Insurance Company Profits are Fat and Healthy." http://aflcio.org/issues/healthcare/upload/facts insurancecompanyprofits.pdf Accessed 7/20/09.

[10] Jack Welch speaking to the Society for Human Resource Management, 6/28/09, quoted by Andrew Leonard. http://www.salon.com/tech/htww/2009/07/14/jack_welch_and_women/index.html?source=newsletter Accessed 7/17/09.

[11] Jennifer MacGillvary and Netsy Firestein, 2009. "Family-Friendly Workplaces: Do Unions Make a Difference?" http://laborcenter.berkeley.edu/jobquality/familyfriendly09.pdf Accessed 7/17/09.

[12] National Coalition on Health Care. http://www.nchc.org/facts/cost.shtml Accessed 7/22/09.

[13] Hewitt Health Care Initiative/AFL-CIO. http://aflcio.org/issues/healthcare/facts_insurancepremiums.cfm Accessed 7/22/09.

[14] CBS News. http://www.cbsnews.com/stories/2009/06/05/earlyshow/health/main5064981.shtml Accessed 7/22/09.

[15] Economic Policy Institute, "Minimum Wage Issue Guide," 2007, www.epi.org/content. cfm/ issueguides_ minwage Accessed 7/22/09.

[16] Testimony of Debra Ness before the Committee on Health, Education, Labor and Pensions Subcommittee on Children and Families, Feb. 13, 2008, help.senate.gov/Hearings/2008_02_13/Ness.pdf, and "The Family and Medical Leave Act Regulations: A Report on the Department of Labor's Request for Information 2007 Update," U.S. Department of Labor, June 2007, at 129.

[17] Jane Waldfolgal, www.bls.gov/opub/mlr/2001/09/art2full.pdf; Jody Heymann, www.iwpr.org/pdf/heymann.pdf ; "Balancing the Needs of Families and Employers: Family and Medical Leave Surveys 2000 Update," conducted by Westat for the U.S. Department of Labor.

[18] www.timeday.org (10/9/2006)

[19] Win-win flexibility: New American Foundation

[20] One sick child away from being fired: When "opting out" is not an option. Center for WorkLife Law.

End Notes for Testimony of Cynthia Thomas Calvert Deputy Director, The Center for WorkLife Law UC Hastings College of the Law 200 McAllister St. San Francisco, CA 94102

[1] E.g., Williams, Joan and Cynthia Thomas Calvert, WorkLife Law's Guide to Family Responsibilities Discrimination (WLL Press 2006 & updates); Joan C. Williams & Stephanie Bornstein, The Evolution of "FReD": Family Responsibilities Discrimination and Developments in the Law of Stereotyping and Implicit Bias, 59(6) Hastings Law Journal 1311 (2008). [2] FRD lawsuits can be brought as sex discrimination cases, family and medical leave retaliation, breach of contract, and other types of lawsuits. FRD can arise at any level of an organization, from hourly shift workers to top management. The number of FRD cases has increased rapidly. In 2006, WorkLife Law reported a nearly 400% increase in the number of FRD lawsuits filed between 1996 and 2005 as compared to the prior decade, 1986 to 1995. WLL is in the process of updating this data. Preliminary results indicate a sharp increase in the number of FRD cases in 2007 (316 cases) and 2008 (348 cases) as compared to 2006 (176 cases). Plaintiffs prevail on motions, resulting in settlements, or win verdicts in approximately 50% of the cases. Settlements and verdicts average $100,000, and WorkLife Law has a database of over 125 verdicts that exceed $100,000; several are multi-million dollar verdicts.

[2] See Enforcement Guidance: Unlawful Disparate Treatment of Workers with Caregiving Responsibilities, Equal Employment Opportunity Commission (2006), available at http://www.eeoc.gov/policy/docs/caregiving.html .

[3] Williams, Joan and Nancy Segal, "Beyond the Maternal Wall: Relief for Family Caregivers who are Discriminated Against on the Job," 26 Harv. Women's L.J. 77 (2003).

[4] Galinsky, Ellen, James T. Bond, and Kelly Sakai, 2008 National Study of Employers, Families and Work Institute.

[5] E.g., L.M. Sixel, *Women's Group to Honor Winner with a Difference,* Houston Chronicle, Houston Chronicle, Jan. 17, 2004, at B1 (Shell's compressed work schedule, flexible work arrangements, and maternity leave programs as among the reasons they received an award from Catalyst for diversity and inclusivity); *see also* Shell Oil's website, http://www.shell.us/home/content/usa/aboutshell /careers/professionals/rewards_benefits/ professional_rew ardsbenefits.html#work-life_balance_5 (listing Shell's work/family programs).

[6] Hotline calls are confidential. In the examples in this section, unless otherwise indicated, facts that would identify the caller have been removed or altered.

[7] In another example of flexible work bias, an employee who recently returned from her second maternity leave was denied a promotion after she said she wanted to cut back her hours to take care of her baby's medical conditions. Another who cut back her hours for childcare reasons was not given any work to do.

[8] *See, e.g.*, WFC Resources, Making the business case for flexibility, available at http://www.workfamily. com/Work-lifeClearinghouse/UpDates/ud0043.htm (collecting studies).

In: Investing in Women for America's Economic Benefit   ISBN: 978-1-62100-053-2
Editors: J. Henrickson and L. O'Connell   © 2012 Nova Science Publishers, Inc.

Chapter 2

THE GENDER WAGE GAP JEOPARDIZES WOMEN'S RETIREMENT SECURITY[*]

The Joint Economic Committee

Equal Pay Day highlights an issue of social and economic significance: the gap between the earnings of men and women. In 2009, women working full-time earned 77 cents for every dollar earned by their male counterparts.[1] That disparity has lasting consequences for the economic security of women that persist long after they have exited the labor force.

LOWER EARNINGS OVER THE COURSE OF THEIR CAREERS JEOPARDIZE WOMEN'S RETIREMENT SECURITY

Families depend on women's earnings for economic security, including during retirement. Data from the Bureau of Labor Statistics' Current Population Survey reveal that the gender pay gap significantly affects women's incomes in retirement. Among women age 65 and older, median income from all sources was $15,209 in 2009—over $10,000 less than the median income for men 65 and older.[2] (See Figure 1.)

THE GENDER PAY GAP AFFECTS SOURCES OF RETIREMENT INCOME DIRECTLY LINKED TO CAREER EARNINGS

Of the multiple sources of income Americans rely on later in life, many are directly linked to a worker's earnings over his or her career. These include Social Security benefits, based on lifetime earnings, and defined benefit pension distributions that are typically

---

[*] This is an edited, reformatted and augmented version of a Report by The U.S. Congress Joint Economic Committee Chairman's Staff Senator Bob Casey, Chairman, dated April 12, 2011.

calculated using a formula based on a worker's tenure and salary during peak-earnings years. The persistent gender pay gap leaves women with less income from these sources than men. For example, older women's Social Security benefits are 71 percent of older men's benefits ($11,057 for women versus $15,557 for men in 2009). Incomes from public and private pensions based on women's own work were just 60 percent and 48 percent of men's pension incomes, respectively.[3] (See Figure 2.) Conversely, older women typically receive larger amounts of income from pensions based on a deceased spouse's work than men do.[4]

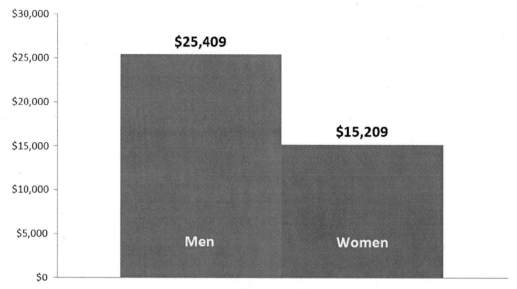

Note: Data exclude individuals who do not receive income.
Source: Employee benefit Research Institute (EBRI) calculations based on data from the Bureau of Labor Statistics Current Population Survey.

Figure 1. Median income for Individuals 65 and Older, 2009.

THE GENDER PAY GAP AFFECTS SOURCES OF RETIREMENT INCOME DIRECTLY LINKED TO CAREER EARNINGS

Of the multiple sources of income Americans rely on later in life, many are directly linked to a worker's earnings over his or her career. These include Social Security benefits, based on lifetime earnings, and defined benefit pension distributions that are typically calculated using a formula based on a worker's tenure and salary during peak-earnings years. The persistent gender pay gap leaves women with less income from these sources than men. For example, older women's Social Security benefits are 71 percent of older men's benefits ($11,057 for women versus $15,557 for men in 2009). Incomes from public and private pensions based on women's own work were just 60 percent and 48 percent of men's pension incomes, respectively.[3] (See Figure 2.) Conversely, older women typically receive larger amounts of income from pensions based on a deceased spouse's work than men do.[4]

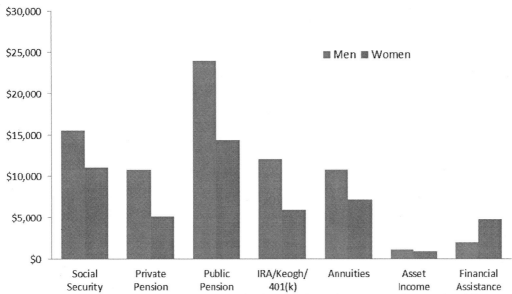

Note: Data exclude individuals who do not reveive income from the source. Private and public person income does not include suvivor's benefits. Financial assistance includes regular assistance from friends and relatives not living in the individual's household, but does not include public assistance.

Source: Employee Benefit Research institute (EBRI) calculations based on data from the Bureau of Labor Statistics' Current Population Survey.

Figure 2. Median Retirement Income from Selected Sources for Individuals 565 and Older, 2009.

THE GENDER PAY GAP LIMITS
WOMEN'S ABILITY
TO SAVE FOR RETIREMENT
IN OTHER WAYS

Lower earnings also affect women's ability to contribute to other retirement-saving plans, including defined contribution pension plans and individual retirement accounts (IRAs). Although not directly based on a worker's earnings, smaller take-home pay translates into less disposable income to dedicate to saving for retirement. Among women 65 and older who receive income from these types of saving and investment vehicles, their income was *half* that of men's. Women also typically received smaller amounts from annuities and private assets.[5]

EARNINGS FOR OLDER WOMEN
STILL IN THE LABOR FORCE
ARE A FRACTION OF MEN'S

With typically less income from other sources, many women remain in the labor force to supplement their retirement income. However, those earnings tend to be a fraction of earnings earned by men. In 2009, women 50 and older working full-time earned only 75 percent of their male counterparts' earnings, leaving a 25 percent gap.[6] Women 65 and older made only 60 percent of the earnings of men 65 or older, leaving a 40 percent gap.[7] Thus, women face both lower retirement income and lower earnings than men when they remain in the labor force to supplement their retirement income.

ADDRESSING THE GENDER WAGE GAP FOR WORKERS OF ALL AGES IS CRITICAL FOR WOMEN'S RETIREMENT SECURITY

Lower earnings over a woman's career can result in smaller private savings to draw upon in retirement, smaller contributions to employer-sponsored retirement plans, smaller Social Security benefits, and smaller paychecks for those women who continue to work later in life. With income that is only a fraction of men's, women 65 and older are more likely to live in poverty and depend on Social Security and financial assistance to make ends meet. Women 65 and older are five times more likely to receive financial assistance than men,[8] and typically draw twice as much income from financial assistance than men.[9] While addressing the gap between men and women's earnings is important for current workers, closing the gap would also bolster women's retirement security.

End Notes

[1] Comparisons for full-time, year-round workers. U.S. Census Bureau. Income, Poverty and Health Insurance Coverage in the United States, 2009. http://www.census.gov/prod/2010pubs/p60-238.pdf This is one widely cited estimate of the gender wage gap that assumes workers work 40 hours per week.

[2] JEC Chairman's Staff calculation based on Employee Benefit Research Institute (EBRI) tabulations of Current Population Survey (CPS) data. Data accessed through EBRI Databook on Employee Benefits, Chapter 7: Sources of Income for Persons Aged 55 and Older. Table 7.4. Available at http://www.ebri.org/publications/books/?fa=databook.

[3] JEC Chairman's Staff calculations based on EBRI tabulations of CPS data. [4]This is true for both public and private pensions. EBRI tabulations of CPS data.

[5] JEC Chairman's Staff calculations based on EBRI tabulations of CPS data.

[6] Joint Economic Committee. *Large Gender Pay Gap for Older Workers Threatens Economic Security of Older Women.* December 2010.

[7] JEC Chairman's Staff calculations based on EBRI tabulations of CPS data.

[8] Financial assistance in Figure 2 includes regular financial assistance from friends or relatives not living in the individual's household and does not include public assistance/Supplemental Security Income, in which the median was $600 for men and $480 for women in 2009.

[9] JEC   Chairman's   Staff   calculations   based   on   EBRI   tabulations   of   CPS   data.

INDEX

D